HIKING IN NORWAY – SOUTH

HIKING IN NORWAY – SOUTH

THE 10 BEST MULTI-DAY TREKS

by Ute Koninx

CICERONE

JUNIPER HOUSE, MURLEY MOSS,
OXENHOLME ROAD, KENDAL, CUMBRIA LA9 7RL
www.cicerone.co.uk

Second edition 2021
ISBN: 978 1 85284 975 7
Reprinted 2024 (with updates)
This completely new guide replaces
Walking in Norway (ISBN: 978 1 85284 230 7) by Constance Roos.

Printed in China on responsibly sourced paper on behalf of Latitude Press Ltd

A catalogue record for this book is available from the British Library.

To my family

Updates to this Guide

While every effort is made by our authors to ensure the accuracy of guidebooks as they go to print, changes can occur during the lifetime of an edition. Any updates that we know of for this guide will be on the Cicerone website (www.cicerone.co.uk/975/updates), so please check before planning your trip. We also advise that you check information about such things as transport, accommodation and shops locally. Even rights of way can be altered over time. We are always grateful for information about any discrepancies between a guidebook and the facts on the ground, sent by email to updates@cicerone.co.uk.

Register your book: To sign up to receive free updates, special offers and GPX files where available, create a Cicerone account and register your purchase via the 'My Account' tab at www.cicerone.co.uk.

Front cover: Hiker scaling the Besseggen ridge in Jotunheimen (Route 1, Stage 1)

CONTENTS

Route symbols on map extracts

trail

alternative trail

route direction

start point

alternate start point

finish point

start/finish point

mountain hut (serviced/self-serviced/unserviced)

other accommodation

trees/forest

fells

high fells/alpine

SCALE: 1:200,000

0 kilometres 2 4

0 miles 2

All maps in this guide are at a scale of 1:200,000 unless otherwise marked

GPX files

for all routes can be downloaded free at www.cicerone.co.uk/975/GPX

Mountain safety

Every mountain walk has its dangers, and those described in this guidebook are no exception. All who walk or climb in the mountains should recognise this and take responsibility for themselves and their companions along the way. The author and publisher have made every effort to ensure that the information contained in this guide was correct when it went to press, but, except for any liability that cannot be excluded by law, they cannot accept responsibility for any loss, injury or inconvenience sustained by any person using this book.

International distress signal *(emergency only)*
Six blasts on a whistle (and flashes with a torch after dark) spaced evenly for one minute, followed by a minute's pause. Repeat until an answer is received. The response is three signals per minute followed by a minute's pause.

Helicopter rescue
The following signals are used to communicate with a helicopter:

Help needed: raise both arms above head to form a 'Y'

Help not needed: raise one arm above head, extend other arm downward

Emergency telephone numbers
If telephoning from the UK the dialling codes are:
Norway: 0047

Police and rescue coordination tel 112; Fires and major accidents tel 110; Ambulance medical emergencies tel 113

Norway - Search and Rescue
South Norway, Hovedredningssentralen Sør Norge, Flyplassveien 160, 4055 Sola
Emergency number: tel 51 51 70 00

Weather reports and warnings
www.yr.no weather information provided by public broadcaster NRK and Norwegian Meteorological Institute; www.varsom.no/en for avalanche, landslide and weather warnings

Always be adequately insured. Mountain rescue is free in Norway, but follow up health costs could be very expensive.

A perfectly still morning in Jotunheimen

ROUTE SUMMARY TABLE

Route	Length (km)	Stages	Max altitude (m)	Ascent (m)	Descent (m)	Page no.
Jotunheimen						35
1 Besseggen	41	3	1743	2060	1990	43
2 Classic	97	6	2469	5220	5225	54
3 Traverse	51	4	2068	2450	2635	83
Rondane						97
4 Summits	85	5	2178	4200	4200	104
5 Traverse	74	4	1429	2440	2510	123
Dovrefjell						149
6 Traverse	80	5	2286	2990	3750	156
Trollheimen						183
7 Trekanten	59	3	1325	2295	2295	190
8 SignaTur	152	8	1669	6750	6750	206
9 Fells to fjord	55	3	1175	1855	2525	235
Ryfylke						247
10 Lysefjord	84	7	1143	5785	5655	254

AUTHOR PREFACE

Hiking in Norway will leave you breathless in so many ways. Its fjords, mountains, moors and glacial valleys, together with the play of wind, light and weather, bring forth dramatic and marvellous sights to hikers wherever they go. The diversity, accessibility and relative ease of navigation are unmatched in Europe. At the same time, you can get a sense of a tantalising wilderness and be as remote and feel as challenged as you desire in this vast and largely unspoilt country.

The hiking season is short, but with the long daylight hours, these summer and early autumn days seemingly go on forever, and are the perfect time for epic journeys through Norway's incredible nature.

No wonder, then, that hiking and an active outdoor life are engrained in Norwegian culture and heritage. The 'right to roam' is given by law to every individual in the country – a public treasure that can be enjoyed and cherished by those who venture out to make it their own.

A good level of fitness is required as well as map-reading skills and the ability and gear to endure changing weather patterns. Otherwise, hiking in Norway in summer does not require specialist equipment and can be done by a variety of people. Chances are, you'll see this for yourself in the evenings. Relaxing together with local Norwegian hikers in the mountain huts adds another dimension to your hiking experience. Exchanging stories and sharing the passion for the natural surroundings over a game of cards or a cup of tea often forms a convivial end to the day.

The treks in this book cover major hiking areas of Southern Norway and as a whole give an overview of the finest multi-day hiking adventures, be they well-known classic treks or lesser-known gems. Hopefully, they will entice you to discover this wonderful country for yourself.

God tur!

Ute Koninx

Langglupbekken waterfall with Rondslottet in the background (Routes 4 and 5)

INTRODUCTION

View over Fannaråkbreen glacier into Sognefjellet (Route 3, Stage 3)

NORWAY – A HIKER'S PARADISE

Southern Norway extends from Kristiansand in the south to Trondheim in the middle of Norway. The fjords and mountain ranges, fish-rich rivers and lakes and superb hunting grounds made the country popular with the earliest tourists and travellers from Continental Europe in the late 19th century. So much so that English mountaineers were among the first to scale many peaks and German aristocracy liked to come for their summer holidays. Much has changed since then – and yet in some ways very little has changed. The natural beauty and magnificent views that attracted the early tourists awe today's hikers as much as if not more than before.

Much of Norway seems untouched by human activity, and once hiking you will invariably learn that it is firmly in the realm of the natural forces that have shaped it: primarily water and wind. Of course, you will not be alone if you are scaling mighty Galdhøpiggen (Route 2, Stage 4), hiking towards the unique Kjeragbolten boulder (Route 10, Stage 4) or crossing the iconic Besseggen ridge (Route 1, Stage 1). They are popular for a reason, but worth your while nonetheless and therefore included within routes in this guide. However, many route stages will have you hiking in solitude for most of the time, meeting few on the trail as you marvel at the panoramas around you.

The stages of each route are designed to end at mountain huts, providing warmth, companionship and comfort at the end of the day. Having said that, it is perfectly possible to hike with a tent, should you wish. Spending time outdoors is part of Norwegian culture.

This guidebook presents a total of 10 multi-day routes, from shorter three-day treks to longer expeditions that require more planning, commitment and stamina. Almost all routes require you to have a head for heights at times. With the exception of the Lysefjord route in Ryfylke that takes you around one of the most beautiful fjords in western Norway, all of the routes are in (high) alpine terrain, with the associated rewards and challenges.

GEOGRAPHY AND GEOLOGY

The Norwegian mountains are often thought to be the remnant of a high mountain range, formed some 450 million years ago and since eroded down to current heights. However, this theory has recently been challenged by the discovery that the continental crust underneath is too thin to have supported such a mountain range, and the scientific community is divided as to the actual origin of the Norwegian mountains.

What we do know is that the mountain range has been shaped and moulded during the Quaternary period of the last 2.5 million years. Southern Norway was covered by immense amounts of snow and ice for half of that time; warmer periods led to glacial movements and snowmelts that needed to be discharged into gigantic rivers, shaping the magnificent landscapes that we can see today. The country is marked by fjords that cut deep into the land, as well as mountain ranges and tundra-like plateaus, permafrost and glaciers, leaving only 4% that can be used for agricultural purposes. It has one of the lowest population densities in Europe, and this is concentrated in coastal

Erratics from the last ice age on the high fells plateau (Route 10, Stage 3)

areas, especially the Oslo fjord. Once you leave towns and villages behind, you will find yourself very quickly in a remote and unspoilt country, with millions of years of geological history under your feet. (If you're interested, for more information see Geological Survey of Norway, www.ngu.no – also in English.)

HERITAGE AND OUTDOOR CULTURE

Norwegians have been living in this rugged and often inhospitable landscape for thousands of years, becoming experts at making a living in harsh and difficult conditions. By the end of the 19th century, all the land suitable for agricultural purposes had been developed, and this often included remote farms in faraway mountain valleys. Today, some of these former summer pastures and alms form part of the vast network of mountain huts around the country. The centuries-old drover trails that connected these hamlets have become part of the network of trails that criss-cross the mountains. While hiking in Southern Norway you will find yourself in some of the most beautiful and varied terrain. Expect to be able to walk over and around mountaintops, around glaciers, along streams and lakes in generally magnificent and stunning scenery, where, depending on the route and time chosen, you might be accompanied by many or by none.

Foraging, fishing and hunting are seen by many as part of the traditional Norwegian way of life. You might well come across hunters and fishermen who will only consume meat or fish that they've caught. Norwegians like to feel connected to nature, and they have a word in their vocabulary that sums up all these experiences into one: *friluftsliv*. While untranslatable, it encompasses all the activities around the outdoors that an individual might enjoy. In the context of hiking in the mountains, this extends to berry picking and other foraging activities, hunting and fishing. The *allemannsretten*, translated as 'public right of access', covers these activities in a law, essentially allowing the individual to walk and hike everywhere in open country and unfenced land, without restriction, regardless of land ownership (search 'right to roam' on the official website of Visit Norway, www.visitnorway.com). Hunting, as well as fishing in lakes and rivers, does require a permit (see information on www.inatur.no). Trout, perch and char are abundant in many lakes and rivers and can supplement your diet on the trail. In Southern Norway you are allowed to pick berries and gather mushrooms for your own consumption (note that this should only be done if you are truly knowledgeable about mushrooms as some are potentially lethal). See Appendix D for more information on the berries that are common in the region.

A quiet, still autumn morning in Visdalen valley (Route 2, Stage 5)

CLIMATE AND WHEN TO GO

Due to Norway's latitude, the mountainous areas described in this book have a climate that is harsher than might be expected for their altitude. Above 600m you are in alpine territory in Southern Norway. This leads to a relatively short hiking season in the mountains, starting at the beginning of July and running to mid September. Depending on winter snowfall and spring temperatures, many hikes can still have snow cover until well into July or even throughout the summer. In June you may find trails and markers hidden under snow, and summer bridges over meltwater rivers not yet installed. For the same reasons, hiking in late autumn, winter and early spring is not advised – in addition to the potential difficulties caused by snow and swollen rivers, many huts are closed over these months.

You will find mid July to mid August to be the busiest times on the trails as these coincide with school holidays and the general 'summer holiday month'. If you prefer quieter trails and have flexibility in your schedule, go earlier or later in the season. The weather might be a bit more unstable, but you will be rewarded with quieter huts and far fewer people on the trails.

Temperatures in summer in the mountains average around 11°C at 1000m, and it is not unusual to have frost at night, while temperatures on warm summer days can also easily reach 20°C. Keep in mind that temperatures fall as you ascend. For every 100m altitude gain the temperature falls by 0.6°C. Any wind that is present will have fewer obstacles in its way and so can further decrease the felt temperature through the windchill factor.

Southern Norway has two main climate zones. The divide runs along the mountain ranges themselves. This leads to large differences in precipitation across some ranges such as Jotunheimen, Dovrefjell and Trollheimen. The western, coastal areas benefit from the Atlantic Gulf Stream and experience generally mild winters. At the same time, they are fully exposed to Atlantic storms and low-pressure systems, and therefore the western mountains receive much more precipitation (typically 1000mm per year) than the eastern areas (typically 400–500mm). In summer, the mountain ranges prevent warm continental winds from reaching the coast, thereby keeping summer temperatures lower along the western parts. The fact that the mountain ranges act as climatic barrier between a coastal and continental climate can give rise to fast-changing weather conditions in the mountains themselves. Be prepared for these. Staffed mountain cabins will generally display the daily local weather report.

The lush valley around Gjende provides for many different insects (Route 1, Stage 2)

GETTING TO NORWAY

Norway is well connected by all means of transportation to Scandinavia and Continental Europe, with networks including plane, ferry, train, bus and car routes. From the UK and the US, direct access is by plane.

Visa

Visitors from the EU/EEA and the US do not need a visa to visit Norway for up to 90 days. US citizens should have a passport that is valid for at least three months beyond the period of stay. They need sufficient funds (NOK 500 per day, unless you're staying with family) and a return airline ticket. You may be asked to prove this when you enter, for example by showing cash, credit cards or documentation of prepaid accommodation and transport. Most people from other countries outside the EU/EEA must apply for a visitor's visa. For information on current visa requirements see www.udi.no/en.

Plane, train and bus

Norway is connected by air to many European and international destinations through the main airports of Oslo, Stavanger and Trondheim, as well as many other smaller airports. Finding a flight is not difficult, but prices can vary significantly based on time of year, time of booking and many other factors. Comparison shopping is recommended (see www.omio.com, for example, which also offers search options for train and bus travel). Airlines flying to Norway include SAS, KLM, Ryanair, Lufthansa, British Airways and many others.

There are some international train connections; these can be researched through websites such as www.rome2rio.com. Travelling by Interrail or Eurail pass (https://eurailgroup.org) can make train travel a cheaper option than flying. Without such passes, travel to Norway by air is likely the cheapest option.

Flixbus (https://global.flixbus.com) is a fast-growing network of European long-distance bus travel that has recently expanded into Norway. It now services Oslo and a few other destinations.

Car and ferry travel

Unless you travel via Sweden, you will have to take a ferry to reach Norway by car. There are several ferry companies servicing the ports of Oslo, Sandefjord, Larvik, Kristiansand, Stavanger and Bergen; these include Colorline (www.colorline.com), Stena Line (www.stenaline.com) and Fjord Line (www.fjordline.com/en). From these ports it is possible to travel onward by private or rental car, bus or sometimes train within Norway. Pricing varies significantly depending on time of booking, and day and time of travel. The most frequented

TOLLS

Norway's extensive road network is part financed by toll stations (about 200) with a 'user pays' principle. Your car will be registered by the toll stations as you pass. Subsequently (some weeks or even months later), you will receive an invoice from Euro Parking Collection (EPC). EPC has been authorised by the Norwegian Public Roads Administration to invoice vehicle owners registered outside its jurisdiction. You can choose to pre-register your vehicle with EPC before entering Norway by car – see www.autopass.no/en – to make the process smoother. Even if you are travelling with a rental or leased car it may be advantageous to register, as otherwise car rental/lease agencies might add their own administration costs to the invoice.

departure ports in Continental Europe are Hirtshals (Denmark) and Kiel (Germany). At the time of writing, there is no ferry connecting the UK to Scandinavia, although operators are always reviewing options.

Given the many options to plan and research car travel, details on how to reach destinations in Norway by car are not detailed in this guide.

GETTING AROUND NORWAY

Once you have arrived in Norway, local transport by train and bus is very efficient and comfortable. Efforts are underway to increase travel by public transport, with websites and apps being developed to facilitate this. Two of these are www.entur.no (English option; app available) and https://ruter.no/en (apps available for route planning and ticket sales). At this point, the user friendliness – especially for English speakers – is still being improved, but no doubt these services will increase ease of planning in the future. In the meantime, the local chapters in this guide provide the information needed.

For travelling by train, use the Norwegian Railways (VY) website at www.vy.no/en. Reservations on trains are highly recommended during high season in the summer months. You might otherwise not be able to board the train, if it is full. Train tickets can be purchased on the website, through VY's mobile app (see website), at ticket desks (only in train stations of the larger cities) or self-service machines at local train stations. VY's call centre has English-speaking staff and can be reached on weekends too (tel +47 61 05 19 10). Ticket pricing will depend on time of day travelling, time of booking and seasonal factors.

Southern Norway has an extensive interregional network of bus lines that connect Oslo in the east to the major cities on the coast. For more information, see for example the NOR-WAY Bussekspress website at www.nor-way.no/en, or www.lavprisekspressen.no (no English-language option but Google Chrome will translate), or again www.vy.no/en for the regional VY bus services. It is advisable to book in advance during the summer months if your itinerary is inflexible and you need to get a particular connection

Train is a favoured mode of transport to Rondane, Dovrefjell and Trollheimen

on a given day. Generally, these buses are reliably on time, comfortable and clean. At least one item of luggage of 20kg will be allowed in the luggage compartment, and some companies allow for more items and heavier bags – best to check on the website when booking. Dogs are allowed by some companies (also best to check first). Most buses have power outlets and some routes offer free Wi-Fi. NOR-WAY Bussekspress is currently rolling out a service by which you can follow the position of any bus in real time.

Apart from these interregional lines, many bus lines operate on provincial and county level. All regional towns that are entry points into the routes described in this guide can be reached by train and/or public bus. Additional information about specific train and bus connections is given in the relevant chapters of the book.

It is of course also possible to travel by plane within the country. At the time of writing, Norwegian, SAS and Wideroe are the main domestic airlines. Norway's extensive road network makes it easy to reach all of the entry points into the routes and some of the mountain huts by car.

HIKING IN NORWAY

The great diversity and range of landscapes that are accessible to the hiker make trekking in Norway a very rewarding experience. The Norwegian Trekking Association (DNT, https://english.dnt.no) is an overarching organisation of the approximately 50 local mountain hiking associations in the country. Together these maintain around 550 mountain huts and around 20,000km of marked trails. The combinations are extensive and limited only by physical and mental endurance. In short, Norway offers a multitude of different, vast landscapes that will have you spoilt for choice and wanting to come back time and again. The https://ut.no website – the Norwegian go-to site for information on outdoor pursuits – has extensive information on every hut run by the DNT or its affiliates and partners. Unfortunately it has recently been redesigned and at the time of writing it appears that the English

DOGS

You can bring dogs along while hiking in Norway, but they must stay on a leash as they might chase reindeer, sheep and other wildlife. They are not allowed inside the main huts, but many huts have separate rooms or other quarters where you and your dog can stay together. For more information visit the https://ut.no website and check out the hut you want to stay in. You should read up on vaccination requirements and other formalities if you are bringing your dog into Norway.

pages have largely been removed. This might of course change again in the future, but in the meantime you will need to use a translating application or acquaintance to get the full benefit of the information provided.

The hikes and treks in this book require a decent level of fitness, the ability to carry a backpack of 8–12kg over multiple days, map and orientation skills, and some mountain and weather experience.

WAYMARKING AND ACCESS

Due to the excellent level of marking, finding your way while hiking in Norway is much easier than in many other parts of Europe. The treks described in this book make use of these marked trails. The marking system uses red waymarkers – usually 'T's. The 'T's are generally painted on trees, rocks or cairns. Other waymarkers include red-topped posts or red-banded trees. Be aware that the mountains are criss-crossed by many trails, some of them unmarked. Unless a cairn is marked by a 'T' it might not be a marker for your trail. The wonderful effort led by volunteers marking hundreds of kilometres every year should not, however, make you complacent. Take a map along and always know where you are. Getting lost could be uncomfortable or potentially dangerous.

Do not add stones to cairns. Cairns are carefully built for stability and visibility. Some routes now have a ban on the building of new cairns as these ancient waymarkers are considered part of the cultural heritage of the country, especially in Jotunheimen.

Close marking with 'T' for the often foggy conditions that prevail on top of Fannaråki (Route 3, Stage 4)

MAPS AND NAVIGATION

The Norwegian government provides the public with free mapping data of Norway. If you are somewhat IT-savvy you can design, download and print your own map at a scale of up to 1:50,000 from https://norgeskart.no (English version available). Geographical detail is continuously updated, and this may include minor changes to heights and spellings. The data in this guide

Skranglehaugan near Dørålseter, a landscape of craters made by ice blocks melting in the glacial moraine (Route 4, Stage 3)

is up-to-date as of late 2019. If you prefer to buy a map, see Nordeca's Norway series. This consists of 195 maps at a scale of mostly 1:50,000, as well as some planning maps at a scale of 1:100,000. Maps are available at www.kartbutikken.no (English option; ships globally) as well as various other online retailers. You should not assume to be able to buy the relevant maps locally in Norway. Outdoors stores have become less reliable in stocking these since the maps have become free to the public. The fully staffed mountain huts often have the maps relevant to their area, but not always.

Most of the maps in this guide are at 1:200,000 – with a small handful at 1:50,000 – and are not intended to be relied on for navigation. Names of places and landscape features mentioned in this guide always feature on the 1:50,000 maps; however, only names printed in **bold** in the text appear on the maps in this guide.

Navigation with GPS route data makes hiking in Norway even easier. Nevertheless, do bring a map, a compass and know how to use both. Your device can run out of battery or the GPS signal could be lost.

ACCOMMODATION

Mountain huts

Norwegians like to hike as light as possible. Most Norwegians will trek with a backpack of about 8–12kg in summer, as they will stay in a hut at night. The huts are positioned such that they can be reached within a day's hike of 4–11hr hiking. The treks covered in this book make use of these mountain huts – see Appendix B for a list of those encountered in this guide and their key services.

There are three types of hut, a common feature being that they are located in stunningly beautiful spots and make you feel welcome and grateful for being in such glorious surroundings. The hospitality and food in some of the fully serviced cabins is exceptional. The three types of cabin are:

- **Unserviced (*ubetjent*)** huts are often small, but offer all facilities needed for heating, cooking and sleeping. They have no pantry, so you'd have to bring along all food. Most unserviced huts are found in Northern Norway. In this guide, there are only a few occasions where you overnight in one of these.
- **Self-serviced (*selv-betjent*)** huts always contain a pantry that allows guests to buy mostly tinned and otherwise non-perishable food by way of an honesty system. These also offer all facilities needed for cooking and sleeping. They are all unique and different from each other but offer both sleeping and living quarters and a service area for rubbish and outhouses.
- In **fully catered (*betjent*)** huts or lodges you can expect full, good-quality catering for breakfast and dinner with the opportunity to prepare a lunch to take along for the day (for a fee, unless you opt for the full-board option). These cabins rarely offer the opportunity to self-cater. In some of the more popular areas, such as Jotunheimen and Rondane, there are mostly fully catered cabins in the mountains. The amenities at these huts are also generally more extensive. There is 220V electricity and often running water for shower and washroom facilities.

The beds and mattresses in all cabins come with quilts and pillows, and use of your own sleeping liner with pillow cover or sleeping bag is compulsory. If you don't have a liner with you, you can generally buy one in fully catered cabins. Additional bedding quilt covers and towels can be hired there for a fee as well.

Booking is possible and often encouraged. Some very popular huts will be fully booked weeks in advance between mid July and mid August (for example Rondvassbu, Gjendesheim and Spiterstulen), so if you know your itinerary you should book ahead. This can be done by directly contacting the relevant hut or on the DNT website. Booking is now compulsory for the Fannaråki mountain hut in Jotunheimen (Route 3). Alternatively, you can book as you move from one hut to the next, if you are hiking between fully serviced cabins. The wardens will do this for you if you wish. Bookings will be held until 7pm on the evening of the day of arrival.

No-one who wants to stay the night in a DNT hut will be sent away. However, while there is a guarantee that you can stay in the hut, there is no guarantee of a bed as these are given out ultimately at the discretion of the hut wardens and according to need. You can be assured, though, that they will do their utmost to accommodate everyone in relative comfort – even if this means tidying up the utilities room and laying out mattresses for guests in there!

In addition to the sleeping quarters that contain mostly bunkbeds, the huts often have lofts with a number of mattresses that can be laid out to make room for everybody. This is generally enough, but on some occasions the living room of a hut might also have some hikers sleeping on the sofas and the floor.

DNT membership

The vast majority of mountain huts are operated by the DNT. It is very advantageous to take out membership of the DNT when coming to hike in Norway. Membership can be ordered online and an app allows for your membership card to be on your smartphone if you wish. The annual fee is dependent on age and family composition – see https://english.dnt.no/join.

Members enjoy substantial discounts on accommodation, fees and food. After about four days of hiking the yearly membership fee will have paid for itself. In addition, discounts are available for private commercial accommodation associated with the DNT, the Norwegian rail card, and even some sports stores.

Staying at a DNT hut

When arriving at a fully serviced and staffed or commercial hut, the 'check-in' is much the same as in a hotel. A room is assigned according to the number of people in the party, the expected number of arrivals, etc. This might or might not be a private room. You will get advice on when breakfast and dinner are served, what is on the menu and other relevant information, such as electricity points and rubbish segregation. Payment is generally only possible by debit or credit card; cash payments are typically discouraged. Upon leaving, guests are obliged to leave the bed as found and generally tidy after themselves.

In non-staffed huts the system is a bit different. While most huts are unlocked, many are not and you will need the universal DNT key to open them (if you are the first to arrive) and lock them (if you are the last to leave). It is a simple universal key that fits the lock on the main entrance of these huts. The key can be ordered online at the DNT's webshop (www.dntbutikken.no) for 100 NOK plus postage, or you can get one in person from a local DNT office, for example in Oslo, Stavanger or Trondheim. You can usually also get it at the main fully staffed DNT mountain huts. Note that you need to be a DNT member in order to get the key. The 100 NOK is a deposit that you get back when you return the key at one of the DNT offices. For further information on how to get and use the key, see https://english.dnt.no/the-dnt-key.

Appendix B has an overview of the huts in this guide that require a DNT key at the time of writing (additionally refer to https://ut.no for up-to-date information).

Hikers resting at Trollheimshytta (Route 7, Stage 1)

Upon arrival, you are obliged to first write yourself into the hut's registration book, including information on where you came from that day and where you are heading next. Only once this is done do you have the right to stay and use the facilities. Then you can go and choose a sleeping quarter or go to your room/bed if you have made a prior reservation. Before leaving, guests must fill out a separate form for payment, including a list of items, if any, taken from the pantry over the course of your stay. You provide payment information (credit card number, address, phone number) and the form is deposited in a safety deposit box. Expect to be charged between two to six weeks later. It is a wonderfully efficient honesty system. At the time of writing, this paper-based payment system is being phased out and an app-based system is taking its place (look for 'DNT Hyttebetaling' on Android and iOS).

When staying in a non-staffed cabin, all guests take care of the amenities together. Often water has to be brought in from a nearby stream or lake, the kitchen has to be shared and arrangements need to be made to accommodate each other's needs. You should clean up fairly quickly after cooking, especially during busy times. While the bigger huts have plenty of pots and pans, cutlery and crockery, it might all be in use. Before leaving the hut, you should sweep and wash the floors of your sleeping quarter, and the common areas also need to be tidied, swept and floors washed. This involves some agreement between the different parties. Aim to leave the hut in slightly better shape than you found it. As long as everybody pitches in, these wonderful huts that sit in the most glorious places can stay viable and will keep welcoming generation after generation of hikers.

Some self-service huts might have a 'cabin warden' during the busy summer season. This guardian is a volunteer that keeps an eye out to make sure everyone is comfortable.

They are often very knowledgeable about the area and the terrain, so will always be a great source of information and will likely have access to the weather forecast. They have the authority to assign rooms and organise the duties around the hut. In other huts a sheet of paper may indicate which rooms should be doing which task (fetch water, attend to the fire, sweep, wash different areas, etc).

Be aware that most huts follow a system of separating rubbish. It is likely you will have to segregate glass and metal, plastic, bio and paper rubbish into different bins. Each hut has a service area where these can be found.

Drying rooms

All serviced huts have a separate drying room that is heated and where you can dry your clothes and equipment. They are a fabulous amenity that you are likely to use at least once. In the self-serviced and unserviced huts, drying takes place in the main room that is heated by a wood-fired stove.

Camping

It is perfectly possible to pitch a tent while hiking in Norway, thanks to the public right of access (see https://english.dnt.no/public-right-of-access). In practice, if you want to pitch your tent close to one of the mountain huts a 150m distance from the hut and its amenities has to be observed. It is also possible to use the facilities of the mountain huts during the day only. This involves a lower fee than staying the night.

Many of the fully catered cabins also offer the option for camping on their grounds with the use of the facilities for a fee that is lower than that for a bed in a dorm. In this case you can also use your camping equipment for cooking your meals. This allows for a stay in the mountains on a much lower budget. The camping fee includes the use of all facilities, such as the drying room, living room, toilets and showers as well as the option to charge your electronic devices.

The many lovely camping spots invite an extra day at leisure, as seen here on Route 5, Stage 4

EQUIPMENT

Norwegian weather in summer is variable and you need to be prepared for this. At the same time, the treks presented in this guide allow you to stay in the wonderful DNT huts along the way, meaning you are not obliged to take a tent, sleeping bag and cooking equipment with you. Your basic backpack should ideally weigh no more than 8–12kg.

Temperatures in summer can be near zero on the high mountaintops such as Galdhøppigen, and can occasionally exceed 30°C in Lysefjorden. As in all mountainous areas, always be prepared for rapid changes in the weather.

The following list covers the basics; anything more is of course down to personal preference:

- An upper-body underlayer of both long- and short-sleeved wool
- A pair of woollen longjohns
- A warm fleece or down jacket
- A pair of long, relatively warm hiking trousers
- Shorts
- Breathable waterproof jacket and trousers
- A warm beanie, scarf and gloves
- Sunhat and sunglasses
- Woollen socks will keep your feet warm even when they're damp
- A good pair of comfortable ankle-high waterproof hiking boots is highly recommended for the treks in this guide
- Gaiters are also recommended
- Comfortable clothes and footwear (such as Crocs or sandals) for the evenings in the huts
- Nightwear
- A sleeping liner for the beds in the huts (this is compulsory); you cannot always rent one, so best to bring your own
- A headlamp is recommended in order to find your way to the hut's outhouse at night
- A towel and basic toiletries
- Sunscreen, mosquito repellent and a tick remover, as well as a basic first aid kit
- Map(s), map holder and compass
- DNT key (see 'Staying at a DNT hut', above)
- Consider investing in a waterproof phone case if yours isn't waterproof – especially if you're dependent on it for navigation and bookings
- Water bottle or bladder and a thermos
- A 45L backpack should cover the above; larger if you want to take more gear like a sleeping bag, books, camera, extra food, spare clothes – and of course if you choose to take a tent
- Waterproof backpack cover (and bear in mind most huts have an excellent drying room where wet and sweaty gear can be hung out for the night)
- A pair of lightweight hiking poles is recommended

For more information go to https://english.dnt.no and search for

On top of Veslesmeden, with (right to left) Rondslottet, Høgronden, Midtronden and Digerronden in the background (Route 5, Extension 2)

'summer hiking gear list'; you'll find an easy-to-follow, tried-and-tested checklist for packing.

WATER, FOOD AND SUPPLIES

At the time of writing it is safe to drink water from the streams that you encounter on the way while hiking. Look for fast-flowing brooks or streams, filtered by a bit of vegetation. Don't take water directly from glacial streams (it contains 'rock flour', which is unpleasant to drink and may contain bacteria), and keep an eye out for animals that might contaminate water sources. You can refill your bottle easily on most hikes; exceptions are stated in the route descriptions.

En route to the hiking areas in the national parks you will pass larger towns or villages. Their supermarkets and often bakeries, cafés and increasingly also sports and outdoors stores are open every day during the summer season. This makes it easy to stock up on food and supplies if needed. Smaller villages and hamlets generally don't have any shopping facilities, but gas stations often have a small convenience store section for a basic supply of snacks.

The fully serviced cabins will have a selection of snacks for sale, such as nuts and chocolate, and provide lunch packages. If you are staying in a self-serviced hut you can buy supplies to take along your treks from the pantry in the hut.

MONEY

The Norwegian currency is called the Norwegian krone (NOK). As at November 2019, £1 equates to roughly NOK 12, €1 to NOK 10, and USD$1 to NOK 9. Norwegians are moving towards a virtually cashless society and are used to paying everything by debit or credit card, even small amounts. In some villages it is not even possible to get cash as there are no ATMs. Credit cards are accepted in all the lodgings described in this guide, including self-serviced and unserviced ones. More and more bank offices are disappearing from the high street in Norway; don't always expect to be able to access one. Therefore, it is advised to bring a small amount of cash with you (some lockers at railway stations still operate on coins) but to rely on your debit/credit card for most transactions.

Norway is not the place for a budget holiday and it is best to get an idea of your likely expenditure before setting out, to avoid unpleasant surprises. At the time of writing, staying in the fully catered cabins covered in this guide will cost between NOK 800 and NOK 1200 per person per night for accommodation with full board (2019 season; consult the DNT website for up-to-date information). This does not include incidentals like alcohol or snacks. A pint of beer will cost NOK 80–100, with a similar price for a glass of wine.

LANGUAGE

Norway has three official languages: two Norwegian languages and a Sámi language that is spoken by the indigenous population. The Norwegian languages are Bokmål and Nynorsk, but every county has its own dialects as well. This can lead to confusion in the writing and pronunciation of town names, mountaintops, rivers, etc. The naming used throughout this book follows the names on the Nordeca maps which in turn are based on the official Kartverket (Norwegian Mapping Authority) names for places, rivers, mountains and so on – though even here there are occasional variations. Locally and in information brochures or other media, places may be spelled in different ways.

In addition, there may be more than one place of the same name. For example, there are many peaks called 'Troll's Head', in varying dialects and spellings. It is important to know in which municipality and county you are looking – details of these are given in the different chapters of the book. If in doubt, consult https://norgeskart.no as it will point out on the map where all the places are located and make finding the correct one easier.

When looking up places – for instance if you're booking bus tickets or consulting an online map – the spelling is important. As an example, the word for 'summer farm' is often used as a suffix for places and can be spelled in a variety of ways, such as *seter, sæter, setre, set* or *sætrin*. Paying attention to these details will make navigation of the online Norwegian resources a lot easier.

English is very widely spoken throughout Norway, so in general communication is not a problem if you speak English.

PHONES AND WI-FI

Many public places offer free Wi-Fi and almost all restaurants, cafés and shopping centres do as well. While hiking in the mountains, phone reception can be intermittent, with a better chance of reception the higher you go. Many lakes in the mountains are used for hydroelectric power generation and will have telecommunications as a result. In their vicinity you can expect to have mobile coverage; this will be 3G or 4G. In the mountain cabins there is generally no Wi-Fi and often there is no mobile reception either. The staff in some lodges do have Internet access and can provide up-to-date weather information.

SAFETY

While all the treks are only a day's hike away from a hut, you still need to be aware of the potential risks. Good preparation and awareness of your surroundings mitigates most of the risks that are due to the terrain or weather. Recognising the signs of exhaustion, keeping hydrated and warm, and taking some high-calorie food rations along should keep you fit and able to complete the hike in safety. The DNT publishes the Norwegian Mountain Code containing a set of nine down-to-earth and sensible rules to follow for safe trips:

- Plan your trip and inform others about the routes you have selected
- Adapt your planned routes according to ability and conditions
- Pay attention to the weather and avalanche warnings
- Be prepared for bad weather and frost, even on short trips
- Bring the necessary equipment so you can help yourself and others
- Choose safe routes. Recognise avalanche terrain and unsafe ice
- Use a map and a compass. Always know where you are
- Don't be ashamed to turn around
- Conserve your energy and seek shelter if necessary

The delta of the Muru river as it flows into Gjende lake; the Nørdre Tjønhollet hanging valley and glacier with cascading stream opposite (Route 1, Stage 2/Route 2, Stage 1)

Weather

Snow on the path is certainly a risk when hiking in early summer and autumn. Many parts of Rondane and Jotunheimen have snowfields that may last all year round and need to be crossed. In early summer, the snow will hide gaps and cracks, and melt-water streams run under it, hidden by thin snow bridges. Be aware of this danger and use a walking pole to probe tricky conditions.

Norwegian mountains experience the same variability of weather as any other high mountain region. Fog, high winds, rain and even snow can move in more quickly than forecasted at any time of year. Sunny summer days can be surprisingly hot, and the long hours of sunlight make for higher-than-expected exposure to sunburn and dehydration. Be prepared for warm and cold, sun and rain on any day.

For up-to-date and local weather information, consult www.yr.no. This service, with an English option available, offers extensive information, including from mountaintops as many peaks have weather stations in their vicinity.

River crossings

In early summer, or after prolonged periods of rain, high levels of water in waterways are common. The more significant waterways on the marked paths have bridges to cross over them. Many bridges are removed before the winter snow and replaced after the

Crossing the Urdadøla requires some careful balancing (Route 2, Stage 6)

snow has melted, once conditions allow. Some minor waterways might become significant after rains, so caution is always needed. Never cross if in doubt; instead search for a place upstream to cross safely.

Stream crossings occur on virtually every hike described in this book, and are generally done without difficulty by rock-hopping. A set of poles can come in handy for balance, and may be essential for some of the deeper, faster-flowing streams. Wading is only called for occasionally. The advice when wading is to either put on sandals, if you have them, or to take your socks off, wade in your hiking boots and put on the dry socks afterwards to warm your feet. Wading in bare feet is risky, as you could easily injure yourself, but more importantly you'll lose feeling (and balance) in your feet fairly quickly due to the cold water. The hike descriptions highlight the more difficult crossings, but yearly rainfall varies and therefore conditions of the streams could differ from those described.

Pests

Mosquitos and midges are present in early summer and can be a source of much irritation, but they do not carry any diseases in Norway. Early summer, shortly after the snowmelt, is the worst time for these. Using mosquito repellent and wearing long sleeves – especially at dusk – can be useful, and if you are very sensitive a hat with a netting might be worthwhile.

Unfortunately, ticks that carry Lyme and other diseases are spreading into Norway. Precautions (repellent, long sleeves) are similar, but in addition it is important to check yourself regularly, especially if hiking through forests. Take a tick remover (typically available at your local drugstore or pharmacy) and read the instructions for how to use it. For more information, see for example the website of the Mountaineering Council of Scotland: www.mountaineering.scot.

The common viper (adder) is the only venomous snake in Norway. It is a passive animal though, and will only strike if it feels threatened. In early summer it might occasionally be found on the trails as the bare earth is warmer than ground with vegetation. The noise and vibrations you make while walking will generally scare the snake away. In the rare case that you are bitten by a viper, you should seek medical attention.

EMERGENCIES

The Norwegian emergency numbers vary for different emergencies. Call 113 for a medical emergency, 110 for fire and major accidents, 112 for the police and rescue operations. There is a comprehensive acute rescue service in Norway and it includes helicopter rescue in the mountains. There is no charge for this service. The Norwegian Air Ambulance Foundation (Norsk Luftambulanse) provides a useful app – 'Hjelp 113' (English version available) – from which calls to all emergency numbers can be made. It provides the operator with important location data in case of a call. For non-life-threatening situations you can contact the local doctor on duty on 116 117, out of normal business hours. Norway has reciprocal healthcare agreements with EU countries; otherwise take appropriate travel insurance.

Be aware that mobile coverage in the mountains is not a given on the hikes presented in this book. Take your own precautions and be prepared.

USING THIS GUIDE

The remainder of this guide is divided into chapters covering the areas of Jotunheimen, Rondane, Dovrefjell, Trollheimen and Ryfylke. Each

The Lysefjord as seen from Bakken (Route 10, Stage 6)

chapter introduces the area in question, giving details of access and other useful information for the subsequent multi-day treks. The routes range from shorter outings that can be done in a long weekend, for example, to expeditions that last five to eight days.

Each route is introduced with some statistical information such as total length, number of days needed to complete it, total ascent and descent. The introductory text gives an overview of the highlights and character of the route and its daily stages, potential extensions, shortenings and other relevant information. Each stage of the route is then described, beginning with start and finish location, total length, duration, ascent and descent as well as maps and height profile. This is followed by an introduction to the stage, and then a detailed description of the trail including points of interest. Features that are included on the map extracts are shown in **bold** in the route description, to aid orientation.

Many routes can be combined to shorten or lengthen your trekking itinerary, and great care has been taken in giving options to extend and combine routes across areas with minimal road transfers.

Grading of hikes and stage timings

There is no consistent scale or set of parameters that is used to grade hikes in Norway across organisations. The Norwegian Trekking Association (https://english.dnt.no) publishes guidelines for guided treks or day trips, while https://ut.no, the online portal for hikes, has its own grading system (although with the recent redevelopment of the site the system seems to be in flux). In addition, official tourism information sites like www.fjordnorway.com publish their own guidelines. All the while, signposts found on the trail will have some colour coding (blue, red and black – for ascending difficulty) to advise the hiker, but with no explanation given for the rationale. Due to this situation, the grading provided in this guide is the author's own, based on information such as **length** (total distance) and **total vertical distance** (being the sum of total ascent and descent during the hike) and the experience of having actually been there.

- **Easy:** the hike is short and terrain is not difficult; length is under 10km and total vertical distance under 500m.
- **Moderate:** the hike's total vertical distance is between 500m and 1500m and the route is no more than 20km long, while the path can be rocky but without scree and there are few streams to be crossed.
- **Challenging:** the hike is for experienced walkers with good stamina. It is typically less than 20km in length and the total vertical distance is above 750m and typically under 2000m. The path involves open terrain, rocky, scree or rugged mountains as well as the crossing of streams, traversing of steep slopes, or long stretches of both loose rock and marshland. There can be multiple ascents and challenges as well as precipitous and exposed sections. The path can include technical challenges that require some scrambling.
- **Very challenging:** the hike is for experienced hikers with good stamina, maps and compass skills. Good-quality gear and sturdy hiking boots are important. The total vertical distance is between 1500m and 3000m and the length of the hike is up to 25km. Any number of streams may be crossed and the route typically includes summit trips with steep ascents/descents on uneven paths. The paths can have precipitous and exposed sections and passages where scrambling is required.

The grading needs to be taken together with the descriptions given for the hikes, where the detail provided gives a better understanding of the demands and challenges than the grading alone. The stated hiking times are without any stops for resting, photography or orientation. Walking speeds are very individual and can vary considerably along the route. Plan for some extra time. The long summer days do help with this, as the danger of having to walk in the dark is reduced.

GPX tracks

GPX tracks for the routes in this guidebook are available to download free at www.cicerone.co.uk/975/GPX. A GPS device is an excellent aid to navigation, but you should also carry a map and compass and know how to use them.

JOTUNHEIMEN

In the Visdalen valley, looking towards Kyrkja and Tverrbytthornet (Route 2, Stage 5)

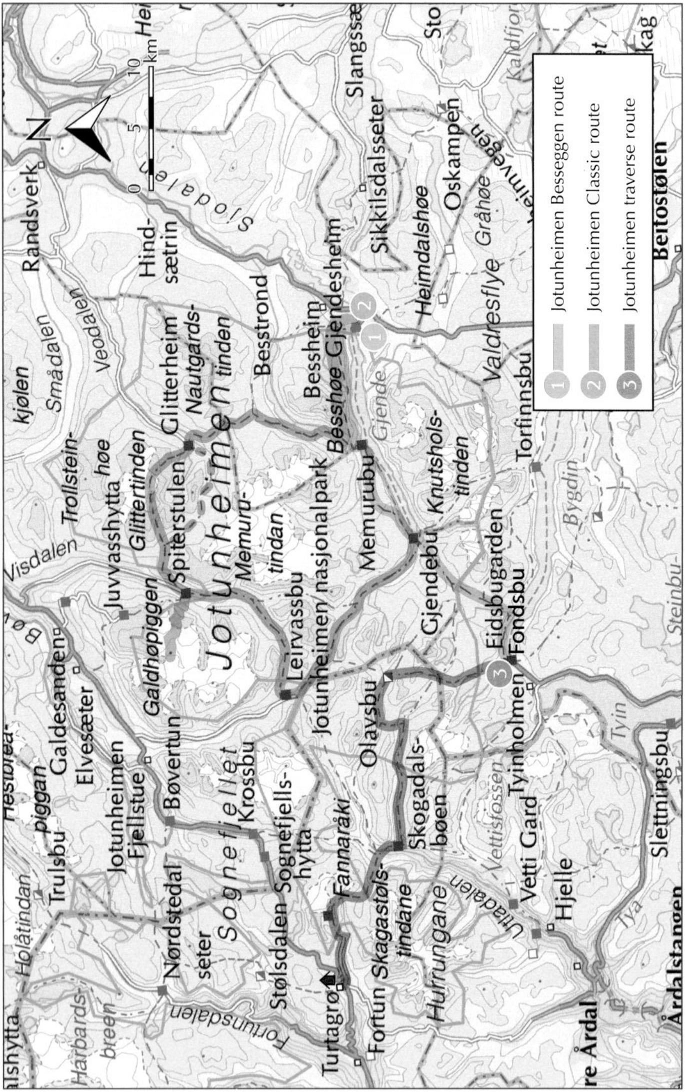
N
0
5
10
km
Jotunheimen Besseggen route
Jotunheimen Classic route
Jotunheimen traverse route
Randsverk
Hind-
sætrin
Sjodalen
Smådalen
Veodalen
Glitterheim
Nautgards-
tinden
Besstrond
Bessheim
Besshøe
Gjendesheim
Sikkilsdalsseter
Heimdalshøe
Oskampen
Gråhøe
Valdresflye
Torfinnsbu
Gjende
Knutsholstinden
Memurubu
Memurutindan
Jotunheimen nasjonalpark
Jotunheimen
Gjendebu
Eidsbugarden
Fondsbu
Bygdin
Tyinholmen
Tyin
Slettningsbu
Beitostølen
Olavsbu
Leirvassbu
Spiterstulen
Juvvasshytta
Glittertinden
Trollsteinhøe
Visdalen
Galdhøpiggen
Galdesanden
Elvesæter
Bøvertun
Jotunheimen Fjellstue
Krossbu
Sognefjellet
Sognefjellshytta
Fannaråki
Skogadalsbøen
Skagastølstindane
Hurrungane
Utladalen
Vettisfossen
Vetti Gard
Hjelle
Årdalstangen
Øvre Årdal
Turtagrø
Fortun
Fortunsdalen
Stølsdalen
Nørdstedal seter
Trulsbu
Holåtindan
Harbardsbreen

Jotunheimen is beyond doubt the most alpine and finest mountain hiking area in Norway, and one of the best known internationally. It is home to the highest peak in Norway and Northern Europe – Galdhøpiggen (2469m) – with Glittertinden (2457m) a close second. Both summits are famed for their stunning views. The name itself, Jotunheimen ('home of the giants'), alludes to this, as well as to the Norwegian mythology around wild landscapes and the imaginary creatures that roam them in search of humans. Around 150 other peaks reach above the 2000m mark, making Jotunheimen the densest agglomeration of summits in Scandinavia.

Jotunheimen lies in central Southern Norway, approximately 300km north of Oslo. The region measures around 65km by 55km and is mostly part of the county of Oppland, with a smaller area belonging to the county of Sogn og Fjordane. In the south, the lakes of Bygdin and Tyin form a natural barrier, and in the west lie the Lustrafjord and Årdalsfjord, both arms of the long Sognefjord. In the east the fertile valleys of Sjødalen and to the north Bøverdalen form a natural frontier.

Part of Jotunheimen, covering $1151km^2$, has been declared a national park, and this is the area on which the hikes in this section are focused. With 50 marked routes in the national park and another 70 routes in the neighbouring areas, Jotunheimen offers a great many hiking options.

The first known visitor to Jotunheimen was the botanist Christen Smith in the early 19th century. Norway was at that time under the Danish crown, and Smith was directed by the Danish king to map the flora of Southern Norway's alpine regions. Few other scientists made the journey into Jotunheimen during this period.

Interestingly, the artists of the Romantic era in Norway put Jotunheimen on the map as a magnificent landscape for the exploration of nature's wonders and forces. These Romantic artists sought to express personal feelings and emotions – a new and novel aspect in art at that time. They immersed themselves in landscapes that would by their untamed and wild nature inspire feelings of both terror and awe. At the same time they sought to capture the uniqueness of these landscapes to create a collective national identity for a country that was still in the process of gaining sovereignty. The paintings by Hans Gude, which can be admired in the National Museum in Oslo, are a fine example of this endeavour. Some other artists are also well known, like the poet Vinje, who is said to have coined the name Jotunheimen; Edvard Grieg, the composer who captured Jotunheimen's local melodies in his *Norwegian Folk Songs*; and not to forget Henrik Ibsen, who described the Besseggen ridge in his *Peer Gynt* play. Together these artists effectively pioneered hiking as a national pastime. While most of us will not have a claim to such fame, Jotunheimen's landscapes are bound to captivate us all. Today Jotunheimen is sought as a hiking destination by people from around the world.

LANDSCAPE AND GEOLOGY

The variety in landscapes is unparalleled, with many characteristics of glacial landscapes visible to the attentive hiker. Jotunheimen still has more glaciers than any other area in Norway: in total they cover about 200km^2. They feed the many lakes and streams on the plateaus in-between the lofty peaks, thus giving the water its characteristic emerald-green colour. During the Quaternary period (roughly the past 2.5 million years), these glaciers formed the landscape we see today. Sometimes they flowed slow and steady, forming wide, open U-shaped valleys like Veodalen around Glitterheim (Route 2, Stage 2), or Leirdalen around Leirvassbu (Route 2, Stage 5); other times they created cols or arêtes like the spectacular Besseggen ridge (Route 1, Stage 1), or pyramid-shaped horns like Kyrkja mountain near Leirvassbu (Route 2, Stage 5). In the Hurrungane massif (seen from Route 3), glaciers forged cirques with sharp, spiky peaks that are less suited to hiking but form the centre of Norway's climbing community. The paths will lead you over the rocky remnants of glacial moraines and past hanging valleys with rivers falling in majestic waterfalls down into the main valley.

PLANTS AND WILDLIFE

Imposing as the geological features may be, the valleys also teem with an incredible diversity of plants, insects and birdlife. No other area of Norway offers as much in terms of variety and contrasts as Jotunheimen. You can be hiking around wind-swept, glacial peaks, whose rocks

Crossing the Skautflye plateau (Route 2, Stage 3A)

Reindeer like the coolness of the snow on a warm day

don't even support lichen growth, only to arrive later at a hut in a valley so lush and full of insects and birds that it looks like a fairy-tale garden. Meanwhile, the population of mammals here consists of mostly small rodents. Common are the lemmings that hurry past along paths. Their highly variable population has given rise to stories and myths since the middle ages. This variability is still not well understood, but in years with many lemmings, all predatory birds have a high chance of healthy offspring. A rare find is the *bjørkemusa*, a small type of mouse and the strangest of all. It hibernates, meaning its temperature drops to 1°C and its heart rhythm becomes irregular and as low as 6 beats/min. Larger predatory mammals such as weasels or wolverines are practically extinct in Jotunheimen. Reindeer in Jotunheimen are almost always domesticated. There are about 2000 individuals and it is quite possible to observe them from nearby.

ACCESS AND SERVICES

The main villages and towns that provide connections to Jotunheimen's mountain huts in the area covered in this guide are Fagernes, Lom, Tyinkrysset and Otta. Otta, Lom and Fagernes have an excellent range of shops for groceries and sports equipment as well as services including banking and medical.

Figure 1 shows a schematic overview of public transport options into Jotunheimen. With a little bit of planning, the area is surprisingly easy to access by train and bus.

Figure 1: Jotunheimen access

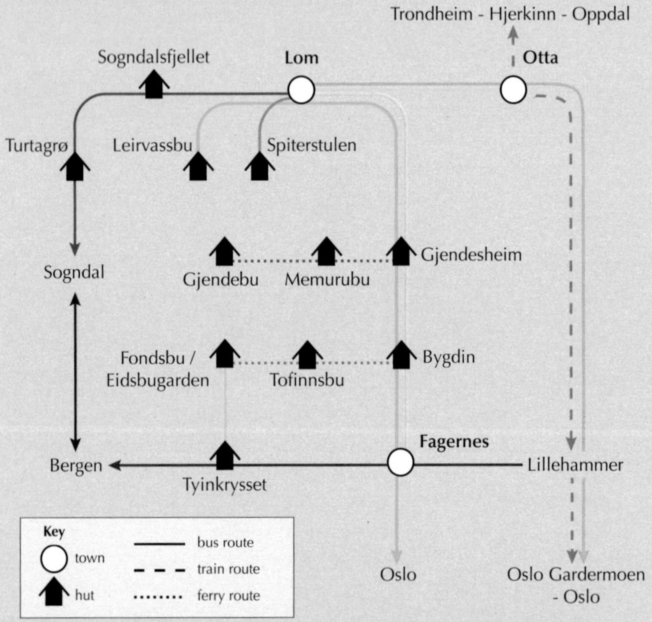

	Line	Connection
– – –	Oslo–Trondheim	Oslo–Gardermoen–Lillehammer–Otta–Trondheim
——	Valdresekspressen NW161	Oslo–Fagernes–Gjendesheim–Lom–(Leirvassbu)
——	Øst-VestXpressen NW162	Lillehammer–Fagernes–Bergen
——	Nordfjordekspressen VY146	Oslo–Gardemoen–Lillehammer–Otta–Lom
——	VY450 + R41/45	Sogndal–Voss–Bergen (bus + train)
——	200	Lom–Turtagrø–Sogndal
——	201	Lom–Spiterstulen
——	143/142	Otta–Lom–(Bismo)
——	137	Lom–Gjendesheim–Bygdin–Fagernes
——	300	Tyinkrysset–Fondsbu–Eidsbugarden
....	Gjendine	Gjende lake ferry
....	M/B Bitihorn	Bygdin lake ferry

The nearest train station is Otta, which is on the Trondheim–Oslo line and is serviced several times a day from both cities. The bus station (*skysstasjon*) in Otta is just outside the train station.

Two long-distance bus companies service the area: NOR-WAY Bussekspress (www.nor-way.no/en) through their long-distance bus lines Valdresekspressen and the Øst-VestXpressen; and Nettbuss (now VY; www.nettbuss.com) runs the VY146 from/to Oslo and the Sogndal to Bergen line.

Local transport

Innlandstrafikk (www.innlandstrafikk.no) is the regional bus company. Typically information on their summer routes appears on their website around February – in Norwegian only at the time of writing. Often regional buses will connect with the train from/to Trondheim/Oslo, boats on Gjende and Bygdin as well as long-distance buses. These connections are stated on the timetables. Since many of the local *'fjell* routes' operate only during the summer months, it is advisable to check details, particularly if you are planning to hike in the shoulder season. See Appendix C for further information on local transport.

Mountain huts

Access to the mountain huts that are relevant to the routes presented varies. The mountain huts of Gjendesheim, Spiterstulen, Leirvassbu, Fondsbu and Turtagrø can be reached by car and public bus. Glitterheim has a car parking lot a few kilometres away from the hut and hikers can rent bicycles to access the hut if they don't want to walk in. Be aware that daily charges

Fantastic views to be enjoyed at leisure (Route 1, Stage 3)

View from Hellerfossen into the valley of Storådalen, with Knutsholstinden and Mesmogtinden rising beyond (Route 2, Stage 6)

might apply for car parking, and that cars might attract a toll payment when access is by small private service road. Memurubu and Gjendebu can be reached by boat, while Olavsbu, Fannaråki and Skogedalsbøen can be reached on foot only.

Memurubu, Spiterstulen, Leirvassbu and Turtagrø are not DNT huts, but you are likely to get a discount as a DNT member. Note that prices are generally slightly higher in these privately run huts. Of all the huts, only Olavsbu, in the heart of Jotunheimen, is a self-serviced hut where you cater for yourself and where you need the DNT key to enter. All other huts are fully serviced. Note that Gjendesheim is one of the most visited DNT cabins in Norway – understandably, given its proximity to the spectacular Besseggen hike and its easy accessibility by car and bus. A reservation in the main season is recommended.

THE ROUTES IN JOTUNHEIMEN

Three Jotunheimen routes are presented in this guide. The Besseggen route (Route 1) takes in the famous Besseggen ridge, then continues along Gjende lake towards Bygdin lake: A short, flexible, but challenging introduction to the Jotunheimen national park. The 'classic' route (Route 2) is a six-day circuit bringing you across the highest tops and along the broad glacial valleys. Both this trek and the Besseggen can be extended with the traverse route (Route 3), which brings you across to the high peaks in the west of the national park. You should feel confident to either follow any of the routes as described or design your itinerary to suit your wishes. For example, Route 1 can be done in a long weekend, while combining Route 2 with Route 3 means you could be hiking for almost two weeks through pristine landscapes.

ROUTE 1

Jotunheimen Besseggen route

Start	Gjendesheim mountain hut
Finish	Fondsbu mountain hut
Distance	41km (25.5 miles)
Ascent	2060m
Descent	1990m
Time	3 days
Extensions	Connects to Route 3 after Stage 3
Variations	The route can be shortened to a one- or two-stage hike by exiting after Stage 1 or 2 by boat back to Gjendesheim.

This route is a perfect introduction to Jotunheimen, especially if you are short on time. At only 4½hr by bus from Oslo, you can be enjoying the Oslo fjords in the morning and experience the Jotunheimen alpine mountains in the afternoon. The route can be exited or entered at any of its three stages, and it can be extended as well, giving a lot of flexibility. It features the famous and memorable Besseggen ridge, while also including much quieter stages, where the great panoramas of Jotunheimen's unique character of high alpine and snow-covered tops, lush and flowering valleys, and steep mountainsides with cascading waterfalls can be enjoyed. Among this wonderful nature stand some of the oldest and most characterful mountain huts in Norway.

The route starts with the unique 'vertigo hike' over the Besseggen ridge between Gjendesheim and Memurubu mountain huts. On a sunny day you'll see the Gjende and Bessvatnet lakes shimmering emerald-green and deep blue. Besseggen, with its spectacular panoramic views, is one of Norway's most famous hikes, and accordingly visited by many. Most hikers walk it in an easterly direction, climbing the ridge, but the author prefers the other direction. Provided you are vertigo-proof, the descent has better views and the significant advantage of going against the crowd. The second stage continues from Memurubu to Gjendebu at the western end of Gjende lake, a day in which you will likely meet far fewer hikers on the trail. Many vistas await you, including that across Gjende lake as well as the high mountain peaks and their various glaciers, such as Knutsholstinden (2341m) and Tjønnholstinden (2331m) – even the Hurrungane range (2406m) in the far west. There are two options for the descent to Gjendebu mountain hut: one is very steep with tight switchbacks that makes use of chains at times, while the other option is a gentler, longer valley walk. Day three of the route takes you to Fondsbu on Bygdin lake – the second large lake in Jotunheimen and just as mesmerising with its emerald-green colour. Along with superb alpine views, lovely meadows and a roaring waterfall, you end at one of the best possible Norwegian mountain huts for afternoon tea.

Access to Gjendesheim is by public express bus (Valdresekspressen) from Oslo or bus from Otta or Lom.

You can shorten this route, both at Memurubu and Gjendebu, by taking the boat on Gjende lake back to Gjendesheim, after Stage 1 or 2. Similarly, if you are prone to vertigo, you can skip the ridge walk and start at Memurubu instead. For boat timings and online tickets see www.gjende.no/en. Booking is recommended in season, and pre-booked ticket holders have priority for boarding. The trek also connects in Fondsbu (at the end of Stage 3) to the Jotunheimen traverse route (Route 3), allowing you to extend by four days. At Fondsbu you can exit by boat over Bygdin lake to Bygdin village (there's a regular summer boat service on the M/B Bitihorn – see https://jvb.no/en) and connect by bus to Oslo; or take the bus to Tyinkrysset for further connections (see Figure 1 for details).

STAGE 1

Besseggen ridge

Start	Gjendesheim mountain hut
Finish	Memurubu mountain hut
Distance	14km (8.75 miles)
Ascent	980m
Descent	965m
Difficulty	Challenging
Time	6hr
Maximum altitude	1743m
Map	Nordeca Jotunheimen Aust 1:50,000 Nr 2503

'Sheer and sharp as the blade of a scythe' (from *Peer Gynt*, by Henrik Ibsen). The hike over the Besseggen ridge is one of a handful of famous 'vertigo hikes' in Norway. The path on the narrowest section of the ridge is steep and airily exposed to Bessvatnet lake (300m below) and Gjende lake (700m below). It narrows to just a few metres in width. If you are happy to use hands and feet at times and are not afraid of heights, this is a once-in-a-lifetime hike and scramble. The views are nothing short of spectacular and unequalled anywhere else in Norway. It has become a popular hike, with around 30,000 visitors a year making the journey. Start early if you want to hike with less company.

In season (June to September), there are mostly day hikers. Most will take the morning boat from Gjendesheim to Memurubu and hike back, in order to climb rather than descend the ridge. The boat also acts as a baggage transport service for trekkers who would prefer to hike the ridge with only a daypack. It will drop your luggage at the quay in Memurubu (leaving it protected under canvas) for you to collect at the end of the hike. See www.gjende.no/en for details.

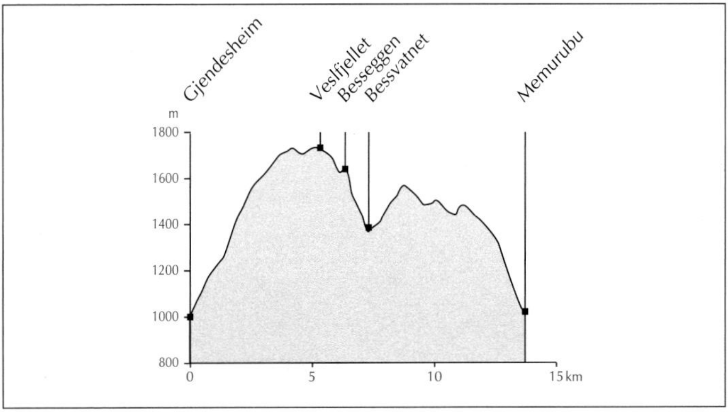

Exit **Gjendesheim mountain hut** and cross over the main service road. The path is well marked throughout. It goes straight and steeply up as you quickly leave behind low-level vegetation. After 1km a signpost marks the split of routes to Memurubu and Bessheim: continue the Memurubu trail, climbing towards the left.

The path ascends steadily for the next 3km, with chains provided at one point to help on slippery rocks. The terrain is covered by mosses and lichen, and the trail is mostly a gravel path. The path reaches the highest point of the stage, marked by a truly humongous cairn, at the top of **Veslfjellet** (1743m).

As you start walking down towards the Besseggen ridge it comes into view slowly, and then suddenly quite dramatically. The panoramic views on a sunny day are really unique and quite magnificent. The **Besseggen ridge** is an arrête and is only a few metres wide at its narrowest point, making it akin to walking on a knife's edge.

The colour of the waters of **Gjende** and **Bessvatnet lakes** give away their origins. Gjende, being fed by glaciers, is a green-and-emerald colour, while Bessvatnet is not glacier-fed and is therefore a deep blue. Bessvatnet is extremely low in nutrients, making it exceptionally clear with water visibility well above 25m.

The lakes are enclosed by high peaks jutting into the sky. Among them are Veslfjellet (1743m) and Besshøe (2258m) as well as Store Knutsholstinden (2341m) and Skarvflytindane (2154m), to name just a few. The rugged Hurrungane range is visible in the far west. Due to the differences in height and orientation, the microclimates around both lakes are quite different, giving rise to great contrasts in early summer, when Bessvatnet can still be frozen while Gjende lake has thawed.

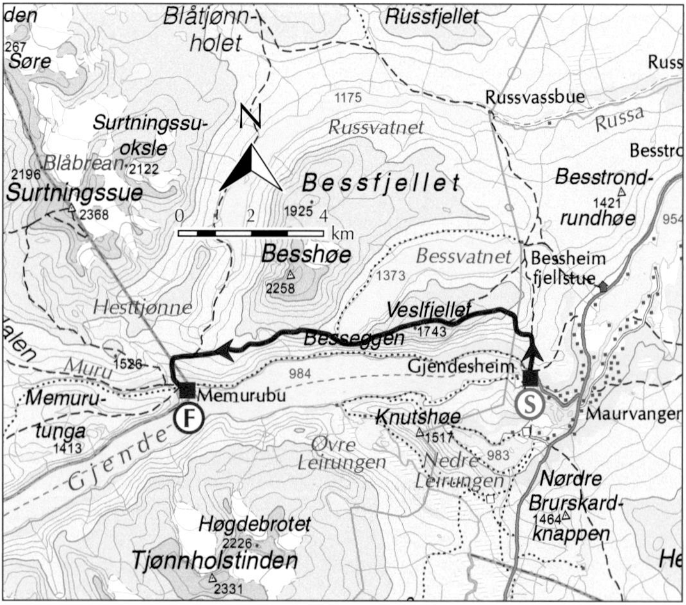

A 'T' marker on the Besseggen ridge

Descend the ridge with care until you reach the shore of **Bessvatnet lake** – a perfect spot for lunch or even a swim on a sunny day. Continuing west, the next 2km towards Memurubu takes you initially through undulating terrain, with a short sharp climb before you meet the signs to Glitterheim and Memurubu huts. As you continue towards Memurubu hut the trail narrows and steepens, especially over the last 2km. Having spent most of the day in the high alpine zone, you finish the hike through dense valley vegetation while descending into the valley and finally reaching **Memurubu**.

STAGE 2

Memurubu to Gjendebu

Start	Memurubu mountain hut
Finish	Gjendebu mountain hut
Distance	10.75km (6.75 miles)
Ascent	640m
Descent	660m
Difficulty	Challenging
Time	4hr
Maximum altitude	1484m
Map	Nordeca Jotunheimen Aust 1:50,000 Nr 2503

With sweeping views over an array of tops above 2000m in all directions, this hike is considered by some to be one of the finest in Jotunheimen. In good weather the Memurubu peaks show in-between their extensive glaciers and seem to be within reach. The descent to Gjendebu is steep and challenging, but this can be avoided by taking a longer route along Storådalen valley (adding 6km/2hr to the stage). Otherwise, this is a short and charming stage, with excellent waymarking making navigation easy.

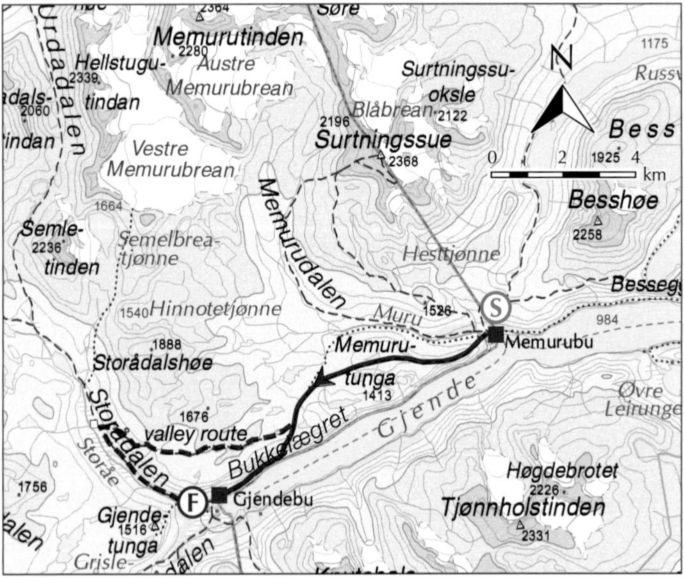

Leave the main hut at **Memurubu** and turn right (or if you arrived by boat, follow the dirt road up until you pass the entry gate to the property). At the signposts, go straight towards Gjendebu mountain hut and shortly after keep left (again this is signposted) to reach the bridge over the **Muru river**.

Pass an unmarked path that leads to the right along the river and continue on the main trail which goes straight up the Sjugurdtinden ridge. The last few metres might be a bit of a scramble. As you gain altitude you will have excellent views of the mountain hut and the milky glacial Muru river emptying into Gjende lake.

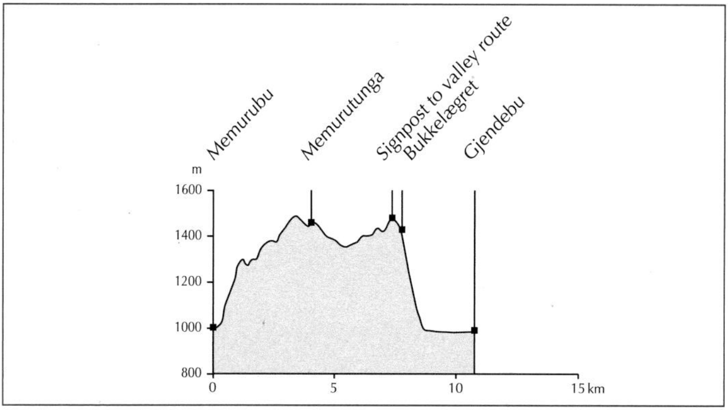

The path continues as a ridge walk, steadily climbing in a series of ups and downs, towards the **Memurutunga plateau**. A short 100m detour that rewards with wonderful views takes you off the marked trail at the highpoint, where you can enjoy truly sweeping panoramas to both the north and south over Memurutindane (2367m) and Surtningssue (2368m), Tjønnholstinden (2331m) and Knutsholstinden (2341m) with hanging glacial valleys over the Gjende lake.

View from the top of Bukkelægret along the lake towards Gjendebu

Over the next few kilometres the trail undulates gently, passing numerous picturesque lakes on the plateau. Ignore a trail on the right, signposted back to Memurubu, and continue straight as the last climb towards the Kjuklingen height begins. At the next signpost you have the choice to reach Gjendebu via the longer, gentler walk that goes down along the Storådalen valley, or tackle the steep descent to Gjendebu via the **Bukkelægret** trail. The valley route is a vertigo-safe alternative; it will add about 6km (2hr) to the day and is not further described here.

This trail drops over the next 500m of altitude in steep, tight switchbacks, with a few sections where you should make use of the secured chains. This can be quite challenging with heavy backpacks and care should be taken in rainy or icy conditions. The marked path is the only route down. Once this descent is behind you, it's a pleasant 2.5km walk along the shoreline to the **Gjendebu mountain hut**. Should you wish, you can leave Gjendebu by boat towards Memurubu or Gjendesheim mountain huts – see www.gjende.no/en for details.

Gjendebu is the DNT's oldest hiking lodge, built in 1871, and you can visit some of the historic buildings on the grounds. That same year, in 1871, a girl named Gjendine was born here. She spent many summers on the pastures throughout her 101 years, and she was persuaded by the Norwegian composer Grieg to sing her lullabies to him, so he could capture the melodies in one of his now best-known compositions.

STAGE 3

Gjendebu to Fondsbu

Start	Gjendebu mountain hut
Finish	Fondsbu mountain hut
Distance	15.75km (10 miles)
Ascent	440m
Descent	365m
Difficulty	Challenging
Time	5hr
Maximum altitude	1374m
Map	Nordeca Jotunheimen Vest 1:50,000 Nr 2505 and Nordeca Jotunheimen Aust 1:50,000 Nr 2503

This third and final stage, which stretches between Jotunheimen's two largest lakes, is a hike of medium difficulty with some more challenging sections. It is easy underfoot as you slowly climb the Veslådalen valley from Gjendebu. The hike then offers phenomenal views as you descend towards Bygdin lake, with a backdrop of the short but powerful Høystakka river thundering downwards. It is worth arriving in Fondsbu mountain hut in time for their delicious afternoon tea offerings of waffles with jam and sour cream or cinnamon buns.

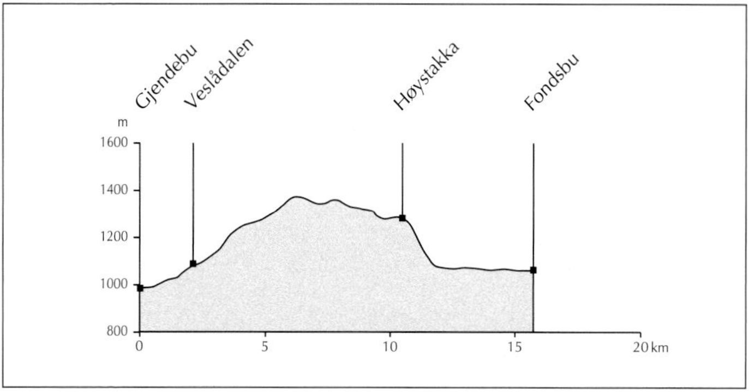

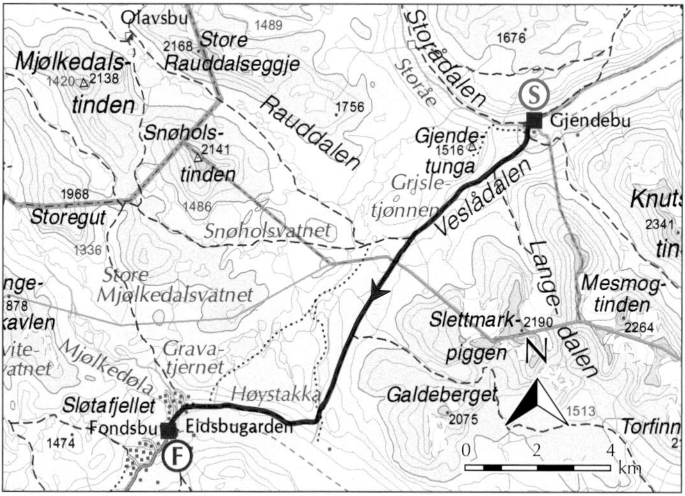

Leaving **Gjendebu mountain hut**, turn left to find a signpost, and take the left fork towards Fondsbu. Follow the path as it crosses the bridge and enters the meadows in the delta of the Storåe river. The few cattle that are often seen grazing in the distance are a reminder of the importance of these summer meadows for farmers in pre-industrial times.

At the next signposted fork, keep right and follow the trail through the dense valley vegetation. You'll pass many delightful campsites along the valley. Make sure to look behind you for wonderful views of Gjende lake, its steep walls and the many high mountains tops rising around it.

Continue gently uphill, heading towards a plateau and col at 1374m – the highest point of the stage. The path is easy going and well-marked; continue past various lakes and turnoffs to other mountain huts. After about 11km the path

Waterfall at Høystakka, high above Bygdin lake

Colourful meadows along the shores of Bygdin lake

crosses the **Høystakka river** over a suspension bridge, then it reaches the steep descent towards Bygdin lake. Fantastic views await at this point, with a roaring waterfall to the left-hand side of the path shortly after the start of the descent.

As you exit this hanging valley onto the north slopes of Bygdin lake, the descent path is initially steep and quite eroded in some sections. Shortly after the steep section you'll find yourself on a pleasant trail again, descending gradually at an angle to the slope towards the lake in a westerly direction.

The last few kilometres follow the contour of the lake. Here the path can be very muddy in places. In summer this last part of the trail takes you through meadows full of wildflowers, where the buzz of bees and other insects is palpable, before bringing you into **Eidsbugarden**.

Eidsbugarden is a small holiday village with its typically Norwegian *hyttes* (cabins) scattered on the mountainside. In the hamlet, a small museum commemorates the poet Vinje (1818–1870), who is said to have coined the name Jotunheimen – 'home of the giants'. He spent many summers hiking and writing in Eidsbugarden.

Follow the T-markings across a bridge and through the village to the **Fondsbu mountain hut**. If you're lucky, the excellent cook will delight her dinner guests with a performance of a beautifully melancholic Norwegian song before serving dessert.

This is the final stage of the Jotunheimen Besseggen route. You can transfer out either by public bus towards Tyinkrysset or by boat towards Bygdin. There you can pick up the Valdresekspressen bus line. Alternatively, you could continue hiking since Fondsbu is also the start of the Jotunheimen traverse route (Route 3).

ROUTE 2

Jotunheimen classic route

Start	Gjendesheim mountain hut
Finish	Gjendebu mountain hut
Distance	97km (60.5 miles)
Ascent	5220m
Descent	5225m
Time	6–7 days
Extensions	From Gjendebu: Route 1, Stage 2 in reverse to Memurubu, then boat to Gjendesheim; or Route 1, Stage 3 to Fondsbu and continue from there on Route 3
Variations	Day hike to Glittertinden with light pack, followed by low traverse to Spiterstulen – see Extension and Stage 3A

The Jotunheimen classic route takes in the three undisputed highlights of Jotunheimen National Park: the hike over the Besseggen ridge, as well as the peaks of Galdhøpiggen (2469m) and Glittertinden (2457m). There has long been debate about which of these summits is the higher of the two, due to the varying thickness of Glittertinden's icecap.

The route has 6–7 stages and almost forms a circle, starting at Gjendesheim mountain hut and ending at Gjendebu mountain hut, at opposite ends of Gjende lake. It begins with the Besseggen ridge hike and then heads into the northern part of Jotunheimen, where Norway's highest peaks await. Two magnificent U-shaped valleys enclose the Galdhøpiggen massif – Leirdalen and Visdalen – both of which are visited on this route. The combination of valley walks in which the high peaks can be savoured from below, and the high routes and ascents, provide the opportunity to enjoy and appreciate the diversity and contrasts in this enticing national park.

Stage 1 comprises the world-famous Besseggen ridge, which is becoming ever more popular among international tourists as well as being a locals' favourite. The long second stage to Glitterheim leaves any day hikers behind and immerses you in the 'home of the giants' as it proceeds amid hanging valleys and alongside large lakes and glacial streams. Two options are presented for the Glittertinden ascent in Stage 3: a full, rewarding but strenuous traverse to Spiterstulen is provided as the main option, while the alternative is a separate summit hike (Extension) to this very attractive peak, done with a light pack and involving a spectacular descent followed by a low route (Stage 3A) over a high alpine, glacial landscape towards Spiterstulen. This option adds an extra day to the route. Stage 4 is the ascent to the top of Norway and Scandinavia, scaling Galdhøpiggen as a day hike from Spiterstulen. Note that you could book a guided glacial tour and climb the mountain from the south in a small group and with a knowledgeable mountaineer instead – an option the author would not hesitate to recommend to those without a fear of heights. Stage 5 takes you along the Visdalen valley and into Leirdalen towards the Leirvassbu hut, which seems incredibly sandwiched in-between all the high peaks and glaciers surrounding it. The trek concludes with a hike to Gjendebu, one of Norway's oldest mountain huts, located in a centuries-old summer pasture. Here you get a glimpse into the life of the people living and working in remote and isolated places while tending to their animals, hunting or fishing to supplement their diets. From Gjendebu you connect by boat back to Gjendesheim mountain hut. (For boat timings and online tickets see www.gjende.no/en. Booking is recommended in season, and pre-booked ticket holders have priority for boarding.)

Except for Glitterheim, all huts can be reached directly either by public bus, car or boat, providing lots of flexibility. You can shorten the route after Stages 3–5 by taking public transport from Spiterstulen or Leirvassbu mountain huts respectively. There are a number of possibilities for extensions as well. From Gjendebu you could walk Route 1, Stage 2 in reverse to Memurubu and take the boat from there to Gjendesheim. You could also connect to Route 1, Stage 3 towards Fondsbu and continue from there on Route 3, which starts in Fondsbu and takes in the western and wildest part of Jotunheimen – the Hurrungane. By doing so, you can explore the whole of Jotunheimen in one grand tour.

STAGE 1

Besseggen ridge

Start	Gjendesheim mountain hut
Finish	Memurubu mountain hut
Distance	14km (8.75 miles)
Ascent	980m
Descent	965m
Difficulty	Challenging
Time	6hr
Maximum altitude	1743m
Map	Nordeca Jotunheimen Aust 1:50,000 Nr 2503

'Sheer and sharp as the blade of a scythe' (from *Peer Gynt*, by Henrik Ibsen). The hike over the Besseggen ridge is one of a handful of famous 'vertigo hikes' in Norway. The path on the narrowest section of the ridge is steep and airily exposed to Bessvatnet lake (300m below) and Gjende lake (700m below). It narrows to just a few metres in width. If you are happy to use hands and feet at times and are not afraid of heights, this is a once-in-a-lifetime hike and scramble. The views are nothing short of spectacular and unequalled anywhere else in Norway. It has become a popular hike, with around 30,000 visitors a year making the journey. Start early if you want to hike with less company. It is possible to have your backpack transported to the destination hut and hike with only a daypack.

In season (June to September), there are mostly day hikers. Most will take the morning boat from Gjendesheim to Memurubu and hike back, in order to climb rather than descend the ridge.

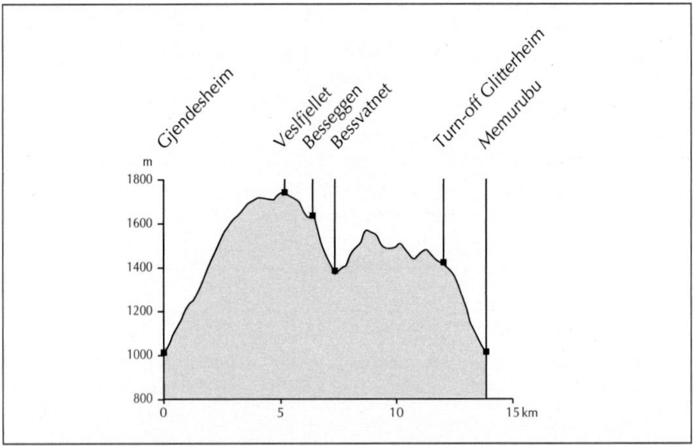

Exit **Gjendesheim mountain hut** and cross over the main service road. The path is well marked throughout. It goes straight and steeply up as you quickly leave behind low-level vegetation. After 1km a signpost marks the split of routes to Memurubu and Bessheim: continue the Memurubu trail, climbing towards the left.

The path ascends steadily for the next 3km, with chains provided at one point to help on slippery rocks. The terrain is covered by mosses and lichen, and

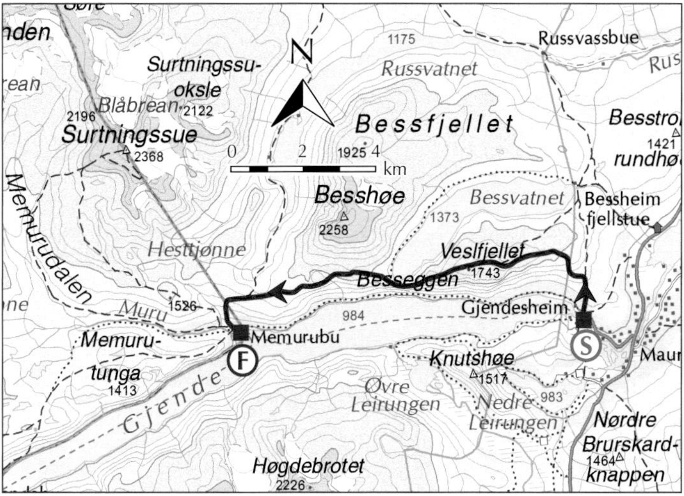

the trail is mostly a gravel path. The path reaches the highest point of the stage, marked by a truly humongous cairn, at the top of **Veslfjellet** (1743m).

As you start walking down towards the Besseggen ridge it comes into view slowly, and then suddenly quite dramatically. The panoramic views on a sunny day are really unique and quite magnificent. The **Besseggen ridge** is an arrête and is only a few metres wide at its narrowest point, making it akin to walking on a knife's edge.

The colour of the waters of **Gjende** and **Bessvatnet lakes** give away their origins. Gjende, being fed by glaciers, is a green-and-emerald colour, while Bessvatnet is not glacier-fed and is therefore a deep blue. Bessvatnet is extremely low in nutrients, making it exceptionally clear with water visibility well above 25m.

The lakes are enclosed by high peaks jutting into the sky. Among them are Veslfjellet (1743m) and Besshøe (2258m) as well as Store Knutsholstinden (2341m) and Skarvflytindane (2154m), to name just a few. The rugged Hurrungane range is visible in the far west. Due to the differences in height and orientation, the microclimates around both lakes are quite different, giving rise to great contrasts in early summer, when Bessvatnet can still be frozen while Gjende lake has thawed.

Bjørnbøltjønne lake with myrull *(cottongrass) flowers*

Descend the ridge with care until you reach the shore of **Bessvatnet lake** – a perfect spot for lunch or even a swim on a sunny day. Continuing west, the next 2km towards Memurubu takes you initially through undulating terrain, with a short sharp climb, and then past the idyllic Bjørnbøltjønne lake, before you meet the signs to Glitterheim and Memurubu huts. As you continue towards Memurubu hut the trail narrows and steepens, especially over the last 2km. Having spent most of the day in the high alpine zone, you finish the hike through dense valley vegetation while descending into the valley and finally reaching **Memurubu**.

STAGE 2

Memurubu to Glitterheim

Start	Memurubu mountain hut
Finish	Glitterheim mountain hut
Distance	20.75km (13 miles)
Ascent	1080m
Descent	700m
Difficulty	Very challenging
Time	8hr
Maximum altitude	1685m
Map	Nordeca Jotunheimen Aust 1:50,000 Nr 2503

Leaving Memurubu and the newly arriving visitors and hikers behind, you move into Jotunheimen's wide valleys, amid craggy peaks and glaciers, steep rock faces, lakes, rivers and waterfalls. The distance covered on this stage inevitably thins the crowds. As you arrive in Glitterheim you might be met by reindeer herds grazing in the Veodalen valley along the river, and you will certainly be met by Glittertinden, Norway's second highest mountaintop, towering above.

The path is generally well marked but is in redevelopment as you ascend from Russvatnet lake to cross over the Blåtjønnae river. Here a new bridge has been built. In the future, it looks like the path will climb gently from Russvatnet towards the bridge.

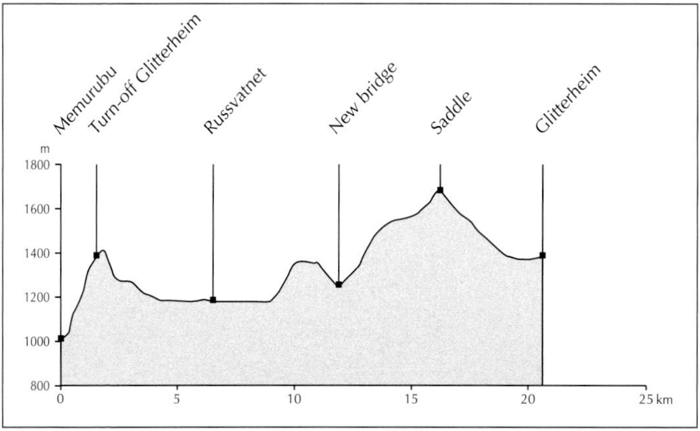

The hike starts with a sharp and steep ascent from **Memurubu mountain hut**. Leave the main building and turn right and right again after the gate. The path quickly ascends beyond the tree line and reaches a turnoff after 2km: left to Glitterheim, right to Besseggen. Turn left towards Glitterheim.

The trail veers to the northeast, descending into a wide U-shaped glacial valley with expansive views into the remote landscape. Find the path between rocks and gravel down towards Russvatnet lake, with Gloptinden (1678m) on your left and the Besshøe (2258m) and its glacier on your right. The trail can be muddy and boggy at times. On reaching the **lake**, the path is less well marked in places. Follow the shoreline to the Sundodden peninsula, which has a sandy beach and makes a beautiful pleasant lunch or camping spot.

The track continues along the lake for another kilometre. At the time of writing, the marked path leads you high up over Russvatnet lake and down again to meet the **new bridge**, after which you have to ascend again. A new trail under development appears to slowly ascend from the lake towards the new bridge.

The rumble of water can be heard from far away and soon becomes a roar as the trail nears the ravine of the wildly flowing **Blåtjønna river**. Its murky waters give away its glacial origins.

From the bridge it is a good 400m climb to the saddle between Vestre and Austre Hestlægerhøe – the highest point of today's stage. Initially the trail is narrow and relatively steep, leading up alongside the ravine, through heather and low vegetation. It levels off and broadens, and shortly afterwards it crosses boulder fields and quite possibly a minor snowfield to reach the saddle at 1685m.

Make sure to look back towards the **panorama** that is left behind. From the highest point, almost all of Russvatnet lake can be appreciated, along with the multitude of peaks around it. Rising high above the dark walls of the Bessfjellet range, Besshøe (2258m) comes into view. There's also Surtingssue (2368m) and Gloptinden (1678m), and to the north behind Russfjellet, Nautgardstinden (2258m). As you approach the highpoint and saddle, the Veotinden peaks and their glaciers appear as well. On perfect days, Galdhøpiggen (2469m) can be seen in the west.

Descend steadily on the other side of the saddle towards Glitterheim, with Glittertinden (2457m) towering above it. The views during the long, gradual descent into the landscape around the large and wide glacial valley of Veodalen are superb. The path is mostly rocky but no longer steep; the last section takes you eastwards of the mountain hut to a bridge crossing of the Veo river. From here it's a 10min walk to **Glitterheim**.

Bridge over the Veo river, with views into Veodalen and Veotinden and the Leirhøe peaks

EXTENSION

Glittertinden summit

Start/finish	Glitterheim mountain hut
Distance	11.75km (7.5 miles)
Ascent/descent	1140m
Difficulty	Challenging
Time	5hr
Maximum altitude	2457m (depending on snow height)
Map	Nordeca Jotunheimen Aust 1:50,000 Nr 2503
Note	This hike is exposed to potentially strong winds and is particularly dangerous in dense fog as the northern edge of Glittertinden is treacherous and can be icy at any time of the year. Do not attempt it in bad weather.

For many years Glittertinden was thought to be Norway's highest peak, and in times of significant snow it still steals the show from Galdhøpiggen. The underlying rock reaches 2452m, and during much of the 20th century the large icecap could measure up to 17m, making the top higher than that of Galdhøpiggen. In recent years, though, the icecap has diminished and is now less than 10m deep, making Glittertinden Norway's second highest peak at officially 2457m. Like Galdhøpiggen, it is relatively easy to access and therefore a much-loved summer hike.

Always ask for advice at Glitterheim mountain hut on snow and weather conditions before setting off. Snowcap conditions at the summit and at the Gråsubrean and Glitterbrean glaciers can vary; they may well change over time and therefore require special consideration. For the descent, either return the way you came or follow an unmarked path that lets you sledge down for a good 2km – an exhilarating and fun-filled ride. The path can be seen but is not marked by red T-markers; there are little stone cairns along the way. See below for the description of this unmarked path. Sledging is done at your own risk; make sure to enquire at the hut about snow conditions before attempting it. You can borrow a small plastic *akebrett* at Glitterheim for the ride.

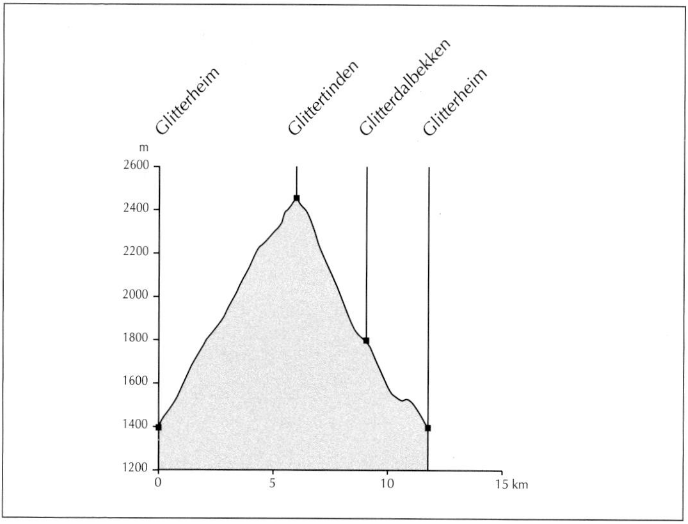

Start from the main building of Glitterheim mountain hut by turning left to the signpost, then turn right and go up the hill out of the valley. After a short ascent through the meadows you'll reach Nedre Steinbuvatnet lake. You can fill your water bottle here before leaving the meadows if necessary.

Follow the path as it veers in a northerly direction and the ground turns to rock and scree. Try not to veer left or right and lose the path; look for the T-markers ahead. Climb steadily, gaining 650m in elevation to reach the edge of the **Gråsubrean glacier**, your goal firmly in sight with its snow-covered peak jutting into the sky.

Once at Gråsubrean the **views** are already spectacular. The characteristically crescent-shaped Glittertinden towers ahead with its vast, expansive eastern slope giving way in a precipice into the glacier below. Glittertinden's cap is crowned by ice and snow overhanging the top, giving rise to a magnificent panoramic display of sky, snow and rock.

Typically, there will be snowfields to cross from Gråsubrean onwards all the way to the top. Many markers may therefore be snow-covered and invisible. Since it is a popular hike there will be a well-trodden path through the snowfields, but caution still needs to be exercised. Continue due west for another

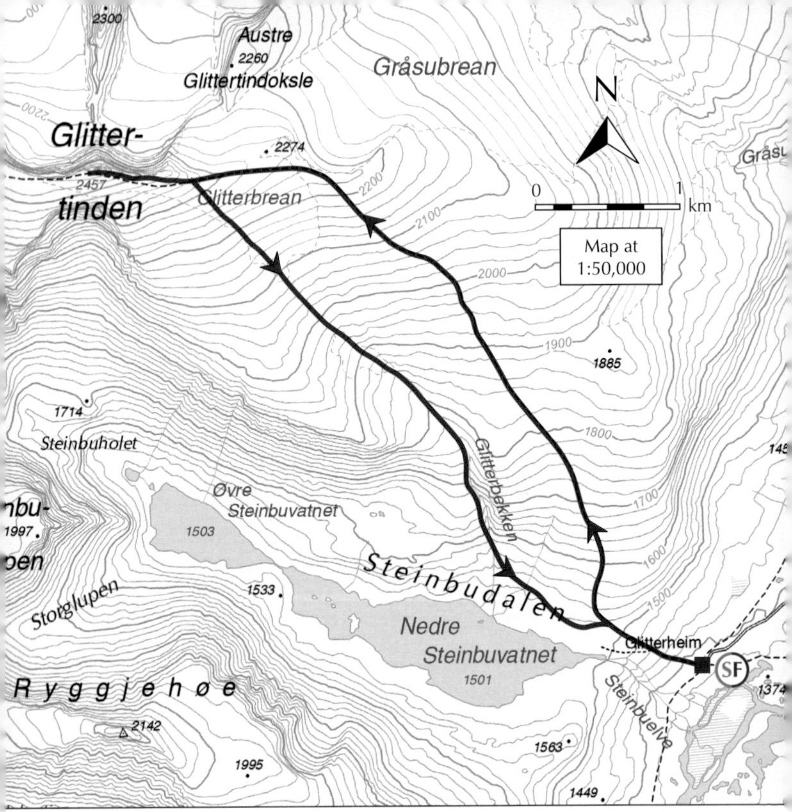

1.5km and about 200m of elevation along the ridge to the top of **Glittertinden**, keeping well clear of the northern overhang.

On a clear day you can see all of Jotunheimen to the south and west, almost like a glaciated seascape upon which its giant peaks show as islands – an utterly majestic and truly panoramic **view**. Towards the north you have views over Grotbrean and Gråsubrean onto Trollsteinhøe (2161m) and Gråhoe (2154m); to the east, the broad expanse of the Veodalen valley and Nautgardstinden (2258m); to the south, Surtningssue (2368m); and last but not least Galdhøpiggen (2469m) in the west. On a very clear day you will be able to see the impressive Hurrungane peaks behind Galdhøpiggen to the west, while on the eastern side the deep Gudbrandsdalen valley dominates the views and the Rondane massif can be glimpsed on the horizon.

From the top of Glittertinden, return the same way for about 700 metres, then turn right towards the valley and down Glitterbrean towards the western side of the Glitterbekken stream valley. The unmarked path runs parallel to the marked ascent and about 500 metres west of it. If there is sufficient snow you can slide down for about 500m of altitude and over 2km until you reach the Glitterbekken stream. Do brake properly before reaching the end of the snow-field! The unmarked path then follows Glitterbekken stream (keep it on your left) until it reaches Steinbudalen valley and Nedre Steinbuvatnet lake. (Being on the south side of Glittertinden, the Steinbudalen valley features a very mild microclimate that makes for comparatively lush meadows and vegetation.) Cross to the left side of the stream and continue on the unmarked path along Steinbudalen until the trail joins the marked path again, bringing you back down to Glitterheim.

Setting out towards Glittertinden, equipped with akebrett

STAGE 3

Glittertinden high traverse

Start	Glitterheim mountain hut
Finish	Spiterstulen mountain hut
Distance	15.75km (9.75 miles)
Ascent	1145m
Descent	1430m
Difficulty	Very challenging
Time	9hr
Maximum altitude	2457m (based on average height of snow cover of the top)
Map	Nordeca Jotunheimen Aust 1:50,000 Nr 2503
Note	This hike is exposed to potentially strong winds and is particularly dangerous in dense fog as the northern edge of Glittertinden is treacherous and can be icy at any time of the year. Do not attempt it in bad weather.

Going from Glitterheim over the top of Glittertinden towards Spiterstulen makes for a true Norwegian *topptur*. It is a strenuous stage that should only be done in the right weather conditions. Glittertinden is very exposed to wind, precipitation and fog; consider the low alternative Stage 3A in poor weather. The approach towards the moon-shaped crescent-top is incredibly photogenic and the views on top are expansive towards the southeast, into the county of Oppland and over Galdhøpiggen and the hundreds of other Jotunheimen peaks in the west. On descent, you might well be by yourself until you reach the crossroads with the low route towards Spiterstulen.

Start from the main building of **Glitterheim mountain hut** by turning left to the signpost, then turn right and go up the hill out of the valley. After a short ascent through the meadows you'll reach **Nedre Steinbuvatnet lake**. You can fill your water bottle here before leaving the meadows if necessary.

Follow the path as it veers in a northerly direction and the ground turns to rock and scree. Try not to veer left or right and lose the path; look for the T-markers ahead. Climb steadily, gaining 650m in elevation to reach the edge of the **Gråsubrean glacier**, your goal firmly in sight with its snow-covered peak jutting into the sky.

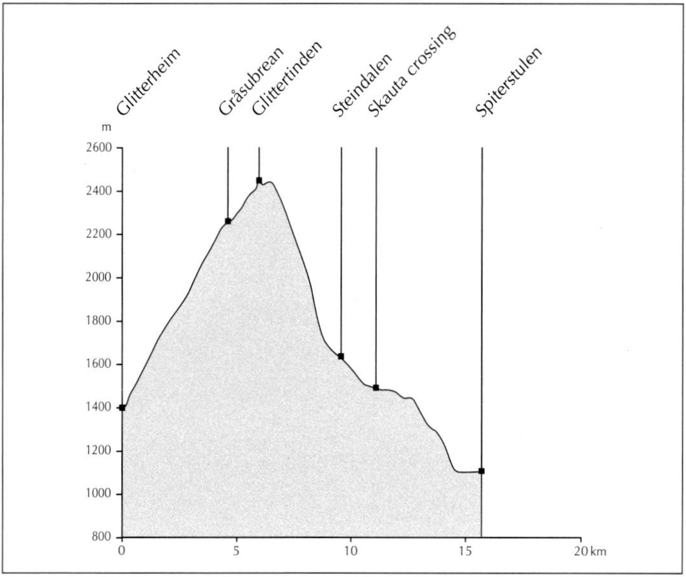
Glitterheim
Gråsubrean
Glittertinden
Steindalen
Skauta crossing
Spiterstulen
m
2600
2400
2200
2000
1800
1600
1400
1200
1000
800
0
5
10
15
20 km

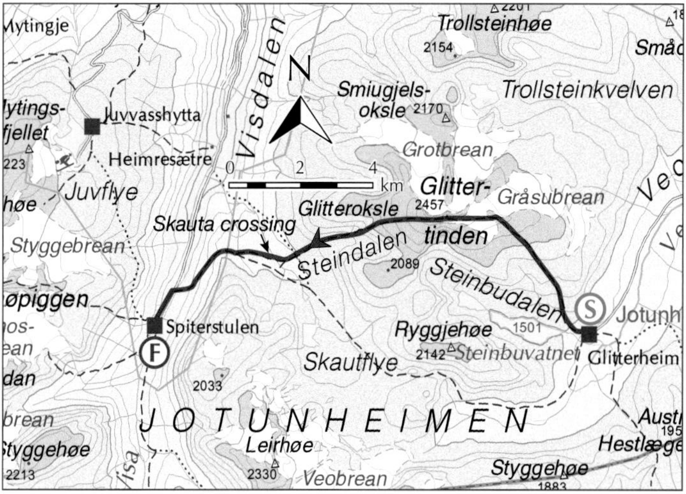
Trollsteinhøe
2154
Smiugjels-
oksle 2170
Trollsteinkvelven
Juvvasshytta
Heimresætre
Visdalen
N
0
2
4
km
Grotbrean
Glitter-
tinden
2457
Gråsubrean
Glitteroksle
Juvflye
Skauta crossing
Styggebrean
Steindalen
2089
Steinbudalen
Spiterstulen
F
S
Glitterheim
Ryggjehøe
1501
2142
Steinbuvatnet
Skautflye
2033
JOTUNHEIMEN
Leirhøe
2330
Veobrean
Styggehøe
Hestlægerhø
2213

The crescent-shaped top of Glittertinden as seen from the Gråsubrean ridge

Once at Gråsubrean the **views** are already spectacular. The characteristically crescent-shaped Glittertinden towers ahead with its vast, expansive eastern slope giving way in a precipice into the glacier below. Glittertinden's cap is crowned by ice and snow overhanging the top, giving rise to a magnificent panoramic display of sky, snow and rock.

Typically, there will be snowfields to cross from Gråsubrean onwards all the way to the top. Many markers may therefore be snow-covered and invisible. Since it is a popular hike there will be a well-trodden path through the snowfields, but caution still need to be exercised. Follow the ridge to the top, keeping well clear of the northern overhang. Continue due west for another 1.5km and about 200m of elevation along the ridge towards the top of **Glittertinden**, where there is a marker.

On a clear day you can see all of Jotunheimen to the south and west, almost like a glaciated seascape upon which its giant peaks show as islands – an utterly majestic and truly panoramic **view**. Towards the north you have views over Grotbrean and Gråsubrean onto Trollsteinhøe (2161m) and Gråhoe (2154m); to the east, the broad expanse of the Veodalen valley and Nautgardstinden (2258m); to the south, Surtningssue (2368m); and last but not least Galdhøpiggen (2469m) in the west. On a very clear day you will be able to see the impressive Hurrungane peaks behind Galdhøpiggen to the west, while on the eastern side the deep Gudbrandsdalen valley dominates the views and the Rondane massif can be glimpsed on the horizon.

Continuing west, proceed downwards, staying well clear of the northern edge. While you are on the snowcap no markings are visible, but this changes as you arrive on the snow-free moraine at the western side. As you continue steeply down you'll come to the escarpment of the **Steindalen valley**. The next 200m of descent is very strenuous over boulders, rocks and scree until you reach the Steindalselve stream, where vegetation makes the going easier. There are superb views over Visdalen and across onto the Galdhøpiggen massif during the descent. Continue along the valley until the route joins the **Skautflye plateau**.

The crossing of the Skauta stream is generally possible via stepping-stones. Pay attention to the 'T' markings here in order to find them on the other side of the stream. A little later the low route path from Glitterheim joins from the left and the trail then heads toward the pass between Skautkampan (1443m) and Skauthøe (1575m). Continue ahead to commence the increasingly steep descent into the **Visdalen valley**. The trail here is still well marked and orientation is easy. Ample vegetation with plentiful wildflowers soon returns as you lose altitude. The track ends on the asphalt service road; walk along this for the last few hundred metres south to **Spiterstulen mountain hut**.

STAGE 3A

Glittertinden low traverse

Start	Glitterheim mountain hut
Finish	Spiterstulen mountain hut
Distance	16.5km (10.25 miles)
Ascent	340m
Descent	625m
Difficulty	Challenging
Time	6hr
Maximum altitude	1680m
Map	Nordeca Jotunheimen Aust 1:50,000 Nr 2503

You are in the midst of a landscape formed by the forces of ice, water and frost, hiking from one vast glacial valley to the next, going over a massive area of till in an extensive, high alpine landscape dominated by Jotunheimen giants. The trail is well marked throughout, but progress over the Skautflye may be slow due to the terrain.

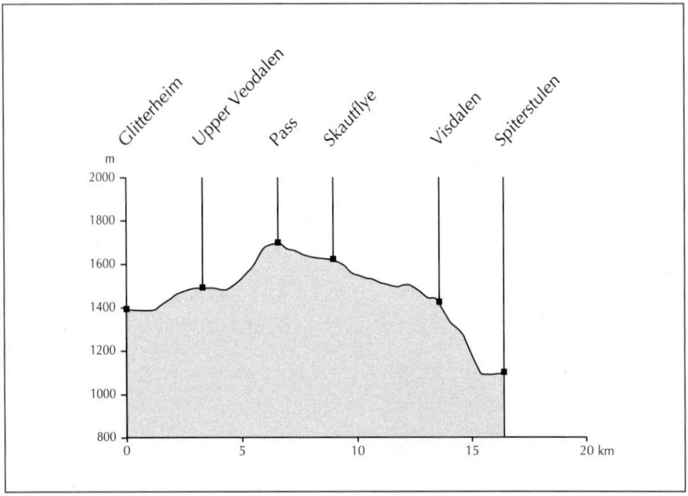
Glitterheim
Upper Veodalen
Pass
Skautflye
Visdalen
Spiterstulen
m
2000
1800
1600
1400
1200
1000
800
0
5
10
15
20 km

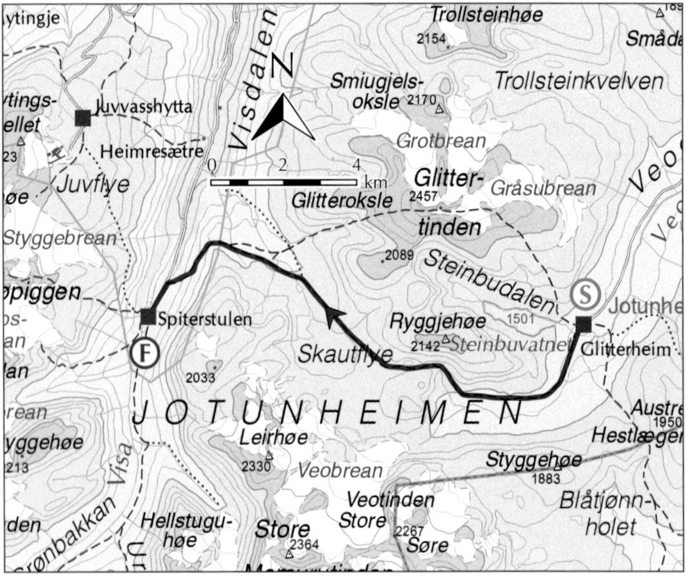
Trollsteinhøe
2154
Trollsteinkvelven
Smiugjels-
oksle 2170
Juvvasshytta
Heimresætre
Juvflye
Visdalen
N
0
2
4
km
Grotbrean
Glitter-
tinden
2457
Glitteroksle
Gråsubrean
Styggebrean
2089
Steinbudalen
S
Spiterstulen
Ryggjehøe
1501
2142
Steinbuvatnet
Glitterheim
F
Skautflye
2033
JOTUNHEIMEN
Leirhøe
2330
Veobrean
Styggehøe
1883
Hestlæger
1950
Blåtjønn-
holet
Veotinden
Store
2267
Søre
Hellstugu-
høe
Store
2364
Visa

The narrow pass at Veslglupen leads out of the Veodalen valley

Exit the hut at **Glitterheim** and turn left towards the signpost. Follow the sign to Spiterstulen mountain hut in a southwesterly direction with the river on your left. The trail starts by crossing several wooden planks over small tributary streams that come down from Nedre Steinbuvatnet lake. (Midges will be abundant on calm days around this area.) Soon the path widens and follows the Veo river glacial valley to its very start. It is well marked and comfortable walking for the first few kilometres.

The upper valley has some very suitable camping spots, and with its meandering river and ample grazing opportunities it often attracts herds of domesticated reindeer. There is no running water on the high plateau on Skautflye, so fill your water bottle before you leave the Veodalen valley. As you proceed towards the end of the valley, the imposing Nørdre Veotinden (2120m) and Nørdre Styggehøbreatinden (2165m) and their glaciers will be your companions until you reach the pass towards Skautflye.

At the end of the valley, the track ascends in a northerly direction towards Veslglupen, between Veopallan (1824m) and **Ryggjehøe** (2142m) – an impossibly narrow, almost threadlike pass forming the end of this wide valley. Continue, passing a series of small, quiet lakes as you traverse over the saddle, clambering over boulders and rocks and possibly the occasional snowfield. This is the highest point of the day.

The trail then descends towards Skautflye, with its thick layer of till moraine that showcases boulders, rocks and gravel of every imaginable size and form.

Progress may be slow as you pick your way among it; your main orientation in this area being the regular T-markers. The path on **Skautflye** is not always visible, and care should be taken in foggy conditions. Make sure to leave one T-marker only once you see the next.

> Skautflye is a Mecca for those interested in **minerals**, with its multitude of different and diverse rocks. If rock classification is not your thing, however, the **views** towards Austre Memurutinden (2301m), Veobreatinden (2183m), the Veobrean glacier and Leirhøe (2330m) are the main event on this stretch as they line up and rise on the opposite side of this very impressive large and mostly flat till. A remote, magnificent, high alpine panorama stretches out all around you.

Skautflye ends when you reach a second signpost towards Glittertinden, where the high route from Glitterheim towards Spiterstulen joins up with this lower route. After the short ascent up the saddle between Skauthøe (1993m) and Skautkampan (1443m) the first panoramic views towards Galdhøpiggen and glaciers appear over the edge of the hanging valley ahead.

Continue ahead to commence the increasingly steep descent into the **Visdalen valley**. The trail here is still well marked and orientation is easy. Ample vegetation with plentiful wildflowers soon returns as you lose altitude. The track ends on the asphalt service road; walk along this for the last few hundred metres south to **Spiterstulen mountain hut**.

STAGE 4

Galdhøpiggen summit

Start/finish	Spiterstulen mountain hut
Distance	12.5km (7.75 miles)
Ascent/descent	1390m
Difficulty	Very challenging
Time	8hr
Maximum altitude	2469m
Map	Nordeca Jotunheimen Vest 1:50,000 Nr 2505
Note	This route is very exposed and should only be attempted in good weather. Poor visibility will make the final ascent close to the glacier treacherous.

This stage takes you to the top of Norway and then down again – a simple description that belies a serious hike, where the challenge is less in the technical difficulty of the path and more in the ever-changing weather conditions. The climb can be hot and sweaty, the top windy and icy. Be prepared. On good weather days, however, you will be on top of Scandinavia enjoying the 360° views.

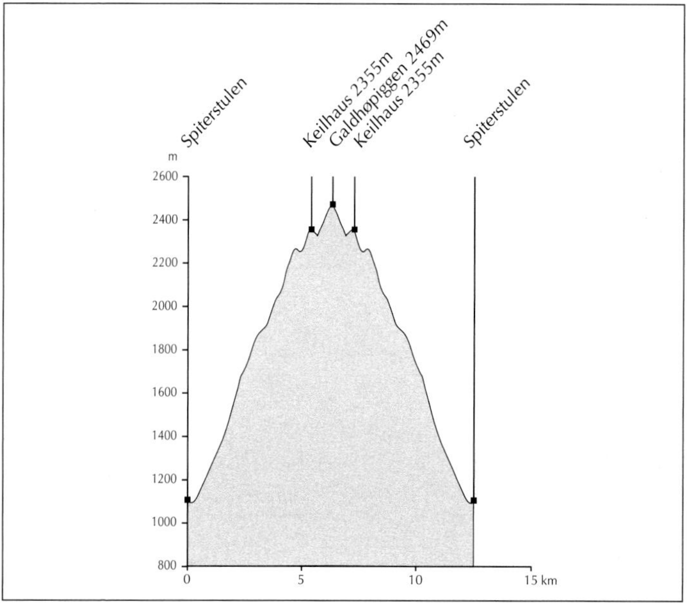

The hiking path from Spiterstulen is generally well marked. Exit the lodge, turn right, and cross the permanent bridge over the Vis river. On the west side head downstream for 100 metres or so and then bear west up the slope. Many paths lead up here, in a steep ascent to about the 1700m mark. Fill your water bottle at around the 1600m mark, when you are still coming across some streams. (There are no more water sources before the summit.)

The ascent from 1800m involves crossing snowfields and boulder fields. The T-markers disappear in places below the snow, but generally there is a

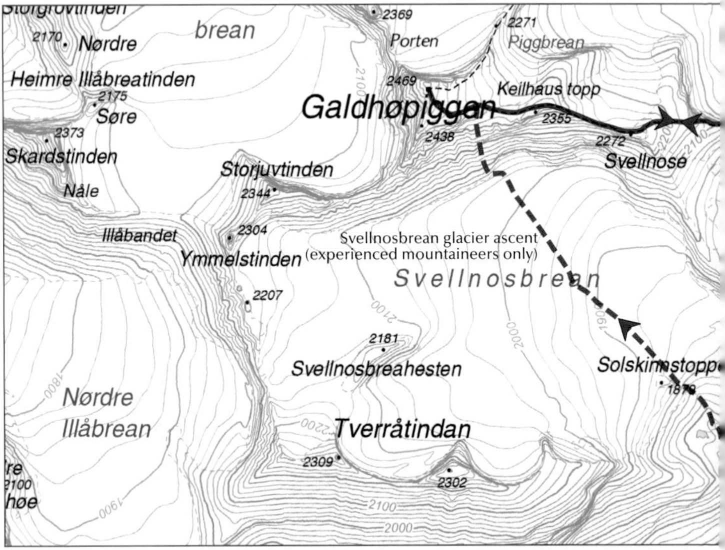

well-trodden trail through the snowfields. Do keep an eye on the T-markers when crossing the boulder fields as it is easy to lose sight of them. Continue ascending to below the dark crest of **Svellnose** (2272m) in a series of more or less sharp zig-zags and over some flatter terraced sections in-between.

At Svellnose you get fantastic views over the **Styggebrean glacier** and you might be able to discern the troupes approaching from Juvasshytta (a mountain lodge) over the very popular northern (guided) glacier walk.

The subsequent ascent to **Keilhaus topp** (2355m) is over a series of ridges. You then descend again for a short stretch towards a saddle, before the final climb towards the top of **Galdhøpiggen**. Make absolutely sure to follow the red markings and posts here in order to avoid going over the Piggbrean glacier, which has potentially dangerous snow bridges over crevasses.

The panorama from **Galdhøpiggen** – Norway's highest summit at 2469m – is simply breathtaking if you're lucky enough to be here on a good weather day. Views can extend to a whopping 5000km^2 and you are truly surrounded by only lesser peaks of all of Scandinavia.

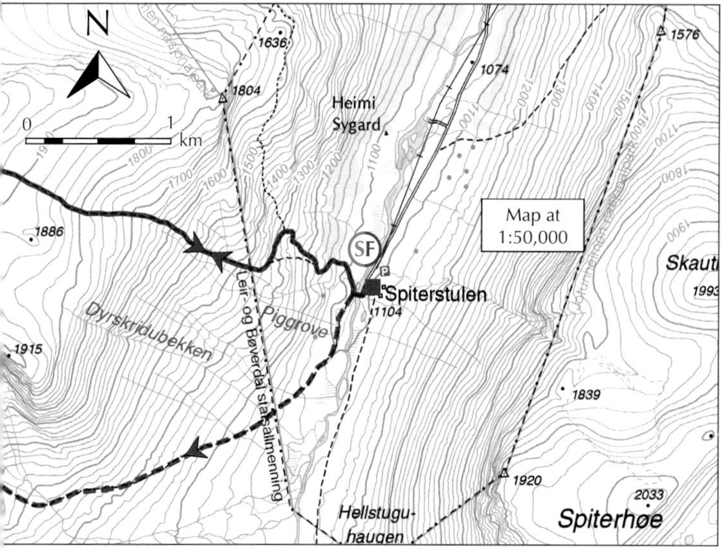

The actual top is 15m behind the small refuge built at the summit. This used to be a small post office, run by the Norwegian Postal Authority – claiming its position as the highest in Northern Europe, naturally. It still sells some essentials like water and chocolate, but more importantly it is a refuge against potentially battering winds on the top.

Alternative ascent via the Svellnosbrean glacier

A more challenging but arguably also more interesting ascent is from the south over Solskinnstoppen (1879m) and the Svellnosbrean glacier. Unless you are a mountaineer, this should only be done with the help and equipment of a mountain and glacier guide. The tour generally can be booked a day in advance at Spiterstulen mountain hut, which is where it starts from. It takes about 1½hr to reach Svellnosbrean, which is crossed and followed by an ascent to the saddle between Keilhaus top (2355m) and Galdhøpiggen peak. Here a 400m-high rockfall at a 45° angle needs to be climbed, which means bouldering using hands and feet. The views along the way are simply phenomenal. This ascent is not to be confused with the northern glacier approach over Styggebrean glacier from Juvasshytta, which takes hundreds of hikers over the top of Galdhøpiggen every day in summer.

Views into Visdalen from the ascent to Galdhøpiggen

The way down from Galdhøpiggen is the same as the way up. Depending on snow conditions, you might find it easier to use or create a slide to sledge down part of the slope below Svellnose. The author made good use of one such snow-field to evade 250m metres in altitude of scrambling down rocks.

STAGE 5

Spiterstulen to Leirvassbu

Start	Spiterstulen mountain hut
Finish	Leirvassbu mountain hut
Distance	15.75km (10 miles)
Ascent	425m
Descent	130m
Difficulty	Moderate
Time	5½hr
Maximum altitude	1487m
Map	Nordeca Jotunheimen Vest 1:50,000 Nr 2505

A valley walk with highly atmospheric views of the surrounding peaks, dramatic cloudscapes, and light reflections on calm days – together presenting a striking natural spectacle. Kyrkja mountain's archetypical pyramid shape dominates vistas to the west as you make your way along on the well-marked trail. The crossing of the Urdadalsbekken river can be a challenge, but otherwise this is a hike of medium difficulty.

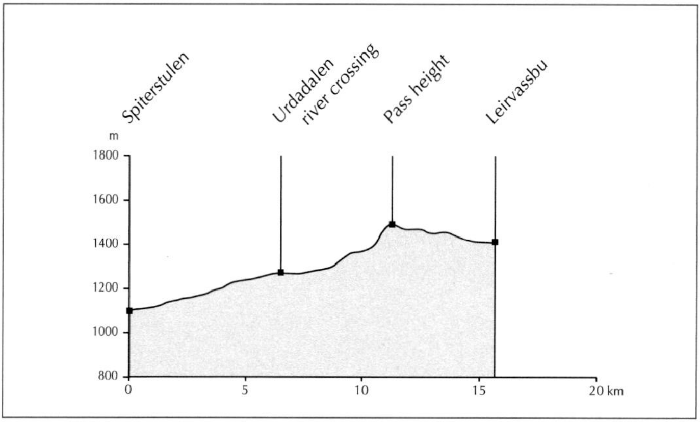

Leave the main cabin of **Spiterstulen**, turn right in front of the signpost and walk through the two gate posts into the Visdalen valley in a southerly direction. The path is comfortable underfoot and follows the wide valley in very gently uphill. Occasionally a small stream needs to be crossed.

The large 'U' shape of the **valley** betrays its glacial origins, and many a 2000m+ mountaintop can be seen on a clear day, such as Styggehøe (2213m) and Store Bukkeholstinden (2213m) in the west, and Store Urdadalstinden (2116m) and Visbretinden (2234m) to the south.

At around the halfway point there is a signpost for the turnoff to Gjendebu, up the **Urdadalen valley**. Keep going straight ahead, and soon afterwards the Urdadalsbekken stream needs to be crossed. You can either wade through it where the T-markers suggest, or you might cross a bit further down where the stream is broader and joins the river downstream.

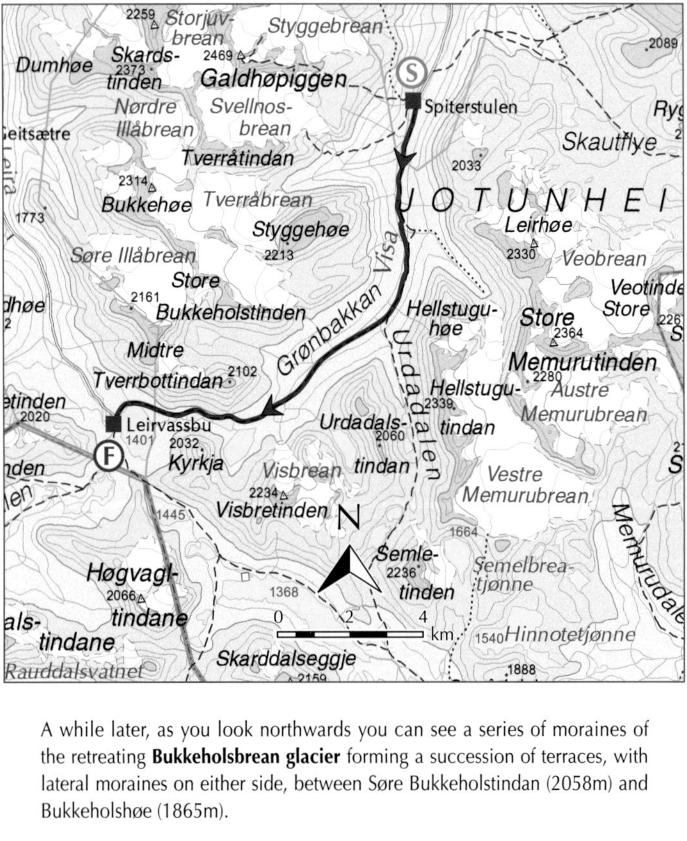

A while later, as you look northwards you can see a series of moraines of the retreating **Bukkeholsbrean glacier** forming a succession of terraces, with lateral moraines on either side, between Søre Bukkeholstindan (2058m) and Bukkeholshøe (1865m).

The striking pyramid-shaped Kyrkja (2032m) forms the backdrop as you continue up the valley towards the pass (1487m) and the highest point of the stage. Here, the two massive glacial valleys that enclose the Galdhøpiggen massif – namely Leirdalen and Visdalen – meet at their narrowest points.

Once over the saddle a series of small paternoster lakes come into view, and there are glimpses a little further afield of the large Smørstabbrean glaciers. The markings along Panna lake are a bit faded at times; stay close to its shore here. Once you've passed beyond Troget lake the path drops down towards Leirvatnet lake. Leirvassbu mountain hut can be seen on the opposite western side of the

Kyrkja has been carved up on three sides by powerful glaciers

lake. From here it's a leisurely stroll along small patches of alpine meadows towards **Leirvassbu** with its own backdrop of peaks such as Stetinden (2020m) to the west and Store Tverrbottinden (2161m) to the north.

Leirvassbu is directly connected to Oslo via the Valdresekspressen bus line. It is a sizable and privately run lodge, well regarded for its traditional Norwegian cuisine. You might observe whole family reunions taking place as Norwegians' love of the outdoors and traditional foods are happily merged here.

STAGE 6

Leirvassbu to Gjendebu

Start	Leirvassbu mountain hut
Finish	Gjendebu mountain hut
Distance	19.25km (12 miles)
Ascent	200m
Descent	610m
Difficulty	Challenging
Time	7hr
Maximum altitude	1541m
Map	Nordeca Jotunheimen Vest 1:50,000 Nr 2505 and Nordeca Jotunheimen Aust 1:50,000 Nr 2503

This stage completes the Jotunheimen classic route with a wonderful valley hike along a series of lakes, streams and waterfalls with the backdrop of a multitude of glacier-covered peaks. Water in its many forms drips, squelches, flows, roars and thunders in the ever-changing spectacular scenery; stream crossings are generally straightforward but may be more challenging early in the season. The trail is well trodden, and although occasionally not well marked it is easy to follow.

The route concludes with a return to Gjendesheim by boat. Boat timings vary throughout the season – see www.gjende.no/en. Pre-booking is possible and encouraged.

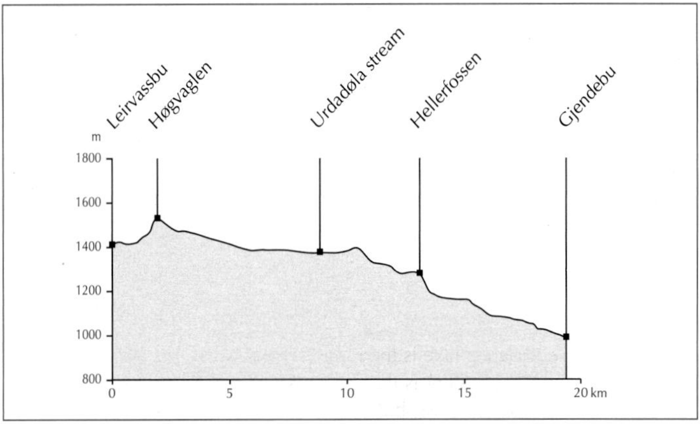

Leave **Leirvassbu mountain hut** from the main entrance, turn left, and cross over the bridge onto the dirt road. Follow the road for a few hundred metres until the signpost to Gjendebu appears. (On the way, a path to the left leads to the top of a hillock, from where you can enjoy the view of Leirvatnet and then rejoin the main route.) Turn left at the signpost and leave the dirt road on a trail that ascends steeply towards the **Høgvaglen pass** (1518m) between Høgvagltindane (2066m) and Kyrkja (2032m), passing an attractive camping spot on the way.

The pass is the highest point of the day, and here the long but generally gentle descent to Gjendebu begins. There are superb views into the length of the Storådalen valley ahead, with the landscape of lakes reaching far into the distance flanked by snowy peaks on either side.

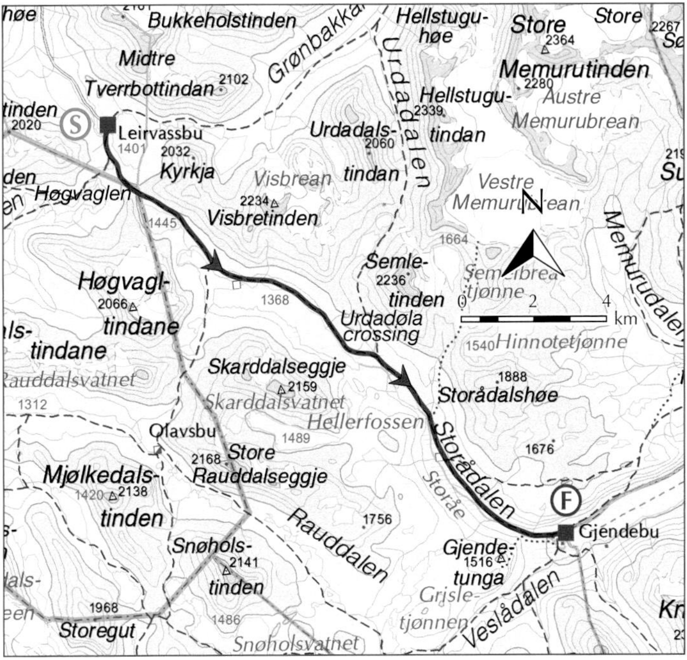

Øvre Høgvagltjønnen lake is the first of many you will pass and the source of the Storåe river. Langvatnet is the next. Most of the streams that empty into Langvatnet will be easy to cross, but conditions can be tricky in the early season depending on snow, ice and meltwater. The Urdadøla stream, feeding the eastern end of Langvatnet, is the largest of these streams. Pick your way with care over rocks and flowing water.

Langvatnet, literally 'the long lake', is about 5km long and is very attractively framed by Skarddalstinden (2100m) and Skarddalseggie (2159m) and their glaciers. Many streams feed it from the Visbrean glacier to the north.

Langvatnet empties into Hellertjønnet, now with a sizeable watercourse. A short while later you will hear the roar of **Hellerfossen waterfall** – a cascade of some 60m. The peaks and glaciers of Knutsholstinden (2341m) and Svartdalspiggen (2174m) rise high and far beyond Gjende lake in the distance.

Hiking along Langvatnet lake towards Gjendebu

The descent alongside the waterfall is steep and slippery but short. The path then follows the left side of the river down into the **Storådalen valley**. Vegetation, shrubs and birch woods and summer pastures return as you near Gjende lake. The path may well be wet and muddy in sections.

The **Storåe river** is a wild and wide alpine stream that rushes through the valley before forming a small river delta at the emerald-green Gjende lake, on the southern side of the Gjendebu hut.

From **Gjendebu mountain hut**, return to Gjendesheim by boat. Alternatively you could continue hiking back east to Gjendesheim (see Route 1), or head west to connect with Route 3.

ROUTE 3

Jotunheimen traverse route

Start	Fondsbu mountain hut
Finish	Turtagrø mountain hotel
Distance	51km (31.5 miles)
Ascent	2450m
Descent	2635m
Time	4 days
Extensions	The route itself is a superb extension to both Route 1 and Route 2
Note	Booking is compulsory at Fannaråkhytta mountain hut

The Jotunheimen traverse route is a four-stage westerly traverse of Jotunheimen, starting at Fondsbu and ending in Turtagrø and featuring the greatest of contrasts en route. It runs along valleys with insect life and flora that seem almost impossibly abundant, while on the other hand your stay at the highest DNT hut, on top of Fannaråki at 2068m, sees you in a barren and stark landscape, with views onto the Hurrungane massif – arguably Jotunheimen's wildest area. Climatic diversity, the variety of rock types, and local snow cover are just some of the factors responsible for this contrast. Fannaråki has virtually zero viability for vegetation growth, while the valley around Skogadalsbøen teems with life.

Starting in Fondsbu, the first stage takes you close by the splendid Mjølkedalsbreen glacier and towards the very heart of Jotunheimen, namely Olavsbu. Its remoteness gives you a real sense of what it is to journey along in this alpine terrain. Here you are surrounded by the untouched and untamed natural world, any road being at least a day hike away. On Stage 2 the route continues towards beautiful Skogadalsbøen, which lies in a fertile valley that is brimming and swarming with birdlife. Stage 3 takes you high towards Fannaråki (2068m) and the highest DNT hut in all of Norway. The hut sits at the edge of the Hurrungane massif and holds the promise of some of the most breathtaking vistas in the country. On a clear day, the rugged and much eroded tops of Skagastølstindane (2387m and 2406m) and their respective glaciers seem just a stone's throw away. The scaling of these tops is the realm of climbers, and not surprisingly Turtagrø is one of the leading centres in Norway for this adrenaline-rich sport. Stage 4 is the final stage of the traverse and descends steeply from Fannaråki towards Turtagrø, with the wild, rugged peaks of the Hurrungane providing a magnificent and imposing backdrop for most of the day.

Access to Fondsbu is by boat over the Bygdin lake (there's a regular summer boat service on the M/B Bitihorn – see https://jvb.no/en), or by bus from Tyinkrysset. Exit from Turtagrø is by public transport, with the bus journey to Lom over the Sognefjellet plateau being one of the most scenic (and highest) alpine drives in Norway.

This route can't be shortened in any meaningful way and is therefore less flexible than Routes 1 and 2. At the same time it is a fantastic extension to both, creating a grand tour in the case of Route 2 and a complete east–west traverse when combined with Route 1.

Note that the DNT hut on Fannaråki is undergoing extensive renovations and upgrades in 2020. Bookings are compulsory as of the summer of 2019. See https://fannarakhytta.dnt.no/engelsk for details. Bookings are also recommended for the hotel at Turtagrø – see https://turtagro.no/english.

STAGE 1

Fondsbu to Olavsbu

Start	Fondsbu mountain hut
Finish	Olavsbu mountain hut
Distance	14km (8.75 miles)
Ascent	750m
Descent	375m
Difficulty	Challenging
Time	5½hr
Maximum altitude	1601m
Map	Nordeca Jotunheimen Vest 1:50,000 Nr 2505
Note	The DNT key is required for access to Olavsbu

Olavsbu lies in the heart of Jotunheimen and is the only cabin in the area that is a day hike from roads of any sort. The fact that it is also a self-service mountain hut adds to the sense of remoteness here. Walking towards Olavsbu gives you an authentic taste of the high mountain terrain, peaks and glaciers of Jotunheimen, with new views opening out at every turn in a truly alpine panoramic setting. This stage features a variety of terrain types. Starting with muddy sections, the largest part of the trail takes you across rocky ground. The trail has been recently redrawn around the lake just south of Olavsbu to improve safety, and it is excellently marked.

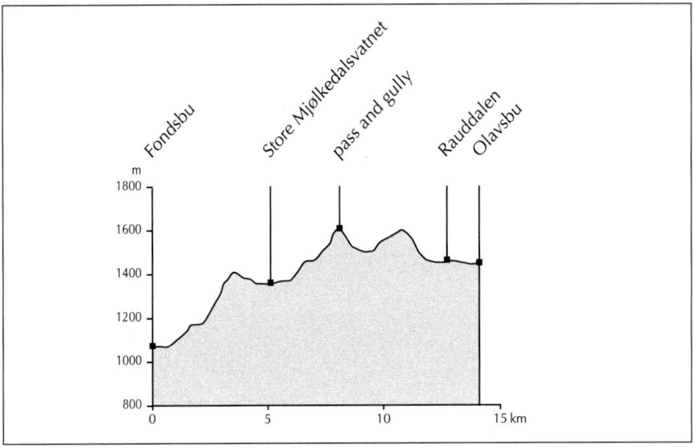

From **Fondsbu mountain hut**, turn left towards the river with Bygdin lake on your right-hand side. Soon you will encounter the first T-marker guiding you towards the bridge that crosses the **Mjølkedola river**. The path will likely be quite wet at the beginning of the stage. A little further on you'll reach a signpost to Olavsbu, with other destinations also signposted. Turn left here and commence the ascent upriver and out of Mjølkedalen.

Continue on the path and cross a rather dilapidated bridge. The track becomes steeper, and soon the muddy ground gives way to a rocky and gravelly path. As you pass a saddle at around 1400m the Mjølkdalsbreen glacier which feeds **Store Mjølkedalsvatnet lake** comes into view.

The approach to and hike around **Mjølkedalsvatnet** is very appealing with extensive views towards the glacier and a series of peaks that surround it, such as Langeskavlen (1878m), Langeskavtinden (2014m), Mjølkedalspiggen (2040m), Uranostinden (2157) and Storegut (1968m).

From here onwards the path is dominated by rocks and boulders of different sizes and shapes until shortly before Olavsbu. The track continues along the

eastern side of the lake and veers north, ascending the valley with Høgbrøgde (1821m) on your right as you climb. Shortly before reaching the highest point of the stage at 1601m you'll pass the turnoff to Skogadalsbøen and other mountain huts. Continue straight at the turnoff and turn east soon afterwards to pass through a narrow gully as you move towards Snøholsvatnet lake.

The path proceeds over scree and boulders. Turn left (north) at the next signpost and continue along the western edge of the lake. You might have to cross some snowfields here. Head up the valley, taking care on the bouldery path which makes for slow progress. The imposing twin peaks of Mjølkedalstinden (highest point 2138m) draw ever closer.

Between unnamed lakes (at 1487m and 1442m respectively) the path crosses some beautiful terraced rocks which might appeal as a resting spot on a summery day, allowing for fantastic views onto the pyramidal peak of Snøholstinden (2141m) and the double peaks of Mjølkedalstinden.

En route through the heart of Jotunheimen

Turn right along the eastern edge of the latter lake (1442m); don't try the shorter trail on the western shore since this has become unstable and unsafe. Descend into **Rauddalen valley**, where the trail joins up with the path from Gjendebu. Continuing northwest, Olavsbu soon becomes visible in the distance, sitting snugly between many high tops such as Rauddalstindene (2157m), Mjølkedalstinden and Snøholstinden. The new path towards **Olavsbu** around the lake just before the hut is excellently marked.

While Olavsbu is the only self-serviced hut in Jotunheimen, it will likely have a hut warden in the busy summer months. As the host, the warden has authority to (re-)assign rooms and organise tasks.

STAGE 2

Olavsbu to Skogadalsbøen

Start	Olavsbu mountain hut
Finish	Skogadalsbøen mountain hut
Distance	17.75km (11 miles)
Ascent	350m
Descent	960m
Difficulty	Challenging
Time	6½hr
Maximum altitude	1617m
Map	Nordeca Jotunheimen Vest 1:50,000 Nr 2505

There could hardly be a more significant contrast of landscapes in Jotunheimen than on this stage. Panoramic views over the glacially formed Rauddalen valley with its string of paternoster lakes are framed by the tops and glaciers of the Mjølkedals and Rauddals ranges. The Skogadalen valley amazes with its abundant, diverse vegetation, giving rise to the impression that you are in a temperate rainforest.

There are two different routes from Olavsbu to Skogadalsbøen. Weather permitting, the high route (as described here) should be chosen. The trail is well marked, the vistas fantastic. The Rauddalen valley walk (18.4km, 6hr, marked) is likely to be muddy and boggy all summer. It is not described here.

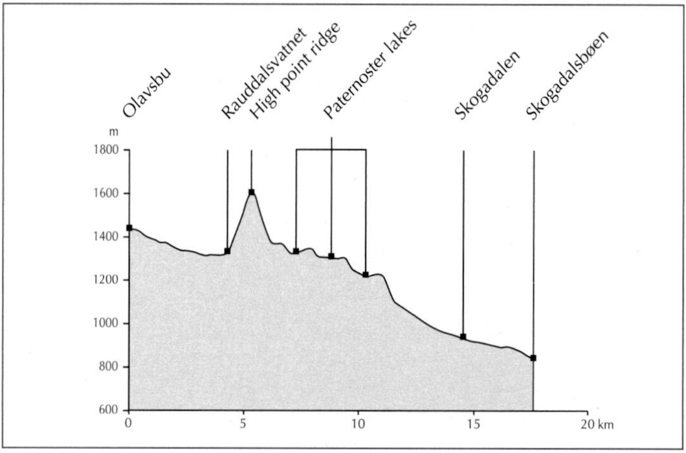

Leave **Olavsbu** and go straight to the bridge across the river. Over the bridge, turn right and follow the path which will stay on the river's true left and the southern side of a series of small paternoster lakes. After a short hour you'll reach a signpost on the edge of **Rauddalsvatnet lake**, pointing you left up a ridge. While the path is generally clear and well marked, it is easy to lose among the boulders. The climb to the top of the **ridge** (1617m) is short and steep.

You are very much rewarded at the top with spectacular **views** along both the Rauddalen and Skogadalen valleys, into the Mjølkedalen valley, and onto the various 2000m+ peaks with their glaciers and lakes. Uranostinden (2157m),

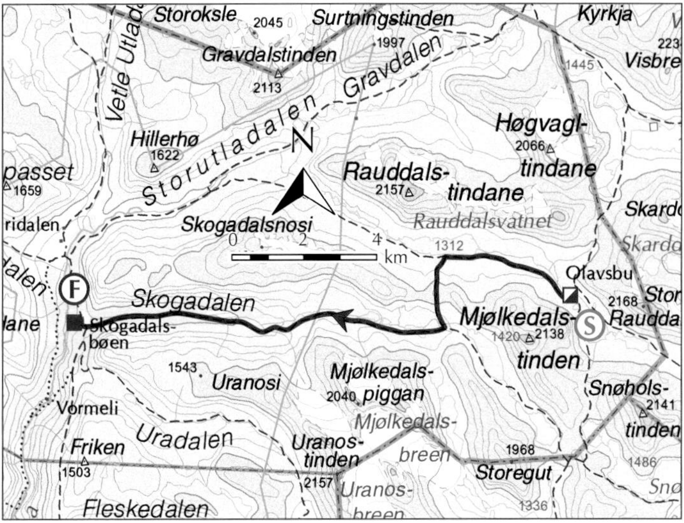

Mjølkedalstinden (2138m) and Stølsnostinden (2074m) are close by while the Hurrungane peaks can be made out a few kilometres away. There is no sign of civilisation in any direction other than the cairns and the dependable T-markers.

Leaving the highpoint of the hike, the descent into Skogadalen valley is steep and at times on loose gravel, but it is well marked. The path leads you to the southern side of the valley across the river and from there it follows the Skogadalen valley down for 12km towards Skogadalsbøen. The path is good, generally dry underfoot, with rocky sections alternating with easy gravel. A steep but short descent takes you into the lower part of the valley.

A large number of **migratory birds** make their annual journey of many thousands of kilometres into Jotunheimen, and you may very well see some of them in the Skogadalen valley. They come to gorge on the abundant insects that are supported by the diversity of plant life. These birds nest in Jotunheimen away from the mammal predators that would hunt them in the warmer climates. Some prefer the wetlands created by meandering rivers, others the peaty marshlands or the dense vegetation of woods. Among the most familiar migratory birds are the meadow pipit, the stone shy, snow bunting and the dunlin, but there are around 70 species that visit Jotunheimen in the summer.

Eye for detail – mosses and fungi

As the view of the wild Hurrungane mountain peaks to the west becomes ever more dominant, the valley itself turns into something akin to a temperate rainforest, with a fantastic variety of plants and flowers. The contrast with the stark, rocky, almost desert-like surroundings of Olavsbu in the morning could hardly be greater.

You arrive at **Skogadalsbøen mountain hut** shortly after having crossed the bridge over the wildly flowing Skogadøla stream. (The stream forms a beautiful and enticing little pool under the bridge and there are some rocky terraces a little further down to dry off after a dip on a sunny day.) Everything about Skogadalsbøen is inviting. The lovely hosts, delicious food and comfortable lounge areas have long made this mountain hut a hiker's favourite.

STAGE 3

Fannaråkhytta: DNT's highpoint

Start	Skogadalsbøen mountain hut
Finish	Fannaråkhytta mountain hut
Distance	11km (7 miles)
Ascent	1335m
Descent	100m
Difficulty	Challenging
Time	5hr
Maximum altitude	2068m
Map	Nordeca Jotunheimen Vest 1:50,000 Nr 2505

This is your chance to overnight in the highest DNT cabin in Norway with its 360° panoramas over the Jotunheimen and Breheimen national parks – ample reward for the 1200m elevation gain.

As you hike further and higher the wild Hurrungane massif and glaciers start to dominate the view to your left, while on your right the peak of Fannaråki reveals itself. On clear days the bright light brings out the contrasts of the landscape on this stretch: blue sky, black rock and white snowfields – minimalistic yet mesmerising. This unique hike ends at the highest point of the stage instead of descending into a valley for the night, providing an extraordinary opportunity to enjoy these high alpine views at dusk and dawn.

Bear in mind that booking is compulsory for Fannaråkhytta, and that at 2068m the nights will likely be cold and windy. July average temperatures are +2.5°C, the annual average precipitation is 1200mm, and it can snow anytime.

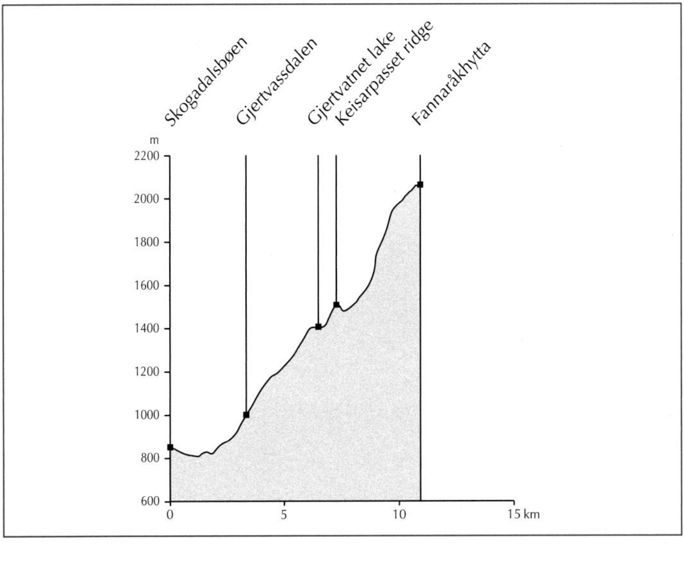

From the main entrance of **Skogadalsbøen mountain hut**, turn left and follow the signs for Fannaråkhytta mountain hut, heading north up the valley. The first 2.5km is a gentle stroll through a birchwood forest. Pass the turnoff to Leirvassbu (through

Gravdalen valley) and Olavsbu (through Rauddalen valley), and soon reach the permanent bridge over the Utla river. After crossing the hanging bridge (shortly after which there are some lovely camping spots) continue straight up **Gjertvassdalen valley** in a westerly direction. Here the climb to Fannaråkhytta starts in earnest. The path is excellent underfoot, soft or a little gravelly with few rocks.

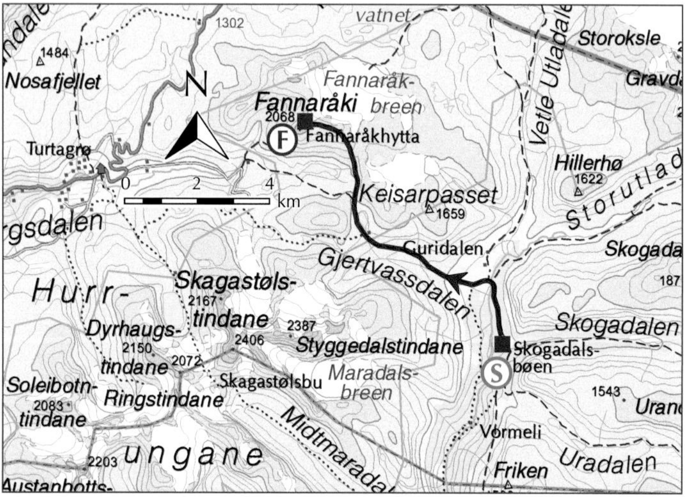

View from the Gjertvassdalen valley onto Styggedalstindane and its glacier

Ascend to Gjertvatnet lake at 1391m and enjoy a short, easy, flat stretch along its shore. After ascending the next ridge (**Keisarpasset**) you'll reach a crossroads: the left-hand option descends to Turtagrø, so turn right to continue up towards Fannaråkhytta. The trail becomes rockier underfoot, with several crossings of snowfields necessary and some steep switchbacks taking you higher up. Note that snow paths change on a yearly basis or even as the season progresses. The path is very well marked though, so keep an eye on the T-markers here.

There's a sign for 'Breføring' (glacier crossing) with marked T-signs leading off to the right (shortly after a glacier/icefield becomes visible to your right behind you). Don't follow this but turn left and up along an also-marked path. Finally, with 250 altitude metres to go, the track flattens, and the final kilometre to the hut and mountaintop is an easy, gradual ascent along the ridge with the Fannaråkbreen glacier to your right. There's a good chance of fog (240 out of 365 days), but if you're lucky, enjoy the views!

There are no streams on top of **Fannaråki**, so rainwater is collected for use as potable water as well as for washing. Needless to say, everyone is asked to use it sparingly and facilities are basic. The whole area is under redevelopment by the DNT during 2020. The vistas make up for any inconvenience! On a clear day, to the south the views to the scraggy and imposing Hurrungane tops are just superb. To the north the Sognefjell plateau, dotted with lakes, is a delightful panorama and the east reveals the magnificent Smørstabsbrean glaciers and tops. Galdhøpiggen and Glittertinden, Norway's highest peaks, can be seen on the horizon behind Smørstabsbrean.

Sunset at Fannaråkhytta

STAGE 4

Fannaråkhytta to Turtagrø

Start	Fannaråkhytta mountain hut
Finish	Turtagrø
Distance	8km (5 miles)
Ascent	15m
Descent	1200m
Difficulty	Moderate
Time	3½hr
Maximum altitude	2068m
Map	Nordeca Jotunheimen Vest 1:50,000 Nr 2505

This stage concludes the Jotunheimen traverse. The hike up from Turtagrø to Fannaråki is very popular; expect to encounter many people on sunny weekends in high season. You will be going against the crowds here. The views onto the wild Hurrungane mountain peaks form a constant yet ever-changing and wonderful backdrop to your descent. The path is well marked and trodden, and quite rocky, until you reach Helgedalen valley. From there it is less well marked, albeit still distinct, and can be wet and muddy.

Turtagrø is sought out by climbers, with the rugged Hurrungane tops being a Mecca for alpinists. A reservation is recommended if you're staying at the Turtagrø hotel/motel – see https://turtagro.no/english.

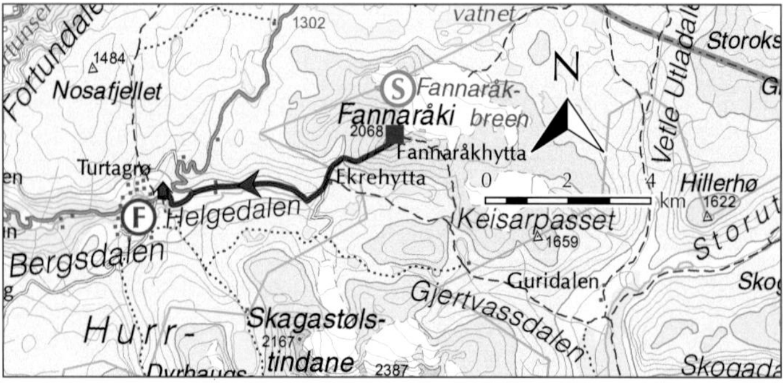

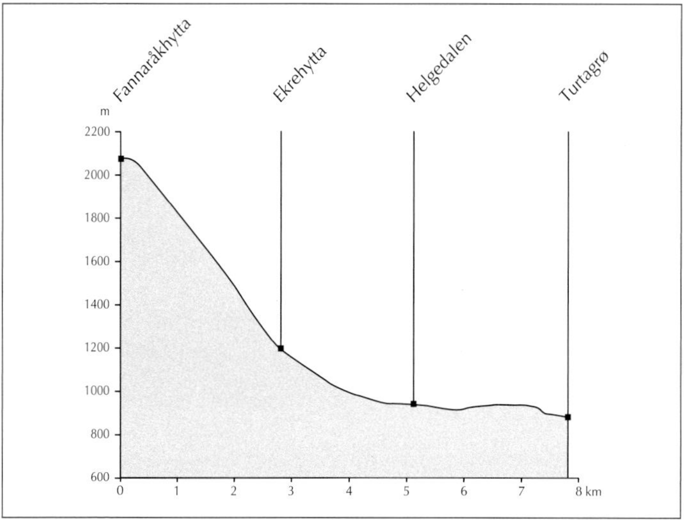

Other descent options

There are alternative ways down from Fannaråkhytta. On most days, guided glacier crossings over the Fannaråkbreen glacier are offered, and you could then continue from the edge of the glacier to Sognefjellshytta or Krossbu mountain huts. This exit is a wonderful option for the vistas it offers towards the northeast.

Descending from Fannaråki, with views towards Lusterfjord in the far distance

Hurrungane as seen from Fannaråken with Store Skagastølstinden and Styggedalsbreen glacier

From **Fannaråkhytta mountain hut**, go south to pick up the path and continue southwest. (The many T-markers are a reminder of the foggy conditions that are so common here; if hiking in fog, do not leave one marker behind before seeing the next.) Soon you will need to cross a snowfield. The steep descent starts immediately down the southwest ridge of Fannaråki mountain, on a well-marked and generally smooth path. It takes many tight switchbacks as it zigzags down the mountain. It's rocky underfoot, with some gravelly sections, and the trail has been worked on in places to avoid further erosion. The descent is relentless over some 850m of altitude, but the views are ever changing. About 100m above **Ekrehytta**, the path veers close to the Steindøla stream and there is a lovely spot to take a break at the side of a cascade.

> Nearby is the sizable **Styggedalsbreen glacier**, with its lake shimmering green. Further away you might see the Lusterfjord and the massive icecap of the **Jostedalsbreen glacier**.

Once you reach Ekrehytta the track starts to flatten out slightly. Continue past the turnoff back to Skogadalsbøen, and join the dirt road down to the Helgedalen valley. From here the remaining 5.7km of the route is mostly unmarked. Follow the road down, or take one of the tracks that shortcut a few of the switchbacks. Close to the cabins in **Helgedalen valley**, follow the road to the parking area or turn left to follow the path through the meadows and along the small gorge that the Helgedalselvi river has carved down to **Turtagrø**. This section can be muddy and wet.

RONDANE

Hiker in the Illmanndalen valley (Route 4, Stage 5/Route 5, Stage 1)

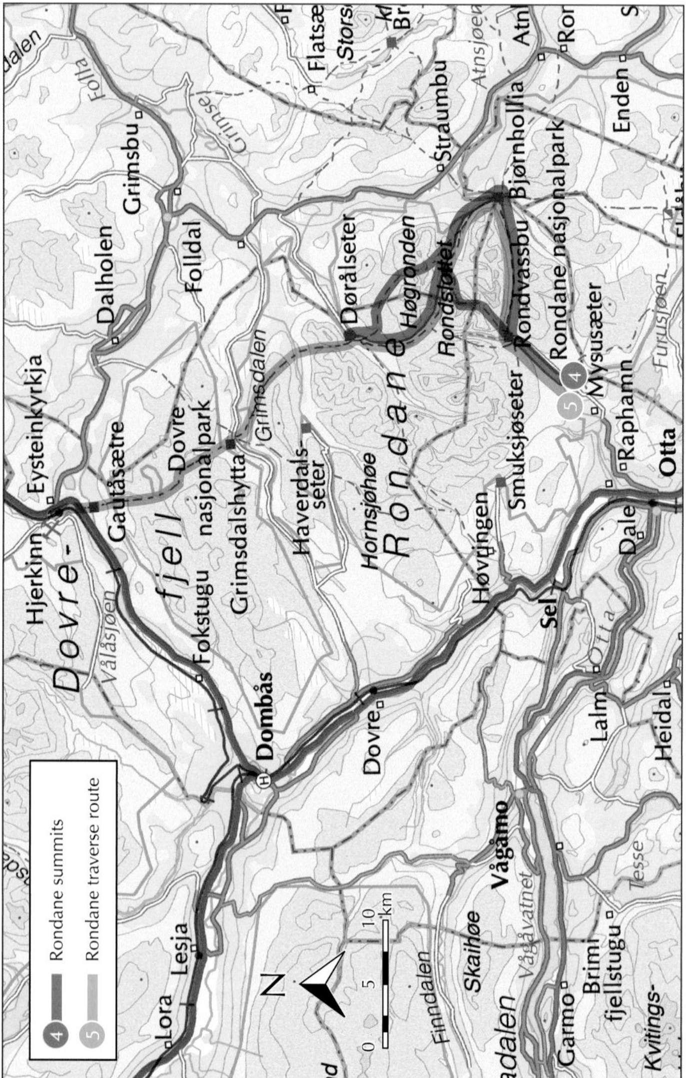
4 Rondane summits
5 Rondane traverse route
N
0 5 10 km
Lora
Lesja
Dombås
Fokstugu
Hjerkinn
Dovre-
fjell
Vålåsjøen
Eysteinkyrkja
Gautåsætre
Dovre
nasjonalpark
Grimsdalshytta
Grimsdalen
Dalholen
Folldal
Grimsbu
Folla
Grimsa
Flatsæ
Dørålseter
Haverdals-
seter
Hornsjøhøe
Rondane
Høgronden
Rondslottet
Straumbu
Atnsjøen
Atna
Bjørnhollia
Rondvassbu
Rondane nasjonalpark
Mysusæter
Smuksjøseter
Høvringen
Enden
Furusjøen
Raphamn
Otta
Dale
Sel
Dovre
Vågåmo
Vågåvatnet
Skaihøe
Finndalen
Lalm
Heidal
Tesse
Garmo
Brimi
fjellstugu
Kvitings-

If you aim to 'collect' the accessible peaks of Norway above the 2000m mark, Rondane National Park is the place to go and get a head start. Within a relatively compact area you could hike and scramble up to about 10 mountains of over 2000m in altitude – five of which are covered in this guide. Rondslottet, 'the Castle of Rondane' (Route 4, Stage 2; and Route 5, Extension 1), at 2178m is the highest peak in the area and is accessible to everyone with a good level of fitness. Rondane is the most continental high mountain area and one of the driest parts of Scandinavia. Annual precipitation averages 200–400mm as opposed to up to 2500mm in Jotunheimen. Rondane is far less known outside of Norway than other national parks; you are more likely to hike alongside locals here then you would in Jotunheimen.

Rondane National Park is Norway's oldest. It was established in 1962 and extended in 2003. Today it comprises an area of about 963km^2 and lies in the counties of Hedmark and Oppland, approximately 300km north of Oslo, 250km south of Trondheim, and 520km east of Bergen on the western coast. The northern part of the national park is the focus of this book. It has a very symmetrical and balanced topography. At its core, three mountain massifs of similar size and height form a triangle: Smiubelgin with Storsmeden (2016m) and Veslesmeden (2015m); Høgronden (2115m) with Midtronden (2060m) and Digerronden (2016m); and Rondslottet (2178m) with Vinjeronden (2046m) and Storronden (2138m). The three massifs are divided by three broad glacial valleys: Døralen running in a northeasterly direction; Illmanndalen to the south and Langglupdalen cutting through the centre. The glacial valleys and mountain massifs are surrounded by a circle of rounded peaks at 1600–1800m.

The area seems at its core largely untouched by humans, and the epic timescale over which change seems to occur comprises the irresistible appeal of this often lunar-like barren landscape. In short, the accessibility of the 2000m+ alpine tops, the well-developed routes, the smaller number of hikers compared to other areas, and lower precipitation together form a very inviting mix for exploring Rondane National Park.

Downstream view of the Storula river towards Rondvassbu (Route 4, Stage 1)

LANDSCAPE AND GEOLOGY

The landscape and landforms in this part of Rondane are unique in several ways. The whole park lies on top of the Norwegian fells, starting at an altitude of 1000m, thus being essentially above the tree line and extending to the top of Rondslottet with its 2178m of altitude. Despite its lack of glaciers, the landscape has a definite alpine character. This is due to the extent and frequency of glacial cirques, the steep and extended slopes, the rocky faces and talus slopes, and the high peaks. At first sight it looks barren, dull and grey due to the vast areas of exposed rocks. It is unlike any other national park as it consists of a highly homogenous bedrock. The bedrock is a metamorphosed sandstone (quartzite) from the Eocambrian period (600 million years old). Some 80% of the minerals found will be quartz, with feldspar accounting for most of the remainder. This makes it primarily a mineral landscape. The seemingly abandoned, predominantly grey rocks above ground have been shaped by glaciations and subsequently by the periglacial processes – mainly the high frequency of frost and thawing cycles that occur in this area of near permafrost – breaking down the rocks into large boulders at first and subsequently smaller rocks. The rocky nature of the landscape and the general poor nutritional content of the rock mean there is much less diversity in the vegetation.

PLANTS AND WILDLIFE

Vegetation is of course still present, notably in the valleys, but is far less diverse than in Dovrefjell or Jotunheimen and is dominated by small shrubs and willow trees. By

Emergency stone shelter on Høgronden (Route 4, Stage 4)

contrast, the slopes and mountainsides are mainly bare or covered by lichen, which shines bright yellow and green when illuminated by the sun in summer, and turns reddish in autumn. The relatively low snow cover and abundance of lichen have attracted reindeer into this area for thousands of years. Lichen forms the reindeer's main diet during the harsh winter months. Together with Dovrefjell, Rondane is home to the last strain of wild reindeer in Europe and their numbers are carefully managed and monitored.

ACCESS AND SERVICES

The main town that provides connections to the Rondane mountain huts that are relevant to the routes presented is Otta, with the train stations at Hjerkinn and Ringebu providing additional exit and entry points. Otta has a good range of shops, among them supermarkets and sports stores.

Figure 2 shows a schematic overview of public transport options into Rondane. Ringebu, Otta and Hjerkinn are all on the Trondheim–Oslo train line and are serviced several times a day, from both cities. The bus station (*skysstasjon*) in Otta is just outside the train station.

Local transport

Innlandstrafikk (www.innlandstrafikk.no) is the regional bus company. The routes presented in this guide start from Spranget near Mysusæter, close to the Rondvassbu mountain hut, which is a short hike away. There's a regular summer bus service from Otta to Spranget. Alternative access to the area is by bus from Ringebu to Straumbu, a short hike away from the Bjørnhollia hut. See Appendix C for further information on local transport.

Mountain huts

The Rondane mountain huts that are visited on the routes in this guide include Rondvassbu, Bjørnhollia, Døràlseter and Grimsdalshytta. Of these, Døràlseter and Grimsdalshytta can be accessed by car, while the other two require a hike from the nearest bus stop or car park. You can hike or cycle into Rondvassbu from the bus stop/car park at Spranget, just 6km away. Bjørnhollia can be reached from the car park in Straumbu, also 6km away. Døràlseter and Grimsdalshytta are accessible by private car only, with no public transport available at the time of writing. All huts are fully catered in the summer season, and except for Døràlseter are DNT-owned. Rondvassbu is particularly popular with families due to its beautiful location at Rondvatnet lake. It boasts extensive camping facilities, and campers can choose to book individual meals or full board just like other guests. Hikers are advised to book ahead between mid July and mid August (see https://rondvassbu.dnt.no/engelsk). As with all DNT huts, no one will be sent away – in fact the author was once given a mattress

Figure 2: Rondane, Dovrefjell & Trollheimen access

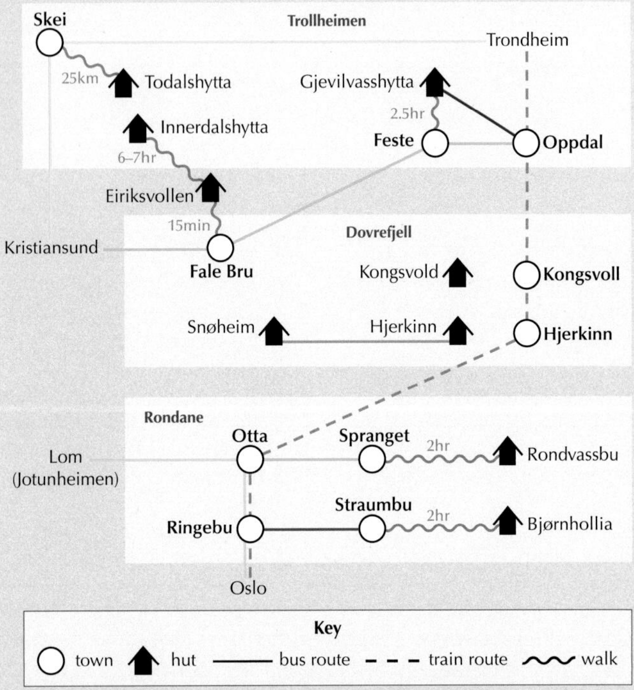

	Line	Connection
– – –	Oslo–Trondheim	Oslo–Gardermoen–Otta–Hjerkinn–Kongsvoll–Oppdal–Trondheim
——	205	Otta–Raphamn–Mysusæter–Spranget
——	206	Ringebu–Straumbu
——	FRAM Ekspress 901	Kristiansund–Fale Bru–Oppdal
——	summer shuttle bus	Hjerkinn–Snøheim (check https://snoheim.dnt.no/eng)
——	580	Oppdal–Gjevilvasshytta (Su, Th)
——	FRAM Ekspress 905	Kristiansund–Skei i Surnadal–Trondheim
——	Nordfjordekspressen VY146	Oslo–Gardermoen–Lillehammer–Otta–Lom

Valley views into Langglupdalen, with Høgronden peak in the distance (Route 4, Stage 3/Route 5, Stage 2)

on the floor of the cleaning supplies room which had been cleared specifically for this purpose!

THE ROUTES IN RONDANE

Two principal routes in the northern Rondane area are presented in this guide: the Rondane summits trek (Route 4) and the classic Rondane traverse (Route 5). Both start from the Spranget parking lot, near the town of Otta. Route 4 is a circular route that takes five days to complete. It goes into the alpine heart of Rondane, taking in its two highest peaks – Rondslottet and Høgronden – as well as two of the park's three glacial valleys. The stages across Rondslottet (Stage 2) and Høgronden (Stage 4) are strenuous and challenging and should only be attempted in good weather. Route 5 takes you from Spranget all across Rondane towards the northwestern corner of the national park and its boundary with Dovrefjell. This route takes 4–5 days. It is an ideal route for those who prefer to explore the high mountaintops on day hikes with lighter packs (using Rondvassbu as a base) and like the idea of connecting to Dovrefjell National Park. There is the possibility of extending either route by 1–2 days by incorporating additional stages onto the peaks of Storronden and Veslesmeden. Route 5 can additionally be extended to include the summiting of Rondslottet as a day hike.

Note that the bridge in Langglupdalen, used on both routes, is a summer bridge only. It's best to enquire (at Rondvassbu or Bjørnhollia mountain hut, for example) before planning a trip in the early season as to whether it has been put in place.

ROUTE 4

Rondane summits

Start/finish	Spranget, parking area (bus from Otta)
Distance	85km (53 miles)
Ascent	4200m
Descent	4200m
Time	5 days
Extensions	1–2 days; up to two extensions possible, visiting additional 2000m+ tops around Rondvassbu mountain hut, one of which could be combined with Stage 1 (weather permitting).

Thousands of years ago it was first the hunters and trappers that were attracted by the bountiful reindeer herds; later poets and painters tried to capture the wild and unforgiving beauty of Rondane. Today, hikers and other sports enthusiasts find their way through these challenging and solitary landscapes, returning time and again, attracted by its dark yet mystical shapes. Rondvassbu's lovely location is in stark contrast to the barren mountaintops around it.

This strenuous five-stage circular route starts and ends at the Spranget car park and bus stop. It explores the high alpine character of Rondane's highest peaks – Rondslottet (2178m; Stage 2) and Høgronden (2115m; Stage 4) – throwing in Vinjeronden (2046m; Stage 2) for good measure. These stages are long and strenuous. Don't let yourself be fooled by the seemingly low altitudes compared to other mountains you might know: the conditions underfoot, steepness of the terrain and exposure to weather make these stages a genuinely alpine experience. They are of course at the pinnacle of Rondane and afford marvellous views on good weather days as well as the satisfaction of having completed them.

Spranget can be reached by bus from Otta. Alternatively, the route can be entered (and exited) at Bjørnhollia. From there it's a 6km marked walk to Straumbu, where public transport is available to Ringebu train station once a day during the summer season. This local bus corresponds with the train to Oslo as well as the long-distance bus to Oslo and Gardermoen airport. The route can be exited at Dørålseter (end of Stage 3), but by private car only. The first stage is short: it only goes to Rondvassbu. It would be quite possible to extend the trek by summiting either Veslesmeden (2015m) or Storronden (2138m) – or potentially both – on the same day (see Route 5, Extensions 2 and 3). The second stage goes over the top of

Vinjeronden to the top of Rondslottet – the 'Castle of Rondane' – and continues on its eastern side to end in Bjørnhollia. Stage 3 provides a respite from climbing as it takes you across northern Rondane to Dørålseter. Stage 4 starts with a crossing of the spectacular glacio-fluvial deposits in the Dørålen valley, and then tests the stamina and calf muscles as it goes over the top of Høgronden. The final 500m vertical ascent of this stage is the steepest of any described in this guide. The stage ends after the long descent once again at Bjørnhollia. Finally, Stage 5 comprises a valley walk through Illmanndalen, passing Rondvassbu and returning to Spranget.

STAGE 1

Entry to Rondvassbu

Start	Spranget parking area and bus stop
Finish	Rondvassbu mountain hut
Distance	7km (4.5 miles)
Ascent	180m
Descent	90m
Difficulty	Easy
Time	2hr
Maximum altitude	1242m
Map	Nordeca Rondane Nord 1:50,000 Nr 2523

From the parking area at Spranget at the entry to Rondane National park you have two choices to reach Rondvassbu mountain hut. The gravel service road is the easy, busy option. To use this, follow it on the true left of the Storula river. However, the author recommends an alternative route which, although unmarked, is easy to find and much more scenic. It is described below.

Rondvassbu mountain hut is very popular with Norwegians in summer. Booking is recommended if you want to stay and explore the surrounding peaks.

The path leaves on the northwest side of the parking lot – do not cross under the barrier. Keep the **Storula river** on your right. After approximately 350 metres there is a bridge; cross here and continue in a northeasterly direction, parallel to the

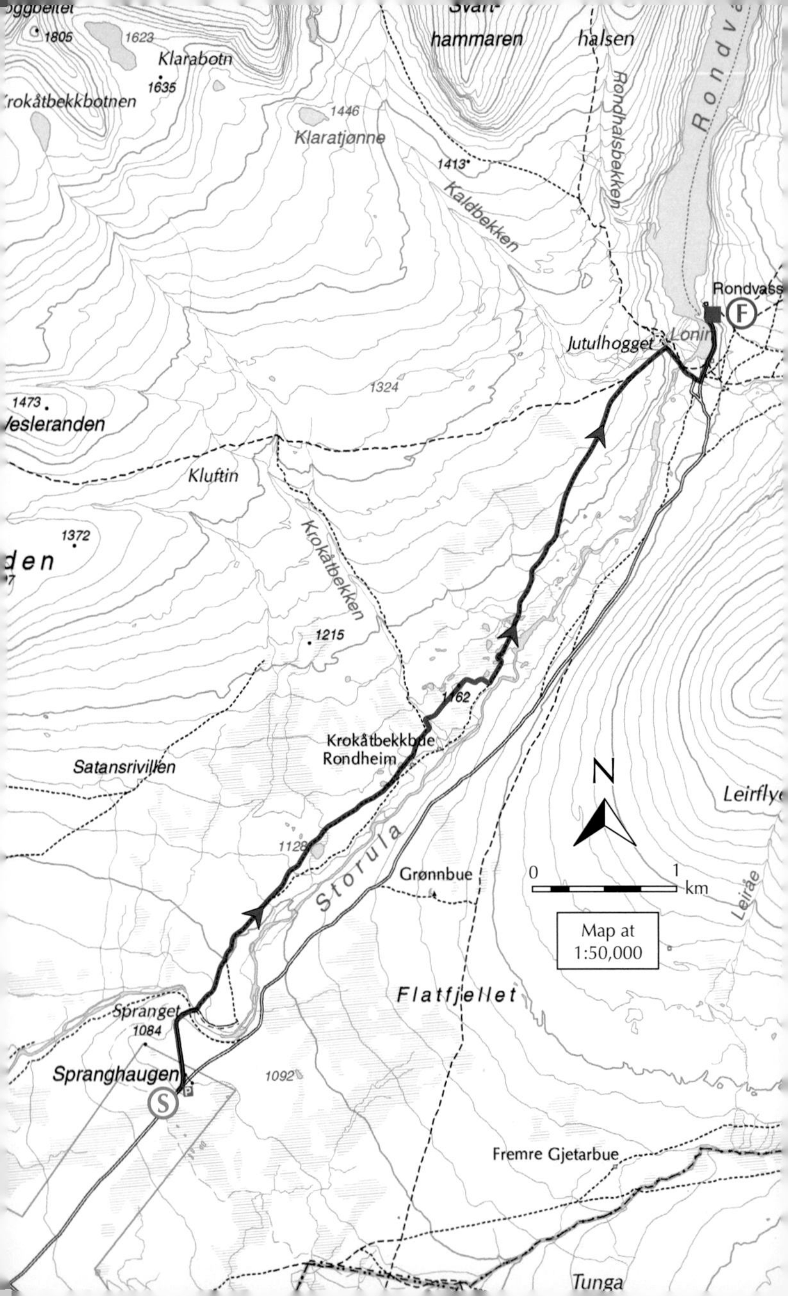

hammaren
halsen
1805
1623
Klarabotn
1635
1446
Klaratjønne
1413
Kaldbekken
Rondhalsbekken
F
Jutulhogget
1324
1473
Kluftin
1372
Krokåtbekken
1215
1162
Krokåtbekkbue
Rondheim
Satansrivillen
1128
Storula
Grønnbue
N
0
1
km
Map at
1:50,000
Leiråe
Flatfjellet
Spranget
1084
Spranghaugen
S
P
1092
Fremre Gjetarbue
Tunga

Approaching Rondvassbu and Rondvatnet lake, with Svartnuten (1842m) towering ahead

river (note that before the bridge another path turns back to Mysusæter). There are many inviting camp spots around the bridge, but if you're camping you need to keep a distance from the Spranget parking area, where camping is not permitted.

Halfway to Rondvassbu, about 200 metres after a little hunting lodge (Rondheim) that you pass on your right, the path forks. Follow the right fork to continue towards Rondvassbu. The trail later joins the paths from the Peer Gynt hut and Veslesmeden and is marked from here. It turns right and goes downhill to reach Rondvassbu with a little U-turn and over a permanent bridge across the river. Follow the trail as it joins the gravel road for the last 300 metres before reaching the **hut**.

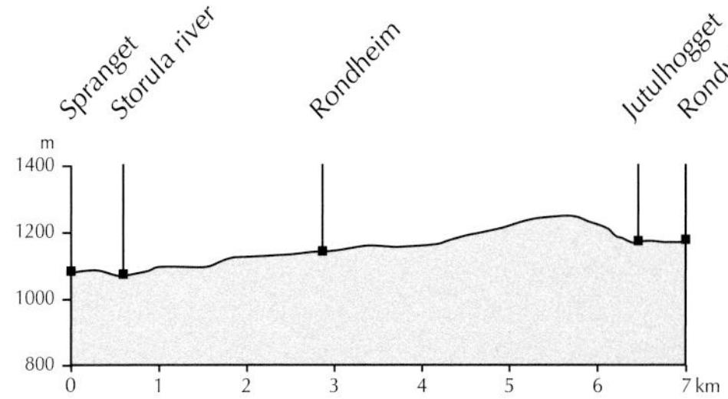

STAGE 2

Rondslottet high traverse

Start	Rondvassbu mountain hut
Finish	Bjørnhollia mountain hut
Distance	17.75km (11 miles)
Ascent	1350m
Descent	1610m
Difficulty	Very challenging
Time	10hr
Maximum altitude	2178m
Map	Nordeca Rondane Nord 1:50,000 Nr 2523

This stage takes you up and over Vinjeronden (2046m) and Rondslottet (2178m), into the Langglupdalen valley and finally to Bjørnhollia. It is a long and strenuous hike, with a bit of scrambling required en route to Rondslottet, but on good weather days the views from the summit are phenomenal, reaching into Dovrefjell and Jotunheimen. A steady descent over the eastern ridge leads to the Langglupdalen valley, and the remaining 8km are a comfortable and lovely valley walk – although tiredness and adverse weather could make this last stretch a challenge as well. The hut will be a welcoming sight after a long day of solid hiking.

Exit the **Rondvassbu mountain hut** and take the path straight up the hill, signposted in front of the hut. After a 10-metre scramble up the severely eroded path you'll reach the top of the ridge. Stay on the path as it heads off to the left, now going gently uphill. The wide path is testimony to the popularity of this hike.

Soon you'll reach the fork with the Storronden path. Continue straight ahead to reach the ridge of the Rondholet valley. From here the trail dips into the wide glacial valley, and the layout and views open up in front of you.

The views into **Rondholet** are very 'rondanesque' with the dark, stony tops of Svartnuten (1842m) to your left, Vinjeronden (2046m) in front and the Storronden (2138m) ridge to your right. You are looking into a highly typical albeit small glacial valley, and there are some lovely camping spots around two small lakes.

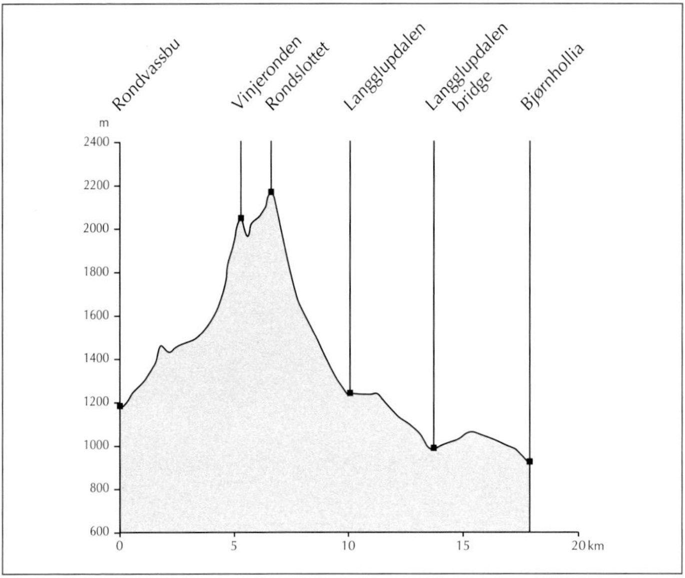
Rondvassbu
Vinjeronden
Rondslottet
Langglupdalen
Langglupdalen bridge
Bjørnhollia
m
2400
2200
2000
1800
1600
1400
1200
1000
800
600
0
5
10
15
20 km

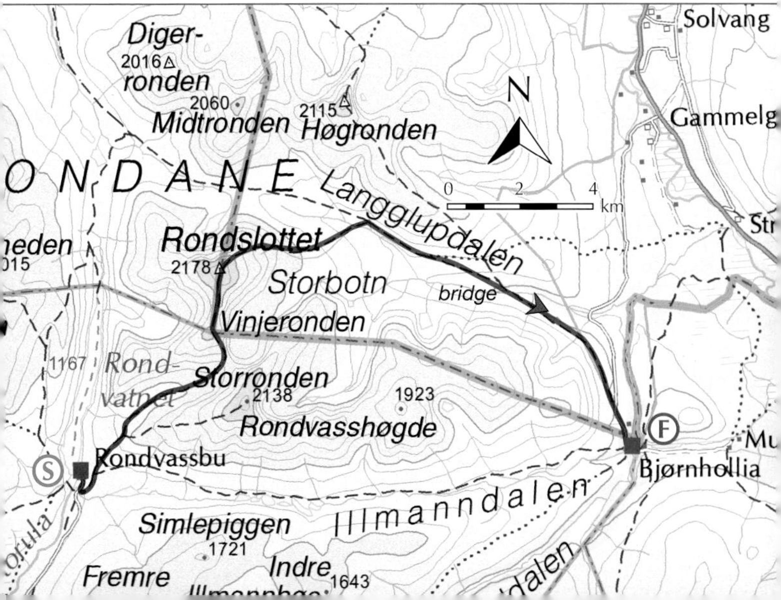
Solvang
Diger-
2016
ronden
2060
Midtronden
2115
Høgronden
Gammelg
N
0
2
4
km
O N D A N E
Langglupdalen
Str
neden
015
Rondslottet
2178
Storbotn
bridge
Vinjeronden
1167
Rond-
vatnet
Storronden
2138
1923
Rondvasshøgde
F
Mu
S
Rondvassbu
Bjørnhollia
Illmanndalen
Simlepiggen
1721
Indre
1643
Fremre
dalen

A hiker descends from Vinjeronden towards Rondslottet

The hike through the valley is smooth and gentle. Be sure to fill your water bottle about halfway up the valley where the path runs right next to the stream; there will be no water until well into your descent from Rondslottet. At the end of the valley the path ascends steeply to a saddle, but remains mostly sand and gravel underfoot.

Two large cairns mark the **saddle**, and the views from here are already spectacular. To your left, Vinjeronden towers above, with Storronden on the other side, and the views into the dramatically steep Storbotn cirque are fantastic, if not a little scary – a reminder not to attempt these hikes in foggy weather.

The way up to **Vinjeronden** is steep but clearly marked. Keep an eye on the red T-markers while you pick your way, using hands and feet to negotiate the boulders. It is a scramble, but you can always find a route. Don't skirt too close to the edge since it's a long, steep drop into the cirque. After about half an hour of scrambling from the saddle you should have reached the top, hopefully with rewarding vistas and an excellent spot for a Norwegian *niste* (picnic break).

Continuing towards Rondslottet, the path dips into a saddle/ridge between **Storbotn** and Styggebotn cirques – at first gently, then steeply down across a relatively narrow and exposed ridge. The final climb to Rondslottet is once more steep, at times airy, and you'll need to pick your way between slabs of rock. Using all fours is recommended until the path levels off just before the top. An enormous square cairn on the top of **Rondslottet** (2178m) welcomes you to the top of Rondane.

From the summit of **Rondslottet** on good weather days, Snøhetta – Dovrefjell's highest top at 2286m – is visible in the northwest, and eastern and northern parts of Jotunheimen are also within range. Needless to say, on a sunny day in summer, the spacious top will be busy.

The hike down from Rondslottet on the northeast side is less steep. Initially, the path skirts the cliffs on the north side of the mountain, but mainly you are walking an inclined plane down towards Langglupdalen valley below. What it lacks in steepness, however, it makes up in length. It is a steady 3km hike down to the Langglupbekken stream, followed by 8km eastwards towards Bjørnhollia. The path crosses the Langglupbekken twice, and at both places there are beautiful camping spots available. Continue on the trail as it skirts Veslsvulten (1579m) and then joins a dirt road for a little while before reaching a turnoff to the left. Take this turnoff and continue for the last 200 metres through the forest down to **Bjørnhollia mountain hut**.

STAGE 3

Langglupdalen

Start	Bjørnhollia mountain hut
Finish	Dørålseter mountain hut
Distance	21km (13 miles)
Ascent	900m
Descent	750m
Difficulty	Very challenging
Time	7½hr
Maximum altitude	1429m
Map	Nordeca Rondane Nord 1:50,000 Nr 2523

This stage corresponds with the second stage of the Rondane traverse route (Route 5, Stage 2).

No other valley stage has such an alpine character as this one, which follows Langglupdalen, cutting across northern Rondane and hiking below the national park's highest peaks. Rondane's highest sheer wall (700m) – the north face of Rondslottet – is an impressive sight, and the slow-weathering rock faces seen all along the hike make it a geologically interesting experience. The end of the stage features a magnificent example of glacial landscaping.

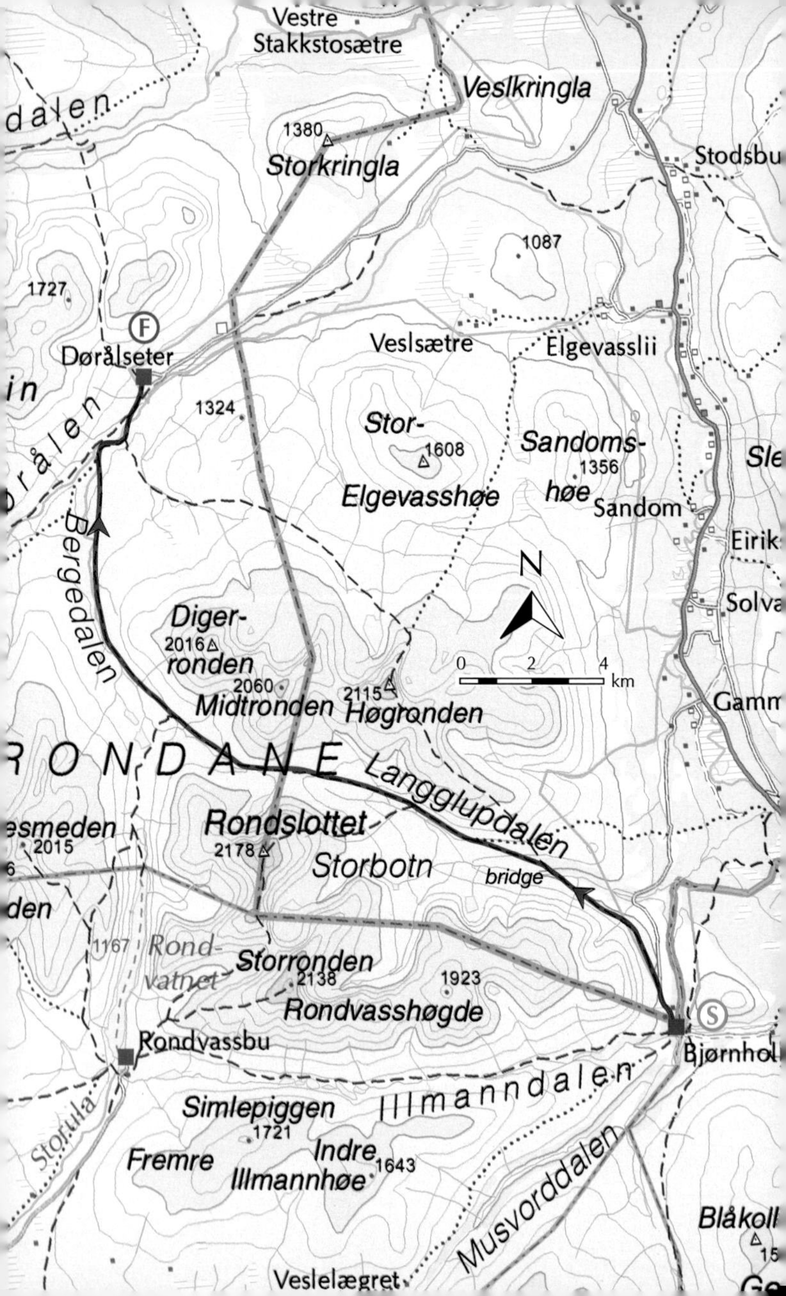

Vestre
Stakkstosætre
Veslkringla
dalen
1380
Storkringla
Stodsbu
1087
1727
Dørålseter
Veslsætre
Elgevasslii
in
Dørålen
1324
Stor-
1608
Elgevasshøe
Sandoms-
1356
høe
Sandom
Sle
Eirik
Bergedalen
N
Diger-
2016
ronden
Solva
0
2
4
km
2060
Midtronden
2115
Høgronden
Gamm
RONDANE
Langglupdalen
esmeden
2015
Rondslottet
2178
Storbotn
bridge
den
1167
Rond-
vatnet
Storronden
2138
1923
Rondvasshøgde
Rondvassbu
Bjørnhol
Illmanndalen
Storula
Simlepiggen
1721
Fremre
Indre
1643
Illmannhøe
Musvorddalen
Blåkoll
15
Veslelægret

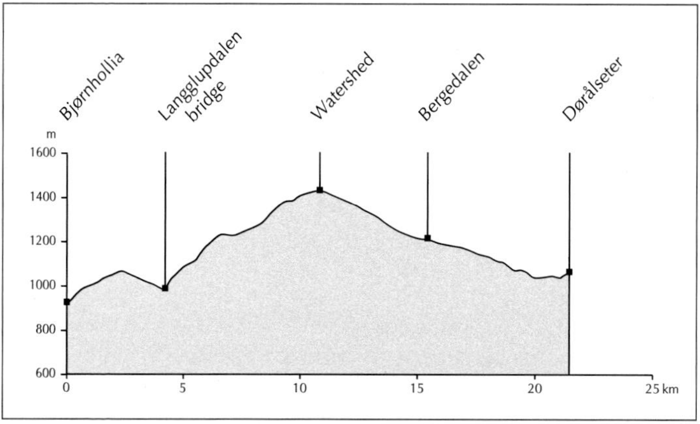

Starting from the **Bjørnhollia mountain hut** reception, move across the outdoor area towards the large tree that bears all the signs to huts and tops. Turn right at the gate in the direction of Rondslottet and Dørålseter. The path is well marked from the start. Soon you find yourself on a service road and then the T-markers lead you towards the left up the hill. The path on this stretch is at first sandy and pleasant underfoot, but later showcases once more a variety of stones, rocks and pebbles. Initially you head in a northerly direction, with superb vistas to the east over the Atna river valley opening up. (The large wooded areas there form an interesting contrast to the area you're hiking in, which is much more void of vegetation.)

Continue on the trail as it skirts the eastern side of Veslsvulten (1579m) and then turns westwards into Langglupdalen before meeting the Langglupbekken further upstream. At the bridge you have a fantastic view over a waterfall with Rondslottet in the background. If you don't mind the roaring of the river and waterfall you could find some delightful camping spots here, and in any case the area certainly invites for a rest.

Cross the bridge over Langglupbekken, then a short, steady climb in a northerly direction takes you a little higher over the stream to reach a crossroads indicating left for Dørålseter and right for Høgronden. Take the left. From here, a good gravelly path – at times rocky or stony underfoot – leads slowly but surely up the Langglupdalen valley towards the pass.

Rondslottet, on the opposite side of the valley, is a constant companion during this part of the hike. The river is now well below you but plenty of feeder streams cross the path, so refilling your water bottle is not a problem. The higher you get, the better the views towards the Rondslottet massif – especially the cirque of Langbotn underneath Storronden and next to it Storbotn, beside Vinjeronden: impressive sculptures formed long ago by glaciers.

Soon (at about the 8km mark) you pass the turnoff towards Rondslottet (see Stage 2) and can see that path snaking up the mountainside along the northern edge of the slope. Continue your ascent up the valley, crossing scree slopes and boulder fields which may slow your progress. The path soon reaches the pass and the highest point of the day at 1429m.

Take a moment to enjoy the **views**. You'll see the steepest and highest wall of Rondane on the northern side of Rondslottet, falling 700m. The outflow of the cirque's tarn flows towards Bergedalen (since you have passed the watershed). To the northeast, Høgronden (2115m), Midtronden (2060m) and Digerronden (2016m) are in view. Opposite, to the west, the scraggy tops of the Smedhamran range contrast with the rounded forms of the three 'ronden' tops.

Passing several signposts towards Rondvassbu and Veslesmeden, keep right towards Dørålseter and move into the **Bergedalen valley**. The path becomes easier again underfoot, with less scree to negotiate. A few kilometres before Dørålseter the valley opens up as the Bergedalsbekken stream joins the larger Døråe river. The landscape changes quite dramatically here. The Bergedalsbekken stream has cut a small but steep ravine into the rock.

At the end of the last ice age a huge chunk of ice blocked and slowed the flow of the glaciers coming down from the southern tops, thereby depositing vast amounts of sand, gravel and small rocks, and forming **terraces**. These terraces appear on the last kilometres before Dørålseter. They are hundreds of metres high and are a magnificent reminder of the glacial natural history. Eight thousand years of vegetation growth have hardly had an impact on the upper slopes. The humus layer is thin and vulnerable and it almost seems like you could be standing on a dune.

Descend towards the **Døråe river** along an easy sandy path. After passing the sign for the high route to Høgronden (Stage 4) the path crosses the river, and **Dørålseter** is only a few minutes away. There is a choice of two privately owned accommodation options – Øvre Dørålseter and Nedre Dørålseter – both friendly, welcoming huts that cater to hikers and provide DNT discounts.

STAGE 4

Høgronden high traverse

Start	Dørålseter mountain hut
Finish	Bjørnhollia mountain hut
Distance	20km (12.5 miles)
Ascent	1280m
Descent	1430m
Difficulty	Very challenging
Time	9hr
Maximum altitude	2115m
Map	Nordeca Rondane Nord 1:50,000 Nr 2523
Note	This stage should be avoided in poor weather due to the steepness of the rocky terrain.

This stage over the top of Høgronden (2115m) should only be done in good weather. The final 500m of ascent to the summit is the steepest of any described in this guide. However, the path is well marked, and the vistas over Rondane and into Jotunheimen are ample reward.

Do not underestimate this mountain, especially when carrying more than a light backpack. In wet weather the rocks become treacherously slippery. The descent, while less steep, is no less challenging.

Leave **Dørålseter mountain hut** and retrace your steps towards and along the river, following signs for Bjørnhollia until you reach the sign for Høgronden, shortly after crossing the bridge. Ascend steeply on the path up the sandy slopes of the glacial terraces and towards the edge of an area called **Skranglehaugan**.

At Skranglehaugan there are some more unique **glacial landforms**. The now-pockmarked landscape used to be full of large 'dead' ice blocks that had become detached from the glacier. As they melted, they left behind large cauldron-like indentations in the landscape. Some of them have become small tarns, but high along this path they look just like craters.

The path continues steadily and is relatively easy going (albeit long), first up the lovely **Vidjedalsbekken stream**. Many birds can be observed in this oasis-type landscape along the river valley. Refill your water bottle often, as you never know when the last opportunity will present itself.

Imsdalen
Sætri
Vestre
Stakkstosætre
Veslkringla
dalen
1380
Storkringla
Stodsbue
1087
1727
S
Døràlseter
Veslsætre
Elgevasslii
1324
Stor-
1608
Elgevasshøe
Sandoms-
høe
1356
Sandom
Vidjedalsbekken
Skrangle-
haugan
Eiriks
N
Diger-
ronden
2016
1460
Solva
0
2
4
km
2060
Midtronden
2115
Høgronden
shelter
Gamm
RONDANE
Langglupdalen
Rondslottet
2178
Storbotn
smeden
2015
bridge
den
1167
Rond-
vatnet
Storronden
2138
1923
Rondvasshøgde
F
Rondvassbu
Bjørnholl
Illmanndalen
Simlepiggen
1721
Storula
Fremre
Indre
1643
Illmannhøe
svorddalen
Blåkolle

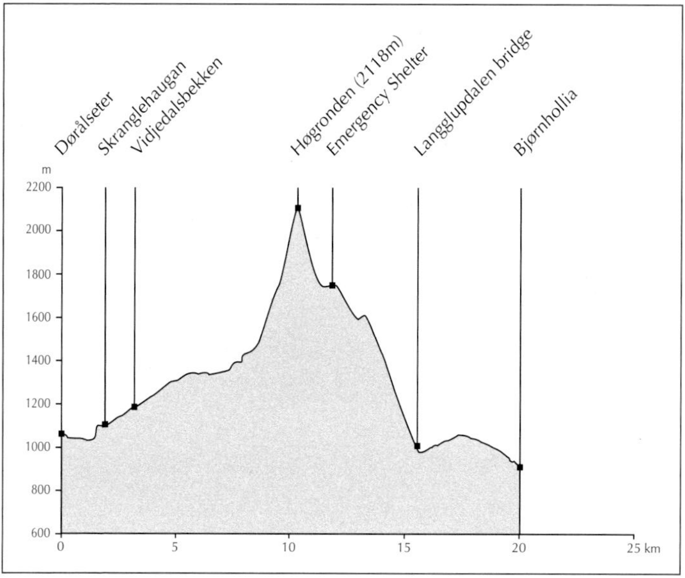

Neverbutjønne lake was dry when the author hiked this stage, making it possible to walk over the stony lake bed. Otherwise take the obvious route around the water. The well-marked path becomes stonier as you gain height. As Midtbotn cirque and its **lake** (1460m) between Høgronden (2115m) and Midtronden (2060m) come into view, the challenge of the ascent towards Høgronden becomes apparent. Pass Midtbotn on its northern side and ascend towards the ridge. The approach to Høgronden summit begins at around 1600m. These last 500m in particular are extremely steep and need to be approached with care.

A group of hikers on their way towards Høgronden

Far-reaching views from Høgronden towards Atnadalen

From the top of **Høgronden** the views on a good day are truly expansive. Only Rondslottet (2178m) and Storronden (2138m) on the opposite side of Langglupdalen are higher, and so you can look down on many of Rondane's other tops. Midtronden (2060m), Veslesmeden (2015m) and Trolltinden (2018m) can be seen. Further away in the west, Hornsjøhøe (1567m), and further to the northwest Gråhøe (1663m) and Kattuglehøe (1553m) near Grimsdalshytta are in view too. To the east is the wide valley of Atna, and in the north Folldalen. In short, a panorama that needs to be savoured.

The path down is again steep for the first 400m, but it is well marked and takes a careful route. No hand support is required generally. Just after this steep section you'll come to a rudimentary stone **emergency shelter**. These structures were traditionally used by hunters and trappers, and this one on Høgronden has recently been renovated. It is not particularly comfortable, but in an emergency you'd be grateful that it's there.

As you continue downwards, the trail flattens out a little over a saddle at Søre Oksle (1779m) before resuming a straight 700m descent over rocks, slate and small boulders. This part of the hike is described as 'the leg-eater' in Norwegian hiking folklore, and by the end of it you might see why.

Down by Langglupbekken at the summer bridge is the first opportunity to fill your water bottle after the long ascent and descent. From here it's a much easier path for the 4.5km to **Bjørnhollia mountain hut**. At the end of this stage you can exit Bjørnhollia by hiking to Straumbu (6km/2hr); there is public transport from Straumbu in summer. The described route, however, continues towards Spranget, through Illmanndalen and via Rondvassbu mountain hut.

STAGE 5

Illmanndalen

Start	Bjørnhollia mountain hut
Finish	Spranget – bus stop and car park
Distance	19km (12 miles)
Ascent	490m
Descent	320m
Difficulty	Challenging
Time	6hr
Maximum altitude	1301m
Map	Nordeca Rondane Nord 1:50,000 Nr 2523

The trek's final stage comprises two sections. The first goes from Bjørnhollia towards Rondvassbu through the narrow valley of Illmanndalen, with fairly high ranges either side concentrating focus on the immediate landscape. Once past Rondvassbu, the second part of the stage is through a much larger valley. You move downstream, following the course of the Storula. This sometimes fast-moving stream has carved a surprisingly steep canyon into the bedrock. Spranget and the adjacent parking area form the end of this stage and route. Public transport is available from the car park to the bus terminal and train station in Otta.

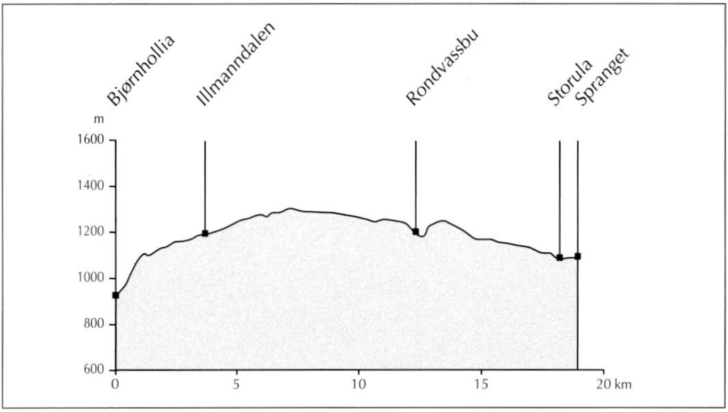

Leave the hut at **Bjørnhollia** and walk past the large tree with all the signposts to different locations. Exit through the gate on the western side of the property and follow the sign to Rondvassbu. Go uphill, ascending 200m in altitude on the south side of Veslsvulten (1579m).

As you climb you'll pass through a birch forest which, given the landscapes seen earlier on this trek, will almost seem lush. Throughout the hike a few small streams need to be crossed, none of which should pose a challenge. This section of the hike simply follows the valley between **Rondvasshøgde** (1951m) to the north and **Illmannhøe** (1643m) and **Simlepiggen** (1721m) to the south. 'Illmanndalen' means something akin to 'valley of the man of bad character', who is thought to have lived in this valley in earlier times.

After the watershed the path gently descends, and you pass a series of **lakes**. Around two-thirds of the way along the valley (9km from the hut), the path forks. The right fork continues to Rondvassbu mountain hut, while the left takes you to the southernmost end of Rondvatnet lake (just a few hundred metres south of the hut on the gravel road between Spranget and Rondvassbu). You can take either, depending on whether you want to take a break at Rondvassbu mountain hut or not.

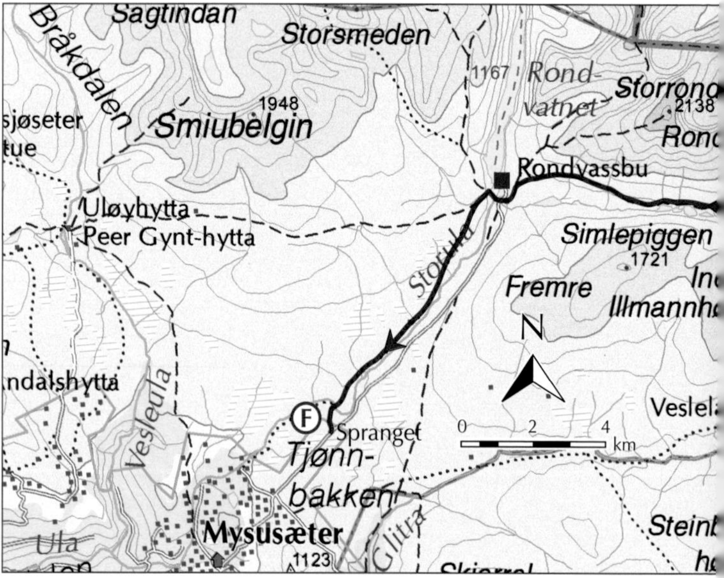

> The fantastic **views** onto the large glaciofluvial fan-like deposit at Jutulhogget, at the end of Rondvatnet lake, give a hint at the size of the glaciers and rivers that drained here after the last ice age. Today only the short Kaldbekken stream drains into the Storula river.

The southern fork (that ends at the southernmost point of the Rondvatnet lake) brings you to a major crossroads of paths. Here you have two choices to reach Spranget, both ending at the car park and bus stop. The fastest and less scenic option is the 6km gravel service road, which goes on the eastern side of the **Storula river**.

The second option is more attractive and quieter and is described here. While it is unmarked, it is not difficult to find and navigate. To continue with this option, cross the bridge at the southern tip of **Rondvatnet lake** and follow the signs to 'Peer-Gynt hytta'. Turn left at the junction just before the next bridge. Continue on this path for about 300 metres as it ascends out of the valley, and then you will notice a well-trodden path forking away from the main marked path. Take this well-trodden but unmarked path to the left. It will bring you towards the **Storula river** and follows the river on its true right. After approximately 5.5km the path meets a service road that leads you over a bridge and towards the car park and bus stop at **Spranget**.

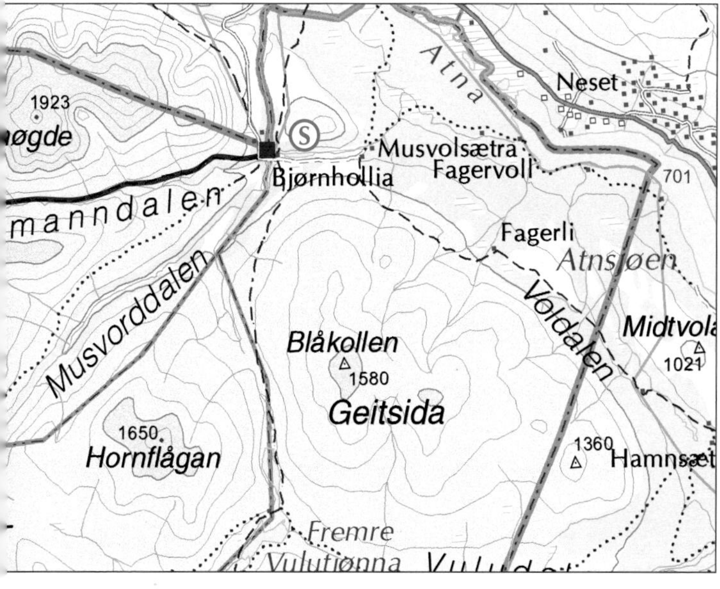

A group of hikers in the Illmanndalen valley, with Simlepiggen mountain in the background

ROUTE 5

Rondane traverse route

Start	Spranget, parking lot (bus from Otta)
Finish	Hjerkinn railway station
Distance	74km (46 miles)
Ascent	2440m
Descent	2510m
Time	4 days
Extensions	1–3 days. Up to three extensions possible, visiting individual 2000m+ tops around Rondvassbu mountain hut. The route can be extended north into Dovrefjell National Park by continuing on Route 6; either walk from Hjerkinn to Kongsvoll or take the train (20km).

This classic four-stage trek explores Rondane's glacial valleys and ends in Dovrefjell National Park, with some remarkable contrasts of landscape encountered en route. The harsh, barren and unforgiving eastern and northern walls of Rondslottet face the west of Høgronden, which, while less steep, is just as barren with only lichen growing on its higher slopes. This makes the thin strips of vegetation along the valley floors of Illmanndalen and Langglupdalen appear all the more precious and vulnerable. The sheer expanses of rock make way for the gentle rolling fells of Dovrefjell as you continue north – a remarkable change of landscape within just a few kilometres.

Weather and fitness permitting, the route allows for individual extensions towards four of the 10 mountaintops in this area above the 2000m mark. Hence personal preferences can easily be taken into account when planning the route. These top-tour extensions include hikes up Rondslottet (2178m; Extension 1) and Vinjeronden (2046m; also Extension 1), Veslesmeden (2015m; Extension 2) and Storronden (2138m; Extension 3), using Rondvassbu mountain hut as a base. Each of these extensions rewards with wonderful views, reaching far and wide. Note that Rondvassbu mountain hut is very popular with Norwegians in summer; booking is recommended if you want to stay and explore the surrounding peaks.

The main route starts from Spranget at the bottom of the triangle that is formed by the three central mountain massifs of Rondane National Park: Smiubelgin, Rondslottet and Høgronden. Stage 1 passes Rondvassbu and continues along the lovely and water-rich Illmanndalen valley towards Bjørnhollia mountain hut. Stage 2 follows the full length of the Langglupdalen valley, with striking and extensive views of the Rondslottet and Høgronden massifs on either side. It continues along the Bergedalen gorge towards the phenomenal glaciofluvial deposits near Dørålseter mountain hut – well worth exploring at leisure on an evening's stroll. At the start of Stage 3, heading towards Grimsdalshytta, you exit through the narrow Dørålsgluppen gorge, at the edge of Rondane's massive glaciofluvial valleys. From here the route continues across the gentler forms of the more rounded peaks of Dovrefjell National Park. You'll see the landscape changing from alpine to high fells and mountain plateaus as you cross increasingly fertile valleys, the greater diversity due to the change in bedrock in Dovrefjell.

The main route ends on the fourth day in Hjerkinn at the train station. The trek could be exited early at Bjørnhollia (end of Stage 1) by way of a 2hr hike to Straumbu. Public transport is available from Straumbu (summer schedule only), while Dørålseter and Grimsdalshytta can be reached by private car. Hjerkinn station boasts a heated waiting lounge area and restroom facilities for guests. Trains to Oslo or Trondheim have up to three daily departures. At Hjerkinn it is also possible to catch a shuttle bus to Snøheim mountain hut in Dovrefjell National Park (in season only). It's also possible to connect to the Dovrefjell traverse route (Route 6) by either taking the train north to the next station in Kongsvoll or hiking a marked route between Hjerkinn and Kongsvoll stations (20km).

STAGE 1

Spranget to Bjørnhollia

Start	Spranget – bus stop and car park
Finish	Bjørnhollia mountain hut
Distance	19km (12 miles)
Ascent	320m
Descent	490m
Difficulty	Challenging
Time	6hr
Maximum altitude	1301m
Map	Nordeca Rondane Nord 1:50,000 Nr 2523

The first stage of the Rondane traverse is long but without much change in elevation. The first leg in particular, from Spranget to Rondvassbu, is so easy underfoot that you will be able to look around while hiking rather than having to stop to enjoy the views. The most dramatic view of the stage is at the start of its second leg and is not a mountaintop: once you've crossed the bridges over the Storula river near Rondvassbu, and after the short, steep ascent at the eastern edge of Illmanndalen, make sure to turn around and enjoy the incredible vista onto the large glaciofluvial fan-like deposit at the southern tip of Rondvatnet lake.

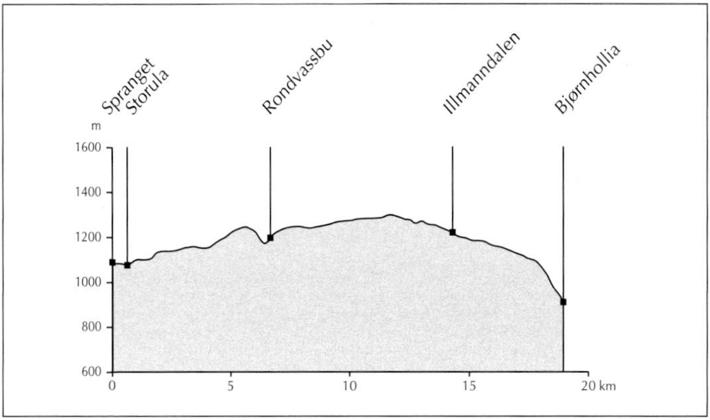

The path leaves on the northwest side of the parking lot – do not cross under the barrier. Keep the **Storula river** on your right. After approximately 350 metres there is a bridge; cross here and continue in a northeasterly direction, parallel to the river (note that before the bridge another path turns back to Mysusæter). There are many inviting camp spots around the bridge, but if you're camping you need to keep a distance from the Spranget parking area, where camping is not permitted.

Halfway to Rondvassbu, about 200 metres after a little hunting lodge that you pass on your right, the path forks. Follow the right fork to continue towards Rondvassbu. The trail later joins the paths from the Peer Gynt hut and Veslesmeden and is marked from here. It turns right and goes downhill to reach Rondvassbu with a little U-turn and over a permanent bridge across the river. Follow the trail as it joins the gravel road for the last 300 metres before reaching the **hut**, which offers refreshments to hikers throughout the day.

From here the route retraces itself for 300 metres and then continues onward towards Bjørnhollia, along the Illmanndalen valley. Leave Rondvassbu hut, turn right and follow the dirt road until you reach the signposted tracks to Bjørnhollia to your left. Go up the slope, and after a short climb the path levels and the first of many lakes in the Illmanndalen valley comes into view. As you'll discover, the valley is dotted with a pleasing string of lakes. **Illmanndalen valley** and Bjørnhollia form a little oasis of vegetation in this otherwise stark Rondane mountainscape.

The trail takes you all along the valley with **Rondvasshøgde** (1951m) on your left, and **Simlepiggen** (1721m) and **Illmannhøe** (1643m) on your right. It is a well-worn, wide and signposted path that slowly becomes smaller but remains obvious. It is usually sandy or gravelly and is comfortable underfoot. At almost halfway you approach the watershed. From here it's slightly downhill for the remainder of the hike. After the watershed, a small stream develops that gathers speed and is creating a minor canyon. Cross over scree that has been deposited across the valley by a glacial moraine; some rock hopping is required here.

As you descend you'll notice an increasing amount of vegetation, primarily on the south-facing slopes. The birch and beech woods hold the warmth, resulting in a pleasant microclimate around Bjørnhollia. Over the last kilometre the path drops quickly in height and descends towards **Bjørnhollia**, although progress may be quite slow when bilberries and blueberries are in season in August. There are plenty of nice camping spots in the vicinity, but remember the camping fee if you are staying close to the hut.

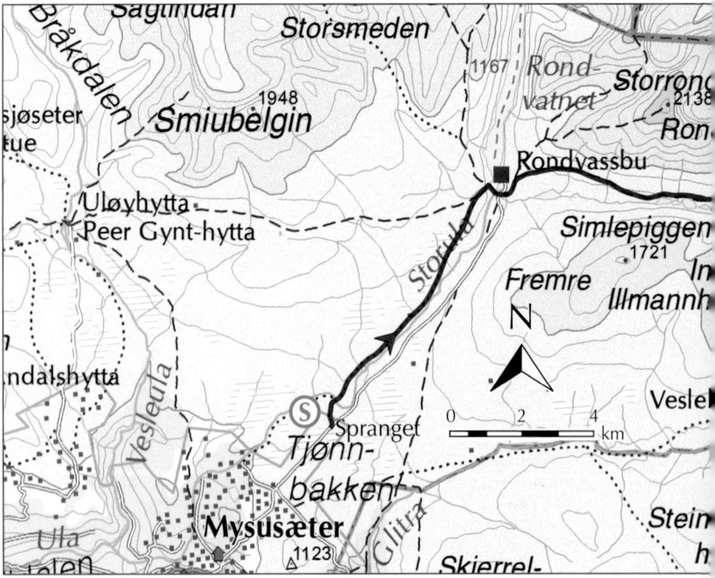

Jutulhogget: a prime example of a glaciofluvial deposit into Rondvatnet lake, with Rondvassbu hut on the lower right

STAGE 2

Langglupdalen

Start	Bjørnhollia mountain hut
Finish	Dørålseter mountain hut
Distance	21km (13 miles)
Ascent	900m
Descent	750m
Difficulty	Very challenging
Time	7½hr
Maximum altitude	1429m
Map	Nordeca Rondane Nord 1:50,000 Nr 2523

No other valley stage has such an alpine character as this one, which follows Langglupdalen, cutting across northern Rondane and hiking below the national park's highest peaks. Rondane's highest sheer wall (700m) – the north face of Rondslottet – is an impressive sight, and the slow-weathering rock faces seen all along the hike make it a geologically interesting experience. The end of the stage features a magnificent example of glacial landscaping.

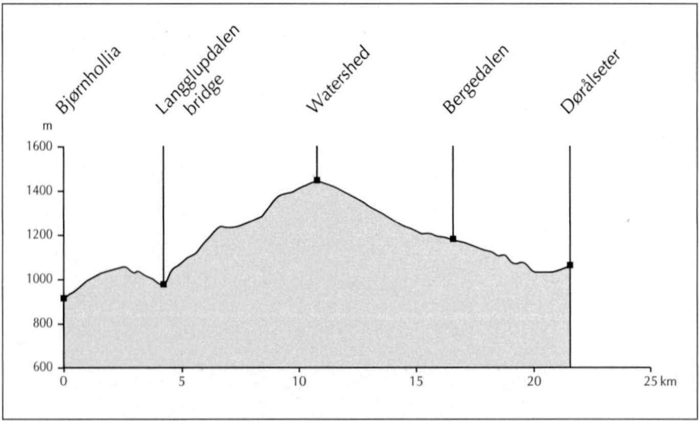

Vestre
Stakkstosætre
Veslkringla
1380
Storkringla
Stodsbuøye
1087
Veslsætre
Elgevasslii
1324
Stor-
1608
Elgevasshøe
Sandoms-
1356
høe
Sandom
Eiriksrud
Solvang
N
0
2
4
km
Diger-
2016
ronden
2060
Midtronden
2115
Høgronden
N D A N E
Langglupdalen
Rondslottet
2178
Storbotn
bridge
1167
Rond-
vatnet
Storronden
2138
1923
Rondvasshøgde
Rondvassbu
Bjørnhollia
Illmanndalen
Simlepiggen
1721
Fremre
Indre
1643
Illmannhøe
Musvorddalen
Blåkollen
1580

Starting from the **Bjørnhollia mountain hut** reception, move across the outdoor area towards the large tree that bears all the signs to huts and tops. Turn right at the gate in the direction of Rondslottet and Døralseter. The path is well marked from the start. Soon you find yourself on a service road and then the T-markers lead you towards the left up the hill. The path on this stretch is at first sandy and pleasant underfoot, but later showcases once more a variety of stones, rocks and pebbles. Initially you head in a northerly direction, with superb vistas to the east over the Atna river valley opening up. (The large wooded areas there form an interesting contrast to the area you're hiking in, which is much more void of vegetation.)

Continue on the trail as it skirts the eastern side of Veslsvulten (1579m) and then turns westwards into Langglupdalen before meeting the Langglupbekken further upstream. At the bridge you have a fantastic view over a waterfall with Rondslottet in the background. If you don't mind the roaring of the river and waterfall you could find some delightful camping spots here, and in any case the area certainly invites for a rest.

Cross the bridge over Langglupbekken, then a short, steady climb in a northerly direction takes you a little higher over the stream to reach a crossroads indicating left for Døralseter and right for Høgronden. Take the left. From here, a good gravelly path – at times rocky or stony underfoot – leads slowly but surely up the Langglupdalen valley towards the pass.

Rondslottet, on the opposite side of the valley, is a constant companion during this part of the hike. The river is now well below you but plenty of feeder streams cross the path, so refilling your water bottle is not a problem. The higher you get, the better the views towards the Rondslottet massif – especially the cirque of Langbotn underneath Storronden and next to it Storbotn, beside Vinjeronden: impressive sculptures formed long ago by glaciers.

Soon (at about the 8km mark) you pass a turnoff towards Rondslottet and can see that path snaking up the mountainside on the right-hand side of the opposite slope. Continue your ascent up the valley, crossing scree slopes and boulder fields which may slow your progress. The path soon reaches the pass and the highest point of the day at 1429m.

Take a moment to enjoy the **views**. You'll see the steepest and highest wall of Rondane on the northern side of Rondslottet, falling 700m. The cirque's tarn flows towards Bergedalen (since you have passed the watershed). To the northeast, Høgronden (2115m), Midtronden (2060m) and Digerronden (2016m) are in view. Opposite, to the west, the scraggy tops of the Smedhamran range contrast with the rounded forms of the three 'ronden' tops.

Passing several signposts towards Rondvassbu and Veslesmeden, keep right towards Dørålseter and move into the Bergedalen valley. The path becomes easier again underfoot, with less scree to negotiate. A few kilometres before Dørålseter the valley opens up as the Bergedalsbekken stream joins the larger Døråe river. The landscape changes quite dramatically here. The Bergedalsbekken stream has cut a small but steep ravine into the rock.

At the end of the last ice age a huge chunk of ice blocked and slowed the flow of the glaciers coming down from the southern tops, thereby depositing vast amounts of sand, gravel and small rocks, and forming **terraces**. These terraces appear on the last kilometres before Dørålseter. They are hundreds of metres high and are a magnificent reminder of the glacial natural history. Eight thousand years of vegetation growth have hardly had an impact on the upper slopes. The humus layer is thin and vulnerable and it almost seems like you could be standing on a dune.

Descend towards the **Døråe river** along an easy sandy path. After passing the sign for a high route to Høgronden the path crosses the river, and **Dørålseter** is only a few minutes away. There is a choice of two privately owned accommodation options – Øvre Dørålseter and Nedre Dørålseter – both friendly, welcoming huts that cater to hikers and provide DNT discounts.

Evening colours from Dørålseter mountain hut, looking southwest towards Nordre Smedhammern and the Smedbotn cirque

STAGE 3

Dørålseter to Grimsdalshytta

Start	Øvre Dørålseter mountain hut
Finish	Grimsdalshytta mountain hut
Distance	16km (10 miles)
Ascent	730m
Descent	800m
Difficulty	Challenging
Time	6hr
Maximum altitude	1388m
Map	Nordeca Rondane Nord 1:50,000 Nr 2523

A farewell in style to the rocky boulders and steep climbs of the Rondane heartland, and a slow change of surroundings towards the gentler hills that are characteristic of the Dovre. This stage is truly between two hiking worlds.

Note that the initial ascent involves a scramble up and over rock falls from both sides of the Dørålsglupen gorge. Due to its narrow, shady nature, snow and ice can be present well into summer and extra care is needed when navigating potentially icy, slippery stretches.

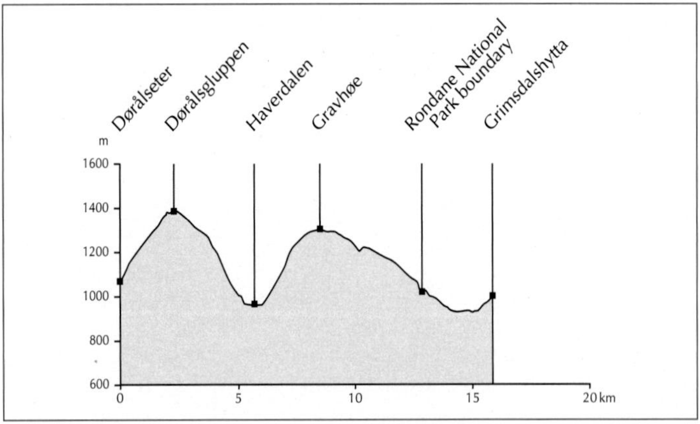

Exiting **Øvre Døralseter hut**, turn right and follow the T-marked path uphill towards Grimsdalshytta. The path takes you steadily up the **Dørålsglupen gorge**, a narrow V-shaped gorge between the tops of Stygghøin (1727m and 1639m). The narrowest part involves a 400m scramble which is slippery when wet – take good care.

> **Dørålsglupen** seems like a gigantic, dark gate between two worlds. Ice carved this canyon into the mountains, with steep walls either side, and scree and rockfalls have filled the valley to form a characteristic V-shape. Water is still a constant companion underneath the rock bed, often invisible but noisy. A dramatic exit from Rondane.

Ascending Døralsglupen, a narrow scree-filled gorge

Once at the saddle, the rock hopping continues, but soon panoramic views into Haverdalen valley open up, and you'll see the path ascending towards Gravhøe (1488m) on the other side of the valley. The descent towards Haverdalen is stony underfoot and the trail meets a stream that you more or less follow steeply down into the valley. At first you walk in the actual stream bed (you should be able to keep your feet dry by stone-hopping), and later the path leads along the escarpment higher up.

At **Haverdalen**, cross the Haverdalsåe river over a somewhat unstable looking bridge. (It seems perfectly safe though.) On the other side the path becomes easier underfoot and progress will be faster. The surrounding views into the birch woods and fertile valley form a welcome contrast to the earlier sections of the stage. Here and there, delightful patches of green invite for a rest.

The path climbs further towards Storkollen top (1306m) and around it, crossing a large and fairly even plateau between **Gravhøe** and Gravhøtangen (1291m). Here the trail will be wet and marshy in places.

In good weather, fantastic **views** deep into Dovrefjell will be the reward from the hike's highpoint. Folldalen valley can be seen, with the towering peak of Snøhetta (2286m) to the northwest.

The Grimse river valley comes into view and the trail descends into birch woods again, with many flowering plants in the undergrowth. Drop into the valley and cross the **Grimse river** over a sturdy bridge, where there is a reasonably large campsite with basic facilities. (A small fee is charged and can be paid onsite.) **Grimsdalshytta mountain hut** is just a short walk up the service road. This large, warm and welcoming hut will be a delight to the weary hiker, especially after a rainy day.

The fertile **valley** of the Grimse river is to this day an important summer pasture. It is also the natural barrier between Rondane and Dovrefjell national parks. There are many natural, historical and cultural sites in this traditional mountain valley. A 2.8km circular walk called Barthstigen, from the campsite at the Grimse river crossing, features information panels, should you have energy to spare.

STAGE 4

Grimsdalshytta to Hjerkinn

Start	Grimsdalshytta mountain hut
Finish	Hjerkinn (train station)
Distance	17.75km (11 miles)
Ascent	490m
Descent	470m
Difficulty	Challenging
Time	5½hr
Maximum altitude	1340m
Map	Nordeca Rondane Nord 1:50,000 Nr 2523

This is the last stage of the Rondane traverse, ending at Hjerkinn train station. The trail follows gently undulating terrain with the soft-coned mountain shapes typical of Dovre National Park on either side. In good weather it is easy hiking with open views, as the plateau does not have many forested areas. In poor weather it is a more challenging affair. From Hjerkinn it is possible to continue onwards towards the Dovrefjell traverse (see Route 6) and even further towards Trollheimen (see Trollheimen chapter).

You are formally leaving Rondane National Park and entering Dovre National Park as you start the hike from **Grimsdalshytta**. From the main door of the hut, proceed through the gate and cross the parking lot. The path to Hjerkinn is marked by a sign and continues to be well marked throughout. Note that in forested areas, red bands around trees are used as waymarkers, rather than the red T-markers.

The trail ascends gently along the hillside of Kattuglehøe (1553m) and runs parallel to the Tverråe stream, a tributary of the Grimse river. Proceed through the

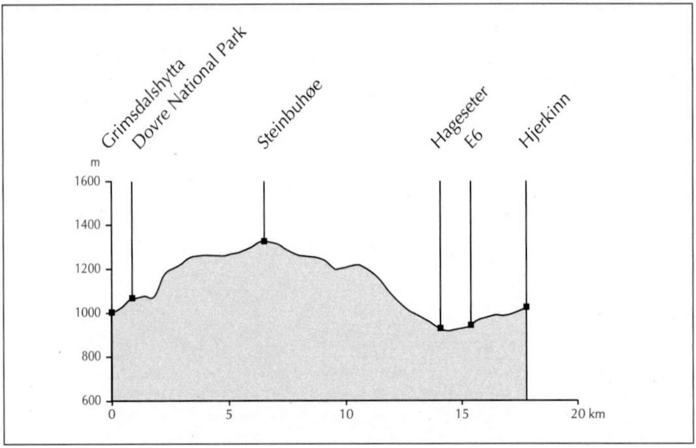

slightly undulating landscape, crossing various small streams along the way. On the whole the path is pleasant and smooth underfoot, dipping at times to cross tributaries. Along the way there are numerous campsites close to streams.

At 5.6km the trail makes a 90° left turn, which is well marked. Here a new route has been set up to skirt the newly created Veslehjerkinntjønnin nature reserve. Shortly after, as you turn right towards the north again, you'll reach the highest point of the day (just below the top of **Steinbuhøe**, 1352m).

Snøhetta (2286m), as well as Svånåtindan (2209m) rise ahead for the first time on this hike, while behind you in the south the many imposingly dark tops of Rondane are still visible. In the east, Mehøe (1425m) and Pikhetta (1510m) complete the stunning panoramic **views**.

The descent into Hageseter is a gentle one on an easy path, crossing a few streams and varying between muddy and gravelly underfoot until you reach the Hageseter campsite and lodgings (formerly **Gåutesætre**). At a crossroads you'll see the sign of the St Olav Way – an age-old pilgrim's road that runs right through Dovrefjell.

The **St Olav Way** is becoming increasingly popular with walkers of all ages, and the section through Dovrefjell forms one of its most scenic parts. You could walk the St Olav Way from here to Kongsvoll (20km, 1 day) – the start of the Dovrefjell traverse (Route 6).

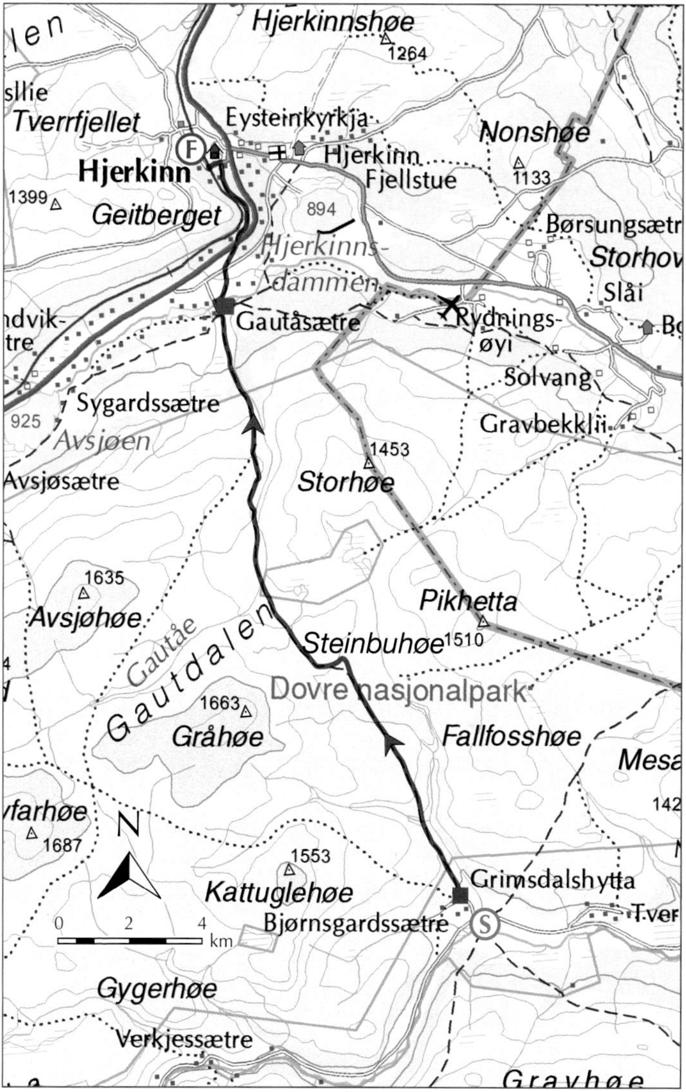
Hjerkinnshøe
1264
Tverrfjellet
Eysteinkyrkja
F
Hjerkinn
Hjerkinn
Fjellstue
Nonshøe
1133
1399
Geitberget
894
Hjerkinns-
dammen
Slåi
Gautåsætre
Rydnings-
øyi
Solvang
Sygardssætre
925
Avsjøen
Gravbekklii
1453
Avsjøsætre
Storhøe
1635
Pikhetta
Avsjøhøe
Gautåe
Gautdalen
Steinbuhøe
1510
Dovre nasjonalpark
1663
Gråhøe
Fallfosshøe
1687
N
1553
Grimsdalshytta
Kattuglehøe
0
2
4
km
Bjørnsgardssætre
S
Gygerhøe
Verkjessætre
Gravhøe

View of Rondane in the south from the highpoint of the stage

Go straight ahead, over the bridge and immediately after turn right towards Hjerkinn. The path meanders through the valley and then rises towards a slope and crosses the major E6 road. Take care here, as cars and lorries go fast and will not be expecting crossing pedestrians.

Continue on the west side of a small picnic area. The path is well marked. From here it is a forest trail towards Hjerkinn. After 45min or so you'll reach the Hjerkinnhus Hostel, which caters not only for pilgrims on the St Olav Way but also to hikers and other visitors. **Hjerkinn rail station** is a further 200 metres to the left, up the road. It has restroom facilities as well as a large, warm and comfortable waiting room. From Hjerkinn there are train connections towards Otta/Oslo as well as Kongsvoll/Oppdal/Trondheim. A regular shuttle bus runs to Snøheim mountain hut from the Hjerkinnhus Hostel in the summer season.

EXTENSION 1

Rondslottet (2178m) and Vinjeronden (2046m) summits

Start/finish	Rondvassbu mountain hut
Distance	13.5km (8.5 miles)
Ascent/descent	1100m
Difficulty	Challenging
Time	8hr
Maximum altitude	2178m
Map	Nordeca Rondane Nord 1:50,000 Nr 2523
Note	This route involves some airy scrambling towards the top of Rondslottet; it should not be attempted in foggy weather.

This extension can be done by staying over at Rondvassbu mountain hut. It is the most demanding of the three extensions presented. Rondslottet, with its supersized cairn at the summit, is a challenging hike but it is especially rewarding in good weather. Being on top of Rondane, all the lesser 2000m+ tops will be in view, and in addition it's possible to see far into Dovrefjell with the Snøhetta mountain in the distance, over 50km to the northwest.

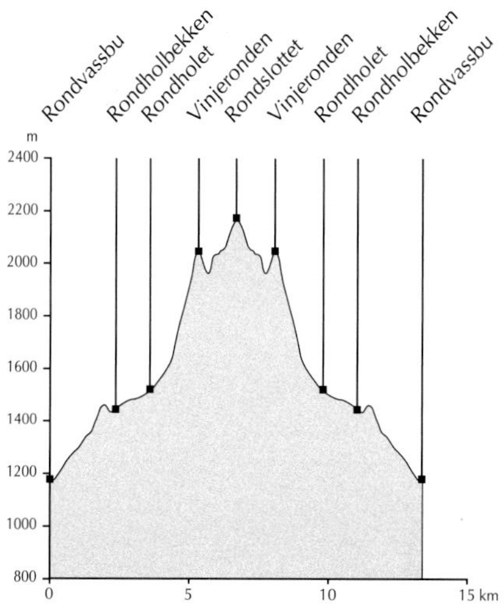

Exit the **Rondvassbu mountain hut** and take the path straight up the hill, signposted in front of the hut. After a 10-metre scramble up the severely eroded path you'll reach the top of the ridge. Stay on the path as it heads off to the left, now going gently uphill. The wide path is testimony to the popularity of this hike.

Soon you'll reach the fork with the Storronden path. Continue straight ahead to reach the ridge of the Rondholet valley. From here the trail dips into the wide glacial valley, and the layout and views open up in front of you.

The views into **Rondholet** are very 'rondanesque' with the dark, stony tops of Svartnuten (1842m) to your left, Vinjeronden (2046m) in front and the

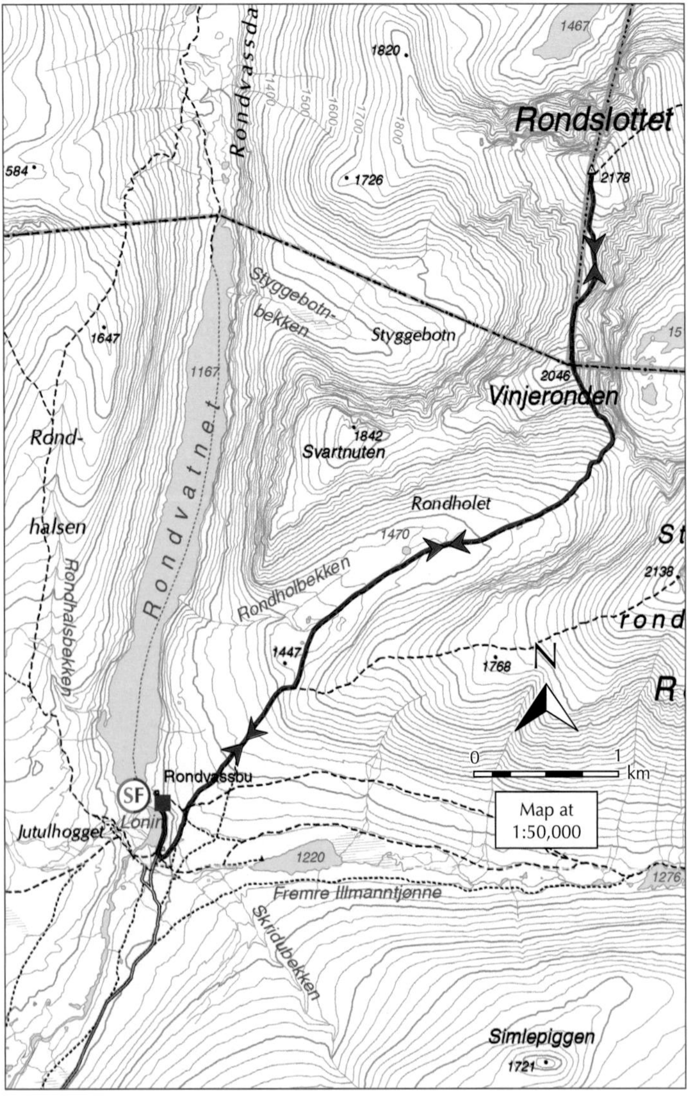
Rondvassda
Rondslottet
1467
1820
1400
1500
1600
1700
1800
584
1726
2178
Styggebotn-
bekken
Styggebotn
1647
1167
2046
Vinjeronden
Rond-
halsen
Rondvatnet
1842
Svartnuten
Rondholet
1470
Rondholbekken
Rondhalsbekken
2138
rond
1447
1768
N
0
1
km
Rondvassbu
SF
Map at
1:50,000
Jutulhogget
1220
1276
Fremre Illmanntjønne
Skridubekken
Simlepiggen
1721

Walking up the Rondholet valley towards the saddle between Vinjeronden and Storronden

Storronden (2138m) ridge to your right. You are looking into a highly typical albeit small glacial valley, and there are some lovely camping spots around two small lakes.

The hike through the valley is smooth and gentle. Be sure to fill your water bottle about halfway up the valley where the path runs right next to the stream; it is the last opportunity until you return down again. At the end of the valley the path ascends steeply to a saddle, but remains mostly sand and gravel underfoot.

Two large cairns mark the **saddle**, and the views from here are already spectacular. To your left, Vinjeronden towers above, with Storronden on the other side, and the views into the dramatically steep Storbotn cirque are fantastic, if not a little scary – a reminder not to attempt these hikes in foggy weather.

The way up to Vinjeronden is steep but clearly marked. Keep an eye on the red T-markers while you pick your way, using hands and feet to negotiate the boulders. It is a scramble, but you can always find a route. Don't skirt too close to the edge since it's a long, steep drop into the cirque. After about half an hour of scrambling from the saddle you should have reached the top of **Vinjeronden**, hopefully with rewarding vistas and an excellent spot for a Norwegian *niste* (picnic break).

Continuing towards Rondslottet, the path dips into a saddle/ridge between **Storbotn** and **Styggebotn** cirques – at first gently, then steeply down across a relatively narrow and exposed ridge. The final climb to Rondslottet is once more steep, at times airy, and you'll need to pick your way between slabs of rock.

Hikers on top of Rondslottet (2178m), with views onto Høgronden (2115m)

Using all fours is recommended until the path levels off just before the top. An enormous square cairn on the top of **Rondslottet** (2178m) welcomes you to the top of Rondane.

From the summit of **Rondslottet** on good weather days, Snøhetta – Dovrefjell's highest top at 2286m – is visible in the northwest, and eastern and northern parts of Jotunheimen are also within range. Needless to say, on a sunny day in summer, the spacious top will be busy.

From the top of Rondslottet, retrace your steps to **Rondvassbu mountain hut**.

EXTENSION 2

Veslesmeden summit (2015m)

Start/finish	Rondvassbu mountain hut
Distance	12.5km (7.75 miles)
Ascent/descent	850m
Difficulty	Challenging
Time	4½hr
Maximum altitude	2015m
Map	Nordeca Rondane Nord 1:50,000 Nr 2523

This summit hike is a wonderful extension and a great option if you want to increase the collection of 2000m+ tops in your book. It is more interesting than the ridge walk up to Storronden, albeit also longer. The last short part of the ascent is steep and airy but you are rewarded with full views into the cirques and subglacial lakes of the Smiubelgin massif. It is also good way to 'warm up' for the more challenging ascents to other Rondane peaks, should you wish to attempt them.

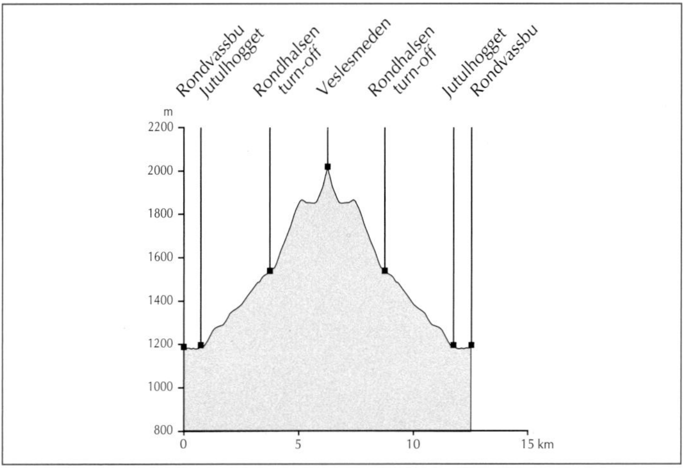

From the **Rondvassbu mountain hut**, exit to the left onto the dirt road. Cross the two bridges over the Storula river and initially follow the signs to Dørålseter. This will take you slowly up the valley along the flank of **Rondhalsen**. The path is easy to walk, wide and good underfoot. After about 1¼hr you'll come to a fork: take the turnoff to the left, which goes to Veslesmeden.

The trail continues in a steady climb that becomes steeper as you go along. The terrain is made up of slabs of stone of varying sizes. The nearly 400m ascent takes you to the top of **Svarthammaren**. Here you walk on the ridge between two cirques that plunge several hundred metres, with the unusual top of Veslesmeden – a dark, huge pile of shale and slate that looks like a gigantic cube – nicely in view ahead. The last ascent is testing on the legs and is quite airy in places, with drops of 500–600m. Care is therefore required as you approach the summit of **Veslesmeden**.

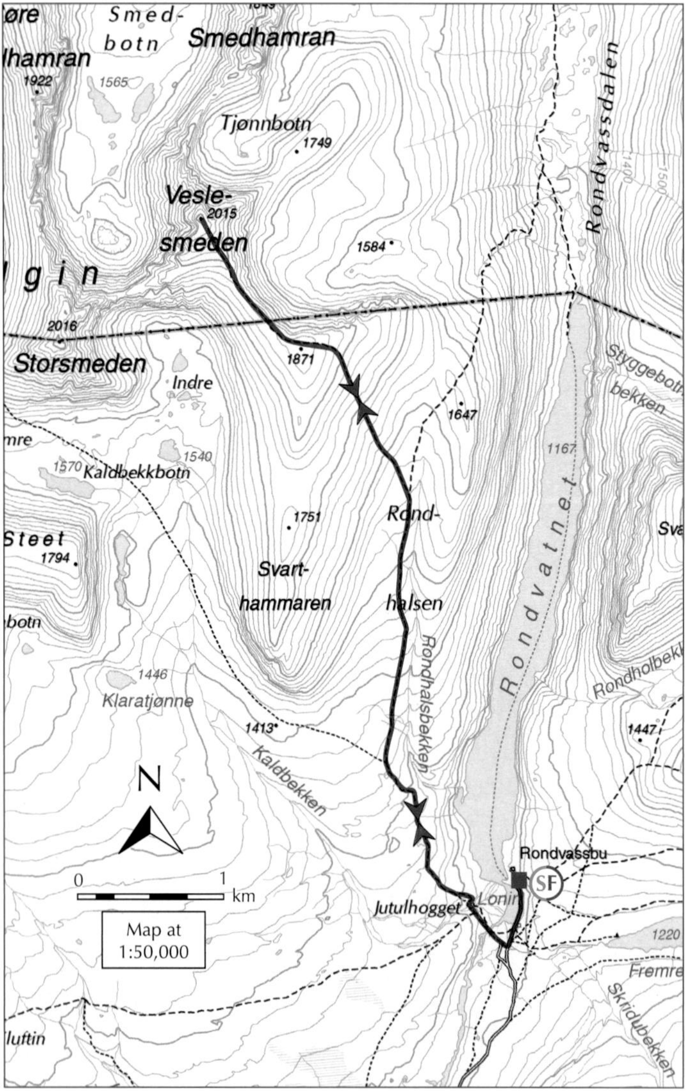
Smed-
botn
Smedhamran
hamran
1922
1565
Tjønnbotn
1749
Vesle-
2015
smeden
1584
Rondvassdalen
1400
1500
2016
Storsmeden
1871
Indre
1647
Styggebotn
bekken
1540
1570
Kaldbekkbotn
1167
1751
Rond-
Steet
1794
Svart-
hammaren
halsen
Rondvatnet
Rondhalsbekken
Rondholbekk
1446
Klaratjønne
1413
1447
Kaldbekken
N
Rondvassbu
SF
0
1
km
Jutulhogget
Lonin
Map at
1:50,000
1220
Fremre
Skridubekken

Just before the final ascent to Veslesmeden

The **views** from the top are phenomenal. You'll see all the way to Jotunheimen and Dovrefjell on a good day, as well as the dark, imposing tops of Rondane, to the north and east. The peaks in the near vicinity are no less dark and impressive, as are the three large cirques that make almost a pyramid out of Veslesmeden: Smedbotn to the west, Tjønbotn to the north and Kaldbekkbotn to the south. All of them fall away steeply for many hundreds of metres, giving the feeling of having reached a truly alpine environment.

Nearby Trolltinden (2018m) is a very airy, unmarked ascent but can be scaled without mountaineering equipment. Guided tours (adults only) are organised from Rondvassbu. A crossing to Storsmeden (2016m) is possible but highly exposed, unmarked and not for the fainthearted.

Having enjoyed the panorama, return to **Rondvassbu** the same way you came.

EXTENSION 3

Storronden summit (2138m)

Start/finish	Rondvassbu mountain hut
Distance	8.5km (5.25 miles)
Ascent/descent	900m
Difficulty	Challenging
Time	3½hr
Maximum altitude	2138m
Map	Nordeca Rondane Nord 1:50,000 Nr 2523

Storronden is Rondane's second highest peak and a relatively easy 2000m+ top to collect, as you climb more or less steadily up the main slope. With a light pack, this hike is rather quick – just under 2hr up and 1½hr down. Be aware that there's no stream to refill your water bottle; you'll need to take enough water with you at the outset.

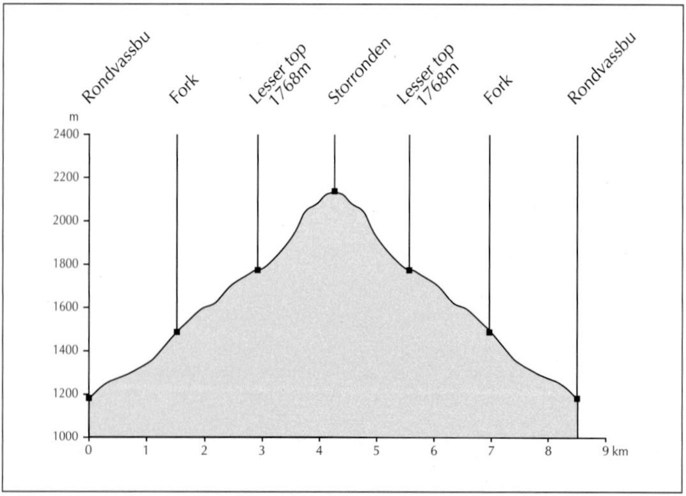

The trail starts pretty much straight up from the exit of the **Rondvassbu hut**. The path scrambles up the hillside and is quite eroded – most people take this shortcut up and down, rather than the minor detour via the Bjørnhollia sign a few hundred metres right up the road. At a fork in the path, Vinjeronden and Rondslottet are signed to the left; take the right fork up to Storronden.

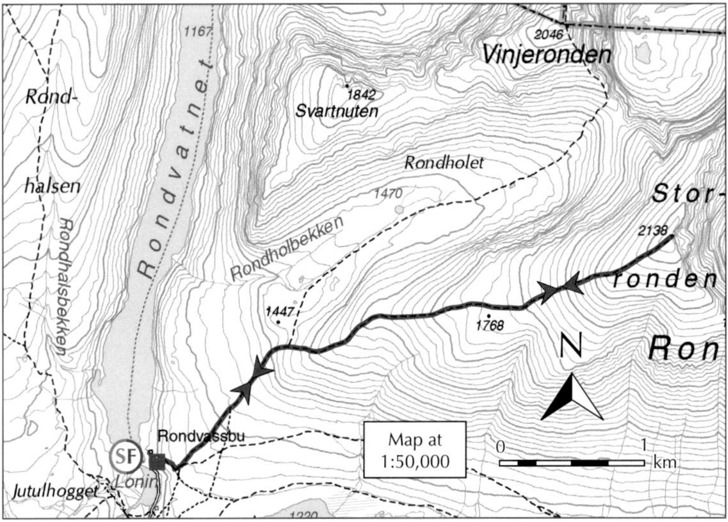

Hikers on their way to Vinjeronden and Rondslottet, as seen from the Storronden fork

Continue straight up the ridge before veering off slightly to the right and then again going straight up the hill. There are only two 5min sections of respite during the ascent where the path levels off briefly. There is a considerable variation in terrain: gravel, sand, pebbles, rocks and stones all find their way under your boots while towering in front and ahead is essentially a large pile of stones. Don't be fooled by several false tops as you climb higher and higher.

Outcrops of stacks of slate announce the vicinity of the summit of **Storronden**, and soon you'll see a somewhat crooked but large cairn.

Storronden is a rather rounded top, as reflected in its name: literally 'the large round'. Like the other Rondane tops its structure has been formed by many cycles of freezing/thawing in this area of near-permafrost. The nutrient-poor rocks weather this way, forming the surfaces of the local tops and surrounding valleys, showing indeed how important bedrock is for vegetation.

The summit is quite wide, with numerous vistas to explore. In good weather you will be rewarded with views into the steep cirques to the east and north (Langbotn and Storbotn, respectively).

The way back is simply the reverse of the outward route, this time with views towards the eastern mountaintops and Rondvatnet beneath – weather permitting, of course. The views into the large glaciofluvial fan deposit into the Rondvatnet lake, close to Rondvassbu, are quite spectacular and unique.

Top tour views from the Storronden cairn

DOVREFJELL

Svøufallet waterfall at Åmotan (Route 6, Stage 4)

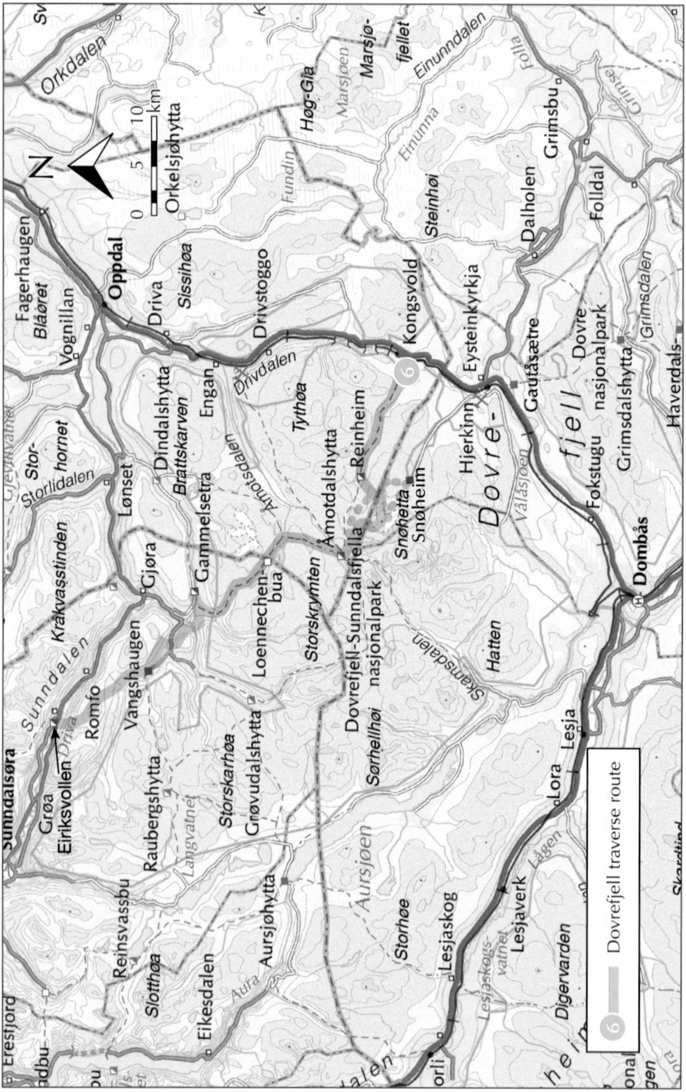
N
0 5 10 km
Orkdalen
Fagerhaugen
Blåøret
Oppdal
Vognillan
Orkelsjøhytta
Høg-Gia
Marsjøen
Marsjø-
fjellet
Einunndalen
Einunna
Folla
Grimsbu
Driva
Sissihøa
Drivstoggo
Steinhøi
Dalholen
Folldal
Kongsvold
Eysteinkyrkja
Drivdalen
Dindalshytta
Brattskarven
Engan
Tythøa
Reinheim
Hjerkinn
Gautåsætre
Dovre
nasjonalpark
Grimsdalen
Stor-
hornet
Storlidalen
Lønset
Gammelsetra
Amotsdalen
Åmotdalshytta
Snøhetta
Snøheim
Dovre-
fjell
Fokstugu
Grimsdalshytta
Haverdals-
Kråkvasstinden
Gjøra
Loennechen-
bua
Storskrymten
Dovrefjell-Sunndalsfjella
nasjonalpark
Dombås
Sunndalen
Romfo
Vangshaugen
Grøvudalshytta
Sørhellhøi
Skamsdalen
Hatten
Sunndalsøra
Grøa
Eiriksvollen
Raubergshytta
Storskarhøa
Langvatnet
Aursjøen
Lora
Lesja
Lågen
Reinsvassbu
Aursjøhytta
Storhøe
Lesjaskog
Lesjaverk
Lesjaskogs-
vatnet
Slotthøa
Eikesdalen
Aura
Digervarden
Dovrefjell traverse route

Grødøla river valley between Vangshaugen and Åmotan (Route 6, Stage 4)

Dovrefjell (also known as 'Dovre') is an extensive and incredibly beautiful high plateau in the very heart of Norway, with the towering 2286m Snøhetta massif as its defining feature. This massif is truly alpine, with rugged peaks and sheer, vertical cliffs. Its valleys, glaciers and snowfields are the equal of any other in Norway. Dovrefjell attracts visitors by rail, road or on foot – over centuries-old paths – from near and far. To Norwegians, there is something immovable and eternal about this ancient landscape that has withstood the forces of wind and weather for millions of years. This sentiment finds expression in the words of the founding fathers of the modern Norwegian state, when upon finishing the writing of the constitution in 1814 they declared their 'unity and loyalty until Dovre falls'.

Dovrefjell stretches from Drivdalen in the east to Romsdalen in the west, with Sunndalen in the north. It forms a rough triangle in which the Dovre and Dovrefjell-Sunndalsfjella national parks are located. The area measures around 54km by 78km and is approximately 350km north of Oslo and 160km south of Trondheim. Today the two national parks and adjacent protected areas cover 4365km^2 and thereby form the largest protected area in mainland Norway, connecting with Rondane to the south. The area reaches across several counties: Oppland, Hedmark, Sør-Trøndelag and Møre og Romsdal.

Due to Dovrefjell's central location along both the north–south and the east–west axes of Norway, it has traditionally been an important mountain range that had to be either crossed or circumnavigated along the adjacent large valleys of Drivdalen or Romsdalen. It is known to have played an important political, spiritual and economic role in Norway's history, possibly as early as the Iron Age. Two prominent examples of this are the

Kongevegen and the Pilgrimsleden. The first of these, the 'King's Way', connected Dovre with Oppdal, almost certainly from the Iron Age onwards. It is believed to have been used by the Viking kings as they travelled the country to assert their authority and meet up with their peers to keep the country unified. The Pilgrimsleden refers to the St Olav Way – the pilgrim path that connects Oslo with the Nidaros cathedral in Trondheim, where St Olav, the Viking king who established Christianity in Norway, is said to have been buried. The St Olav Way has been restored in recent times and allows pilgrims to walk the 643km between Oslo and Trondheim.

Dovre is a meeting point for the oceanic and continental climate zones, and the park forms an area of transition between these two systems. You will feel the differences. West of Snøhetta the terrain is not only harsher and rockier with big elevation differences, but the weather is also less stable with lots of wind and more frequent precipitation than in the east. East of Snøhetta the climate gradually becomes more continental. The winters are dry and cold, the summers can be warm. These areas are on the lee side and often therefore protected from weather fronts. Kongsvoll, for example, has only around 125 rain days a year with precipitation around 475mm annually. Snøhetta itself gets more than double that. Further west, the yearly average can be as high as 1800mm. The difference in bedrock between the west and east also has a large influence on the flora of the park. Eastern parts are rich in plant life due to good-quality bedrock and nutrient soil. Other than in Jotunheimen and Trollheimen, there are no other mountain areas in Scandinavia with such a diversity of plant life.

PLANTS AND WILDLIFE

Together, Dovrefjell and Rondane form the last still largely intact fells ecosystem in northern Europe. The large size of this area allows for the reindeer to roam between their summer and winter territories. The region holds the last viable strain of wild reindeer in Europe. These are wary animals and will flee at the slightest disturbance, running for 3–4km before they settle again. This is especially hard on the young and nursing mothers. If they move too often they will not be able to graze enough to survive the very harsh winters. Therefore, it is crucial to stay on the marked paths in order to minimise disturbance to the herds. There are about 2000 wild reindeer in Dovrefjell and Rondane national parks. The hunting of reindeer has been an integral part of Dovre and Rondane human and cultural heritage. Over the last decades around 1250 hunting pits and old funnelling 'fences' have been mapped. These systems vary in age from between 500 and 1300 years. Hunting wild reindeer is a strictly regulated, sustainable and important element of maintaining a healthy population.

T-markers and Snøhetta are never far away in Dovre (Route 6, Stage 1)

The wild reindeer also encounter their natural predator in the park, that being the wolverine. There are about 20–30 wolverines here – the highest concentration in Norway. It's mostly extinct elsewhere. It's highly unlikely you'll come across these creatures when hiking; they are notoriously shy. You may encounter the arctic fox (if lucky) or its close cousin the red fox (more likely).

The most recognisable mammal of Dovrefjell in the public mind, however, is the musk ox. These are believed to have been native to Scandinavia together with the mammoth and to have been a part of the fauna between the last two ice ages. These large, arctic, thickly coated mammals were hunted to extinction, but were reintroduced into Dovrefjell in the 1950s. This re-wilding initiative seems to have been successful as the musk ox herds are thriving. Their most significant enemy are careless humans that frighten the animals into attacking. Sadly, a few have had to be put down after such encounters. As a rule, stay 200 metres away from the animals and disturb them as little as possible. They can easily be seen from afar and tend to congregate between Kongsvoll and Reinheim.

ACCESS AND SERVICES

The main hamlet and towns that provide connections to the Dovrefjell mountain huts covered in this guide are Hjerkinn, Otta and Oppdal. Otta and Oppdal both have a good range of grocery shops and sports stores as well as services such as banking and medical.

Figure 2 shows a schematic overview of public transport options into Dovrefjell. All three places as well as Kongsvoll are on the Trondheim–Oslo train line and are serviced several times a day from both cities. The bus station in both Otta and Oppdal is just outside the train station.

Figure 2: Rondane, Dovrefjell & Trollheimen access

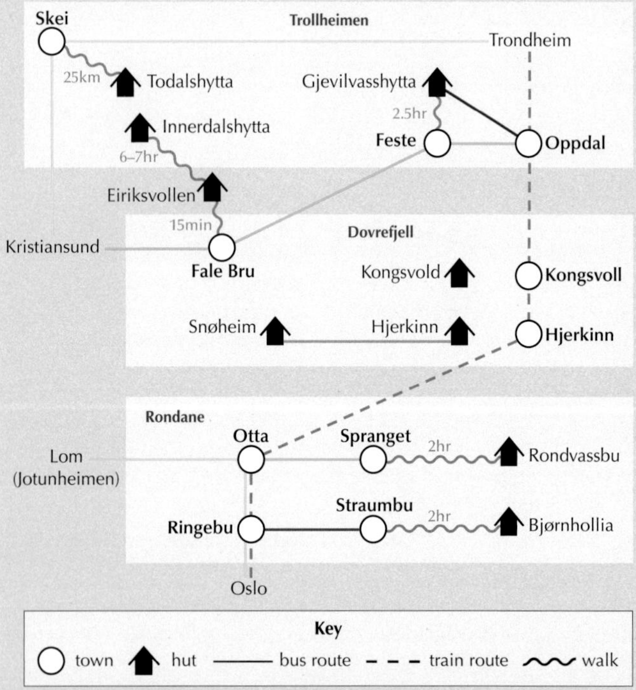

	Line	Connection
– – –	Oslo–Trondheim	Oslo–Gardermoen–Otta–Hjerkinn–Kongsvoll–Oppdal–Trondheim
——	205	Otta–Raphamn–Mysusæter–Spranget
——	206	Ringebu–Straumbu
——	FRAM Ekspress 901	Kristiansund–Fale Bru–Oppdal
——	summer shuttle bus	Hjerkinn–Snøheim (check https://snoheim.dnt.no/eng)
——	580	Oppdal–Gjevilvasshytta (Su, Th)
——	FRAM Ekspress 905	Kristiansund–Skei i Surnadal–Trondheim
——	Nordfjordekspressen VY146	Oslo–Gardermoen–Lillehammer–Otta–Lom

Local transport

There is a very regular bus service between Kristiansund and Oppdal that stops at Fale bru, which is a 15min walk from the Eiriksvollen mountain hut at the end of the Dovrefjell traverse. The service connects to Oppdal train station and is timed in such a way that it corresponds to the trains' departures towards Oslo. See Appendix C for further information on local transport.

Mountain huts

Access to the huts that are relevant to the described route varies. Reinheim and Åmotdalshytta can only be reached on foot. Gammelsetra and Vangshaugen can be reached by private car. Eiriksvollen is only a short walk from the main Rv70 road, along which the public bus runs between Kristiansund and Oppdal, making it a very easy entry and exit point into both Dovrefjell and Trollheimen. Snøheim mountain hut can be reached by regular shuttle bus from Hjerkinnhus Hostel (200 metres from the Hjerkinn train station) in the summer months.

Snøheim is the only fully serviced hut, and Vangshaugen operates as a full-service hut in the high season and a self-service hut otherwise. During the off-season it requires a DNT key for access. Eiriksvollen, Reinheim and Gammelsetra huts also require a DNT key. Åmotdalshytta (at the time of writing) can be accessed without a key. Since the majority of huts are self-service, hiking in Dovrefjell has a different character to Jotunheimen or Rondane. Hikers cater for themselves and share in the organising of duties around the huts. In the busy summer months, some of them, like Reinheim, will have a warden who helps in the organisation of responsibilities and distribution of rooms.

THE ROUTE IN DOVREFJELL

Imagine putting your backpack on, tightening the hip belt as you step out of the train, and starting a five-day hiking trek. It is possible to start the Dovrefjell traverse route directly from the Kongsvoll train station – only 4½hr from Oslo or 2hr from Trondheim. The traverse through Dovrefjell scales Snøhetta and then continues along the high fells, into the deep gorges and terraces around Åmotan, ending at Eiriksvollen mountain hut on the edge of Trollheimen. There's the option of a shorter three-stage route, including Snøhetta, with entry at Kongsvoll and exit via Snøheim mountain hut to Hjerkinnhus Hostel and train station. It is made up of Stages 1 and 2, and Stage 2B hiked in reverse. It is also possible to extend the traverse into both Rondane (walking from Kongsvoll to Hjerkinn) and Trollheimen (hiking from Eiriksvollen to Innerdalen). Both these connecting extensions are single-day hikes.

ROUTE 6

Dovrefjell traverse route

Start	Kongsvold Fjellstue or Kongsvoll train station
Finish	Eiriksvollen mountain hut
Distance	80km (50 miles)
Ascent	3040m
Descent	3630m
Time	5 days
Extensions	Connect to Trollheimen routes to the north, or the Rondane traverse (Route 5) to the south
Variations	In adverse weather, Stage 2A Reinheim to Snøheim (including Snøhetta peak and carrying a light pack), with a low route – Stage 2B – from Snøheim to Åmotdalshytta.

This route makes a full traverse through Dovrefjell and both its national parks. It starts at Kongsvoll, which lies on the Oslo–Trondheim rail line, and ends in Eiriksvollen in Sunndalen on the edge of Trollheimen. Stage 1 starts either from the private lodge and pilgrim's accommodation of Kongsvold Fjellstue, which is a 10min walk from Kongsvoll train station, or from the train station itself. It is a moderate hike to Reinheim, from where Stage 2 takes you over the Snøhetta massif into Åmotsdalen. This stage, over the top of Snøhetta (2286m), is bound to etch itself into your memory, especially on a day with good weather. The views from the top of Snøhetta are simply magnificent and only get better on the exposed descent into Åmotsdalen, with a panorama of glacial lakes and cirques.

Throughout Stages 3 and 4 towards Gammelsetra and Vangshaugen the landscape changes significantly. Stage 3 passes Loennechenbua, DNT's smallest mountain hut, in typical *fjell* landscape. Shortly after, the path descends towards the deep gorges, moraine ridges and terraces formed during and after the ice ages, creating a fan-like river system that converges at Åmotan. Six rivers – Grødøla, Grøvu, Geitåa, Reppa, Skiråa and Linndøla – converge here, becoming the Driva. Three waterfalls roar from afar as they fall into the gorges below. Reppefallet and Lindalsfallet have a height of 110m, while Svøufallet crashes down 156m into the valley, making Åmotan a marvellous and splendid place to linger. Stage 4 takes you from the beautiful old mountain farm of Gammelsetra, near Åmotan, to Vangshaugen, past these waterfalls and through different microclimates on the north- and south-facing valley sides.

Crossing Linndola river, before Gammelsetra (Stage 3)

On Stage 5 the route heads gradually out of Dovre. Once again the rounded tops of Dovre's high plateau are revealed out of Grødalen as you approach the hanging valleys of Trollheimen. The incredibly steep Sunndalen valley forms the natural barrier between the two areas. The route ends at Eiriksvollen mountain hut, which is a leisurely 15min walk from the bus stop at Fale bridge, connecting to Oppdal or Kristiansund. Remember to bring along the DNT universal key for access to Eiriksvollen, Vangshaugen (in low season), Gammelsetra and Reinheim mountain huts.

The route cannot be meaningfully shortened but could be exited at Vangshaugen (Stage 4) or Gammelsetra (Stage 3) by private transport. Reinheim, Åmotdalshytta and Loennechenbua can only be reached on foot. In case of bad weather around Snøhetta, two alternative routes are described so as to avoid the northern descent from Snøhetta to Åmotdalshytta mountain hut, with its exposed sections. See Stages 2A and 2B. By taking these alternatives you can still ascend Snøhetta, but then descend to Snøheim mountain hut and resume the traverse by hiking across to Åmotsdalen via a low route. This would add a day to the itinerary. The alternative low route also creates the option for a short three-stage route focusing on the Snøhetta ascent, by doing Stage 1 and 2 and then returning via the low route (walking it in reverse) to Snøheim and exiting here (by shuttle bus to Hjerkinn, for example).

This superb and strikingly varied route naturally connects to treks in Trollheimen National Park. It is just a day hike from Eiriksvollen to Innerdalen into the heart of Trollheimen (on a marked trail, not presented here). From Innerdalen you can join either the Trollheimen SignaTur route (Route 8) or the Trollheimen fells to fjord route (Route 9).

It could also be an extension of the Rondane traverse (Route 5), which ends at Hjerkinn train station. By either taking the train between Hjerkinn and Kongsvoll or walking along the Kongevegen – the 'King's way' between Hjerkinn and Kongsvoll – these routes could be combined to create an epic traverse all the way from Rondane to Trollheimen.

STAGE 1

Kongsvold Fjellstue to Reinheim

Start	Kongsvold Fjellstue or Kongsvoll train station
Finish	Reinheim mountain hut
Distance	15.25km (9.5 miles)
Ascent	520m
Descent	80m
Difficulty	Moderate
Time	4hr
Maximum altitude	1351m
Map	Nordeca Dovrefjell-Snøhetta Vest 1:50,000 Nr 2829
Note	In low season the Reinheim hut is locked with the DNT key, so remember to take it along.

The first stage of the Dovrefjell traverse starts with a slow and steady ascent through the woods. Once you reach the plateau, the panorama opens up and the views become sweeping and expansive. The path is well marked once you reach the plateau; less so but still noticeable earlier as you ascend through the woods.

Alternative start from Kongsvoll station

It is possible to reach Reinheim by starting directly from Kongsvoll train station. If you are starting from there, with your back to the train track, walk left (north) behind the left station building. Follow the small service road parallel to the line until you reach the bridge over the tracks. Cross over and follow the T-markings from there. This path joins the ascent from Kongsvold Fjellstue once you reach the plateau. It is about 3km (1hr) from the station to the plateau.

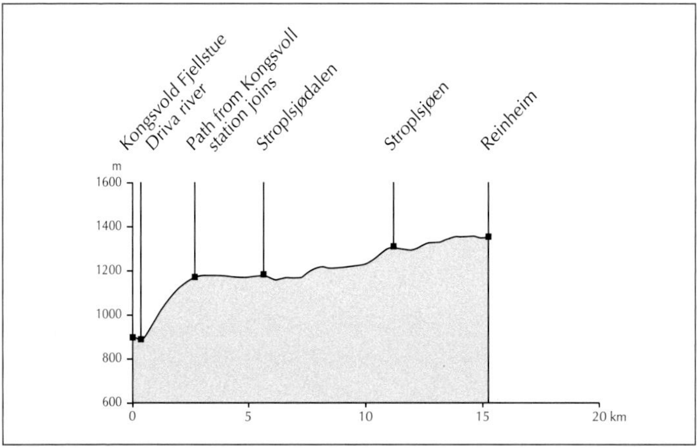

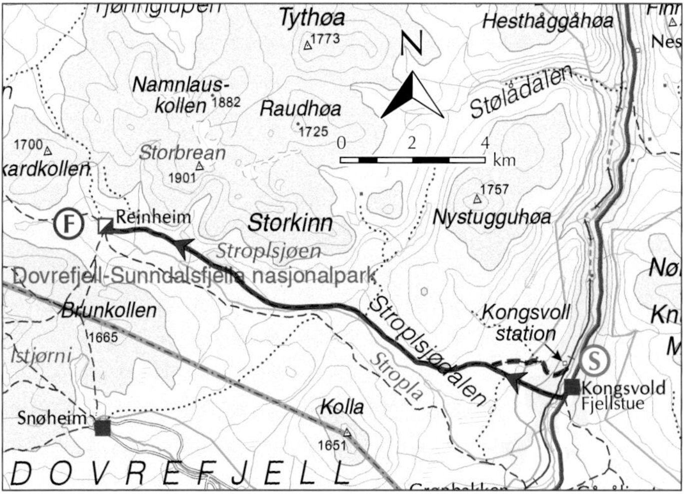

Leaving the main entry at **Kongsvold Fjellstue**, turn left end follow the E6 road for 100 metres towards the end of the parking lot. Cross the road, to the signposted start of the track. The path starts by descending towards the Driva river, crosses the bridge, then continues under the railway line. From there, the main ascent begins. You will gain 300m of elevation during the first 3km, passing through birch woods, heather, bilberry and crowberry shrubs. As you gain altitude the birches disappear and the view opens up to the vast skies and hills of Dovrefjell.

Except for a few tops, the whole of Dovrefjell was covered by an enormous **glacier** during the last ice age. As a result there are terminal moraines of sand, stone and clay in most flat areas of the national park, as found in-between Kongsvoll and Reinheim.

As the path reaches the plateau and levels off, a signpost to Kongsvoll train station appears. If you started at the train station, this is where the trail merges with the main track. Continue ahead, and not long afterwards the snow-capped peak of Snøhetta appears in front. It will stay ahead as a beacon all the way to Reinheim mountain hut. The path on the plateau is relatively wide and mostly small gravel or soft earth.

It is quite possible to spot **musk ox** on this stage. They are known to stay around this area for grazing, and they like to rest among the small sand dunes, at times close to the trail. Be alert and keep your distance (200 metres; wait or take an off-path detour if they are on or close to the path). Musk ox are believed to be native to Scandinavia. They are tundra animals and need an ice-free habitat. In Norway they were hunted to extinction, but reintroduced in the 1950s and the animals seem to be thriving in Dovrefjell.

Hyttewarden *at Reinheim inspecting his cold-smoked trout*

Follow **Stroplsjødalen valley**, sometimes close to the river itself, passing the lakes of **Stroplsjøen** and Stroplsjøtjønna on the way to Reinheim. The openness of the landscape is the reason it can be so unforgiving and harsh: there is no escape, no hiding from wind and weather.

You may encounter **reindeer** here – they pertain to the last strain of true wild reindeer in Europe. Be sure to do your utmost to avoid disturbing them as they will take flight and run for 3–4km before settling again. This is particularly hard on the nursing mothers and the young and can seriously impact their ability to 'fatten up' for the harsh winter months.

As with any path in Norway, you sometimes need to navigate a muddy or rocky section and cross a few streams, but overall it is an easy trail to the hut. **Reinheim** is a self-serviced mountain hut, although in the high season a hut warden will be present.

STAGE 2

Snøhetta high traverse

Start	Reinheim mountain hut
Finish	Åmotdalshytta mountain hut
Distance	12.75km (8 miles)
Ascent	900m
Descent	935m
Difficulty	Very challenging
Time	6hr
Maximum altitude	2286m
Map	Nordeca Dovrefjell-Snøhetta Vest 1:50,000 Nr 2829
Note	The descent from the summit of Snøhetta is exposed and is prone to ice and snow even in summer. It should be approached with care.

In good weather, the Snøhetta massif can be seen from all over Dovrefjell, and its peaks beckon to be climbed as it towers over the whole plateau. Snøhetta is the highest mountain in Norway outside of Jotunheimen.

While deceivingly lovely on a beautiful summer's day, Dovrefjell is considered by Norwegians to be one of their harshest natural areas. In poor weather or in strong winds the traverse to Åmotsdalen can be especially challenging due to its airy exposure and northern orientation. There is no hiding from the elements. The descent from the top towards Åmotsdalen is down the north side of Snøhetta, and therefore the chance of encountering icy patches is much higher – and even a dusting of snow makes the sandstone immediately slippery. Even in August the temperatures here are around freezing and snow can be knee-deep. If the forecast is for particularly poor weather, consider using Stages 2A and 2B as an alternative.

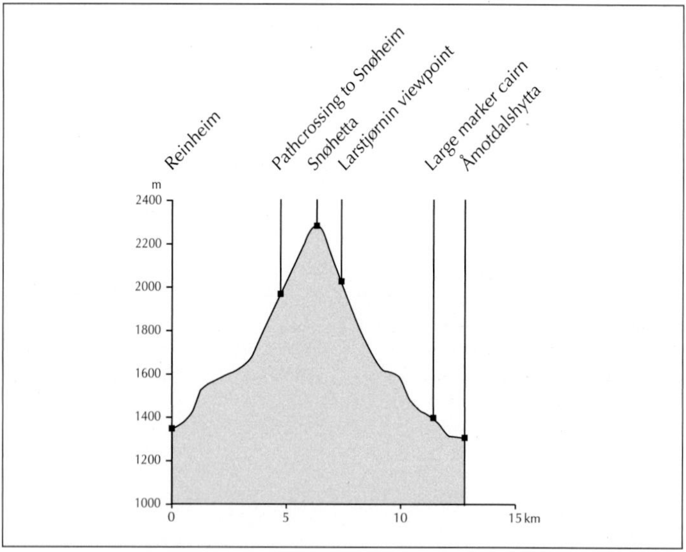

Leaving **Reinheim mountain hut**, turn left, head down to the river and cross the bridge. Start the gentle ascent on a good, wide path, soon passing the turnoff to Grønbakken and Hjerkinn. Continue straight on and in 2km you'll pass the turnoff for the low route to Åmotdalshytta mountain hut. Carry on straight; the trail here is a bit harder to follow, but the general direction is clear, with Snøhetta dominating the view to the southwest.

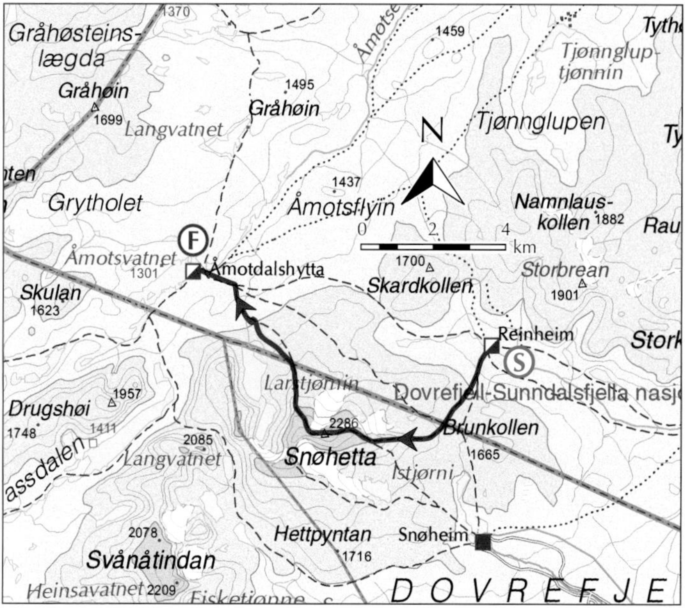

The path steepens and becomes bouldery. Once you reach the ridge, metal poles will guide your way due west. The rocks are not easy on your feet, even on a good day; take care in wet or wintry conditions. The ascent is not steep but it is long and monotonous, and you have to concentrate on selecting steady rocks to stand on. With some 350m of ascent remaining, the path to Snøheim mountain hut joins in. (If you're ascending and then returning to this point before continuing to Snøheim you might want to leave part of your luggage at this crossroads – see Stage 2A.) The final climb continues over boulders and large rocks. It is not unheard of to encounter knee-high snow here even in August; proceed with caution to the top of **Snøhetta**.

On a clear day, the views from Snøhetta's main peak (**Stortoppen**, 2286m) are phenomenal. The western view is taken up by the dramatic cirque formed by the triple Snøhetta peaks – Stortoppen, Midttoppen (2278m) and Vesttoppen (2249m) – as they encircle the glacier. Svånåtindan and its glaciers dominate to the southwest. Rondane is visible in the east, Jotunheimen in the southeast, while the northward vistas stretch to Trollheimen.

Views from the north slope of Snøhetta onto the Larstjørnin lakes

A weather station dominates the summit. Pass it on the right and continue north, picking your way over the narrow, exposed ridge. Keep the steep edge of the ridge well to your left, but at the same time don't venture onto the sloping ice to your right. Choose your way carefully among the rocks, slowly descending around the start of the glacier. At the top of the glacier on the ridge there is another spectacular view into the bowl of the southeast glaciers.

From here, follow the well-marked path over the rocks. The first 300m of descent is steep, on and over boulders, and continues to be well marked. The path stays well away from the edge, although a short (and careful) detour towards the edge of the cirque is very rewarding for its views down onto Larstjørnin. After that, the path eases a bit and becomes rockier until you reach about 1600m and the level of **Larstjørnin lake**. Here the path is flat as you cross the now-dry lake floor to reach the glacial moraine. Another steep boulder-hopping section awaits here and brings you down to the meadow flats below. From here it's easy underfoot and well marked, bringing you to a giant cairn (signposting the low route back to Reinheim) and the **Åmotdalshytta hut** shortly after.

In August you're likely to share the **Åmotdalshytta hut** with both keen fishermen and reindeer hunters. The smells of freshly fried trout and reindeer meat might waft through the hut and make the hiker's fare look quite meagre by comparison. They are unlikely to share their hard-earned meal, but you can certainly expect to share stories!

STAGE 2A

Reinheim to Snøheim over Snøhetta (2286m)

Start	Reinheim mountain hut
Finish	Snøheim mountain hut
Distance	12.25km (7.5 miles)
Ascent	950m
Descent	815m
Difficulty	Challenging
Time	6hr
Maximum altitude	2286m
Map	Nordeca Dovrefjell-Snøhetta Vest 1:50,000 Nr 2829

In good weather the Snøhetta massif can be seen from all over Dovrefjell, and its peaks beg to be climbed as it towers over the whole plateau. However, if the weather deteriorates, with high winds, rain or late-summer snowfall, it is important to assess the feasibility of the traverse over the north towards Åmotsdalen (Stage 2). This stage gives an alternative. The hike to the peak of Snøhetta is included, but the descent is back on the south side and finishes at Snøheim mountain hut. This way the exposed traverse and descent towards Åmotsdalen is avoided. Stage 2B can be taken to reach Åmotsdalen the next day via the low route, in order to continue the Dovrefjell traverse.

Leaving **Reinheim mountain hut**, turn left, head down to the river and cross the bridge. Start the gentle ascent on a good, wide path, soon passing the turnoff to Grønbakken and Hjerkinn. Continue straight on and in 2km you'll pass the turnoff for the low route to Åmotdalshytta mountain hut. Carry on straight; the trail here is a bit harder to follow, but the general direction is clear, with Snøhetta dominating the view to the southwest.

The path steepens and becomes bouldery. Once you reach the ridge, metal poles will guide your way due west. The rocks are not easy on your feet, even on a good day; take care in wet or wintry conditions. The ascent is not steep but it is long and monotonous, and you have to concentrate on selecting steady rocks to stand on. With some 350m of ascent remaining, the path to Snøheim mountain hut joins in. (As you'll be returning to this point, you might want to leave part of your luggage here.) The final climb continues over boulders and large rocks. It is not unheard of to encounter knee-high snow here even in August; proceed with care to weather station at the top of **Snøhetta**.

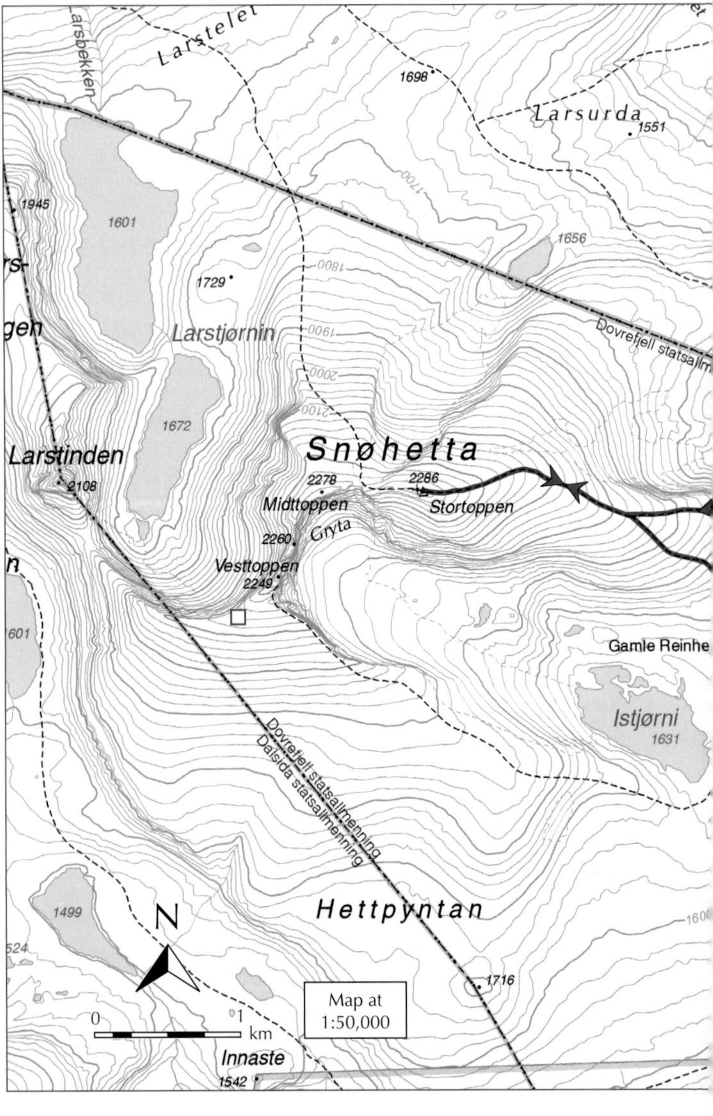
Larstelet
Larsbekken
1698
Larsurda
1551
1945
1601
1700
1656
1800
1729
Larstjørnin
1900
Dovrefjell statsallm
2000
2100
1672
Snøhetta
Larstinden
2108
2278
2286
Midttoppen
Stortoppen
2260
Gryta
Vesttoppen
2249
1601
Gamle Reinhe
Istjørni
1631
Dovrefjell statsallmenning
Dalsida statsallmenning
Hettpyntan
1499
N
1716
Map at
1:50,000
0
1
km
Innaste
1542

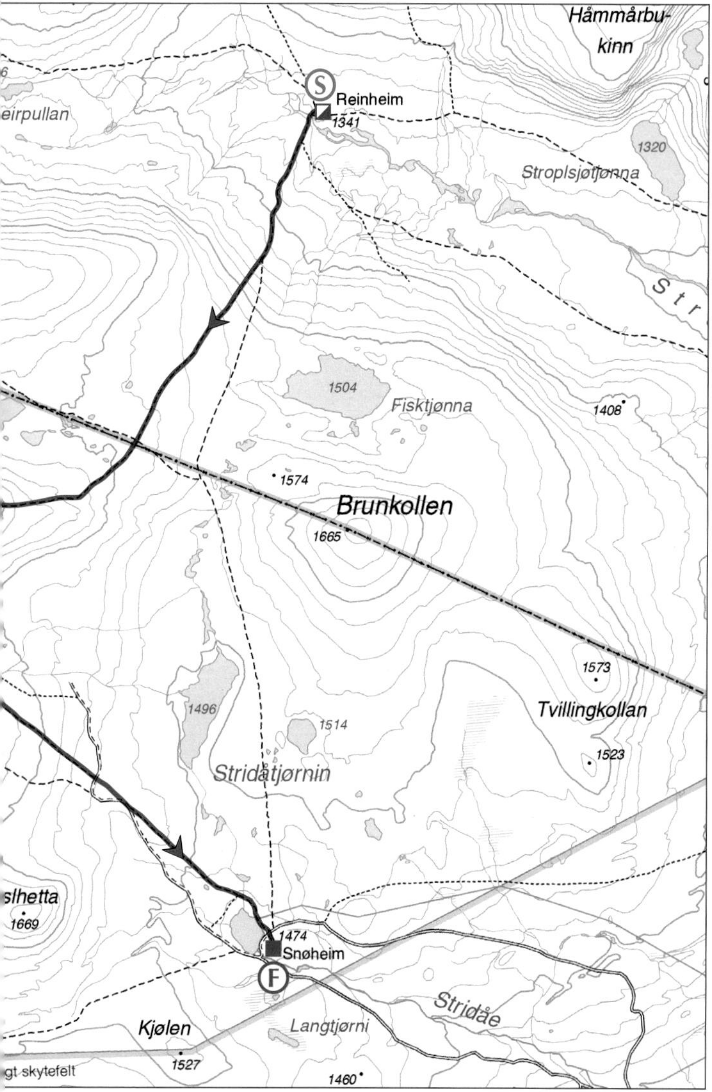

Håmmårbu-
kinn
Reinheim
1341
eirpullan
1320
Stroplsjøtjønna
Str
1504
Fisktjønna
1408
1574
Brunkollen
1665
1573
Tvillingkollan
1496
1514
1523
Stridåtjørnin
slhetta
1669
1474
Snøheim
Stridåe
Kjølen
Langtjørni
1527
1460
gt skytefelt

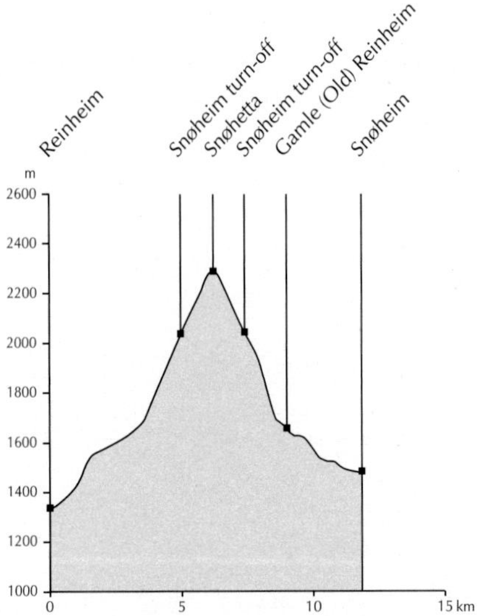

On a clear day, the views from Snøhetta's main peak (**Stortoppen**, 2286m) are phenomenal. The western view is taken up by the dramatic cirque formed by the triple Snøhetta peaks – Stortoppen, Midttoppen (2278m) and Vesttoppen (2249m) – as they encircle the glacier. Svånåtindan and its glaciers dominate to the southwest. Rondane is visible in the east, Jotunheimen in the southeast, while the northward vistas stretch to Trollheimen.

From the summit, retrace your steps to the crossroads to pick up your pack and continue to Snøheim. Follow the path southeast, descending steeply on the rocky, bouldery trail towards the site of **Gamle (Old) Reinheim**, where you reach a plateau. From here the path broadens and eases, and it follows a straight line downhill to the sizable Snøheim mountain hut. The shortest route includes the crossing of a rather large stream, which may be a challenge in the early season. Alternatively, a slightly longer route takes you on the west side of the lake, where you cross the river over a bridge. In season there's a shuttle bus (five departures daily) to Hjerkinnhus Hostel (200 metres from Hjerkinn train station) from **Snøheim** – see https://snoheim.dnt.no/eng for details.

Summit view west into the Snøhetta cirque, Svånåtindan (2209m) in the background

STAGE 2B

Snøheim to Åmotdalshytta mountain hut (low route, east side)

Start	Snøheim mountain hut
Finish	Åmotdalshytta mountain hut
Distance	12.25km (7.5 miles)
Ascent	365m
Descent	535m
Difficulty	Moderate
Time	5hr
Maximum altitude	1725m
Map	Nordeca Dovrefjell-Snøhetta Vest 1:50,000 Nr 2829

From Snøheim there are three options to get to Åmotdalshytta mountain hut. Left and west of Snøhetta, via Svånådalen, which is a very rocky and uncomfortable path; straight northwest over the top of Snøhetta (see Stage 2); and right, towards the north, initially in the direction of Reinheim, along the eastern side of Snøhetta. This stage describes the eastern option.

This alternative stage has two functions within the Dovrefjell traverse route. In adverse weather during the second stage of the traverse, from Reinheim over Snøhetta to Åmotdalshytta mountain hut, it is safer to take Stage 2A to Snøheim mountain hut than to descend on the northern side of Snøhetta. Subsequently, the stage described here will bring you to Åmotdalshytta, from where you can continue the traverse from Stage 3. If, for whatever reason, you have not been able to scale Snøhetta yet, you could attempt to do it from Åmotdalshytta as a day hike, before continuing with Stage 3. In this case the same challenges that are described in Stage 2 would apply.

If you were successful in your top traverse from Reinheim over Snøhetta to Åmotdalshytta but were not intending to do the full traverse, this stage could lead you out of Dovre and back to Snøheim. From here you can catch the shuttle bus to Hjerkinnhus Hostel (located 200 metres from Hjerkinn train station). Note that you would have to hike the reverse of the description given here.

The trail is well marked throughout, and the stage description is kept short as it is not part of the main route.

From **Snøheim** take the path signed initially for Reinheim. About 3km after leaving the hut the path forks; take the left turn towards Åmotsdalen. Shortly after, the trail crosses the path coming from Reinheim towards Snøhetta. Continue straight. From here the trail starts to become rockier and you encounter boulders as you traverse the various moraines coming down from Snøhetta. Gradually ascend to 1725m altitude, passing the lake off the northeast glacier of **Snøhetta**. Beyond that first height, the terrain changes, with different rocks, different layering, glistening with quartz, mica, and pyrite crystals.

Hiking on the eastern side of Snøhetta, on the low route to Åmotsdalen

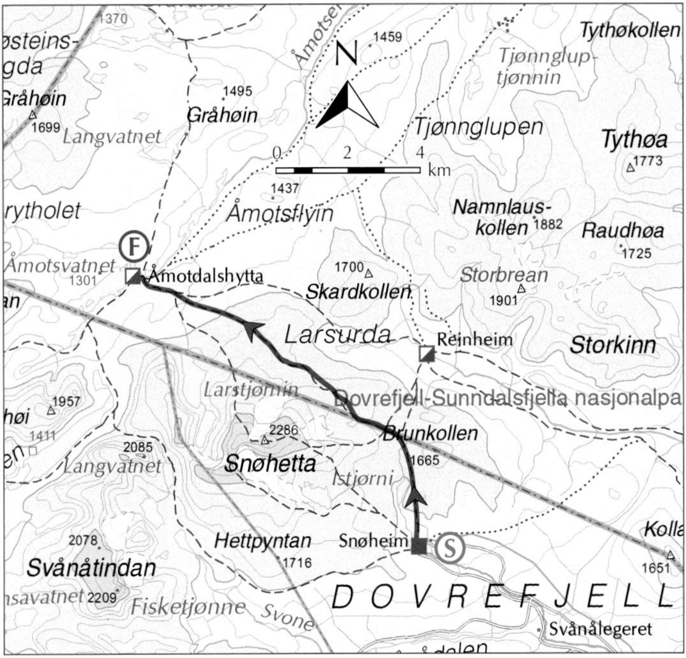
N
0
2
4
km
1459
Tythøkollen
Tjønnglup-
tjønnin
1495
Gråhøin
1699
Langvatnet
Tjønnglupen
Tythøa
1773
1437
Åmotsflyin
Namnlaus-
kollen
1882
Raudhøa
1725
F
Åmotsvatnet
1301
Åmotdalshytta
1700
Skardkollen
Storbrean
1901
Larsurda
Reinheim
Storkinn
Larstjønnin
1957
1411
2286
Brunkollen
2085
Langvatnet
Snøhetta
1665
Istjørni
2078
Hettpyntan
1716
Snøheim
S
1651
Svånåtindan
2209
Fisketjønne
D O V R E F J E L L
Svånålegeret

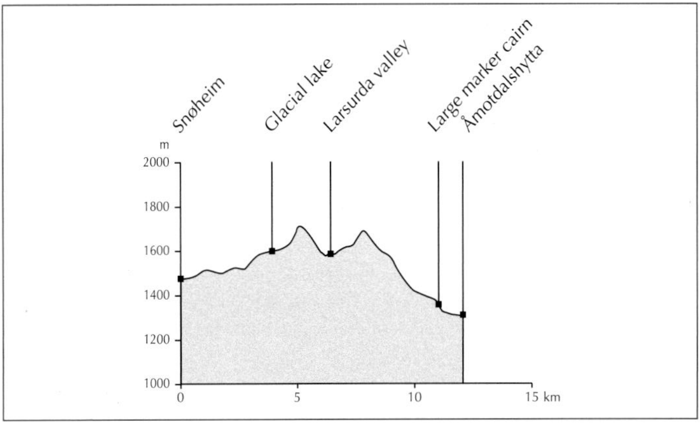
Snøheim
Glacial lake
Larsurda valley
Large marker cairn
Åmotdalshytta
m
2000
1800
1600
1400
1200
1000
0
5
10
15 km

The top of the ridge out of the **Larsurda valley** at 1698m provides a great view to Snøhetta and Larstinden to the south/southwest, including the sparkly green **Larstjørnin lake**. Åmotdalshytta is now visible in the valley below, to the west-northwest, and it is a gentle descent into the Åmotsdalen valley.

A kilometre before you reach the hut you will pass a three-way crossing marked by a large cairn, where the paths join before heading to Åmotdalshytta mountain hut. From here on the path is easy and wide and you will shortly arrive at the **cabin**.

STAGE 3

Åmotdalshytta to Gammelsetra via Loennechenbua

Start	Åmotdalshytta mountain hut
Finish	Gammelsetra mountain hut
Distance	24km (15 miles)
Ascent	350m
Descent	850m
Difficulty	Challenging
Time	7½hr
Maximum altitude	1465m
Map	Nordeca Dovrefjell-Snøhetta Vest 1:50,000 Nr 2829 and Nordeca Trollheimen Sør 1:50,000 Nr 2828

This long stage leads from the heart of wild Dovrefjell towards the fertile valleys around Åmotan. The route is arduous at times, going through boulder fields and along lakes and rivers. It leaves the high fells behind and descends into the forested valleys and summer alms. It is well marked for most of the way.

Åmotsdalen, on the northwestern side of Snøhetta, is veritably in the heart of Dovrefjell, and is only accessible on foot in the summer months. **Gammelsetra**, at the end of this stage, is a mountain farm so old that its age cannot be ascertained. Both give an insight into the formidable endeavours of Norwegian people surviving in this harsh climate. Wild reindeer and mountain trout from Åmotsdalen were prized, and good summers were vital to the survival of farm animals and therefore the people of Gammelsetra.

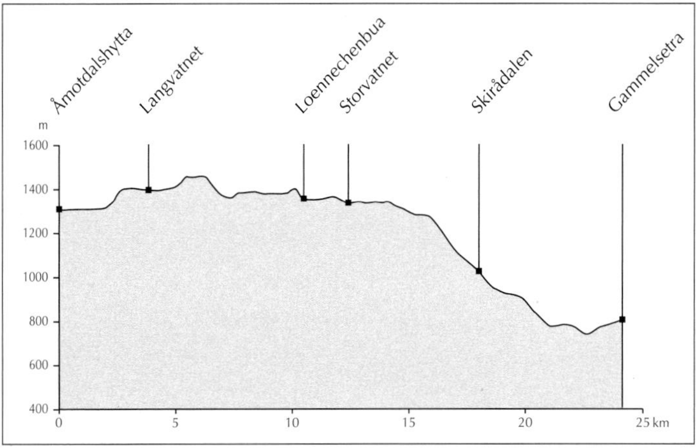

Turn left from **Åmotdalshytta hut**, cross the small stream and take another left at the signpost to Loennechenbua and Gammelsetra. Over the first few hundred metres the path traverses many streams in the valley and therefore can be wet. Soon you start on a gradual ascent on the northwestern side of the valley. The path is rocky here, and very well marked. Continue north on the plateau past lakes and streams and then descend into Urdvasbakken and cross the stream to reach a crossroad with the path to Engan and the Dindalshytta mountain hut.

Snøhetta as seen from Åmotsdalen

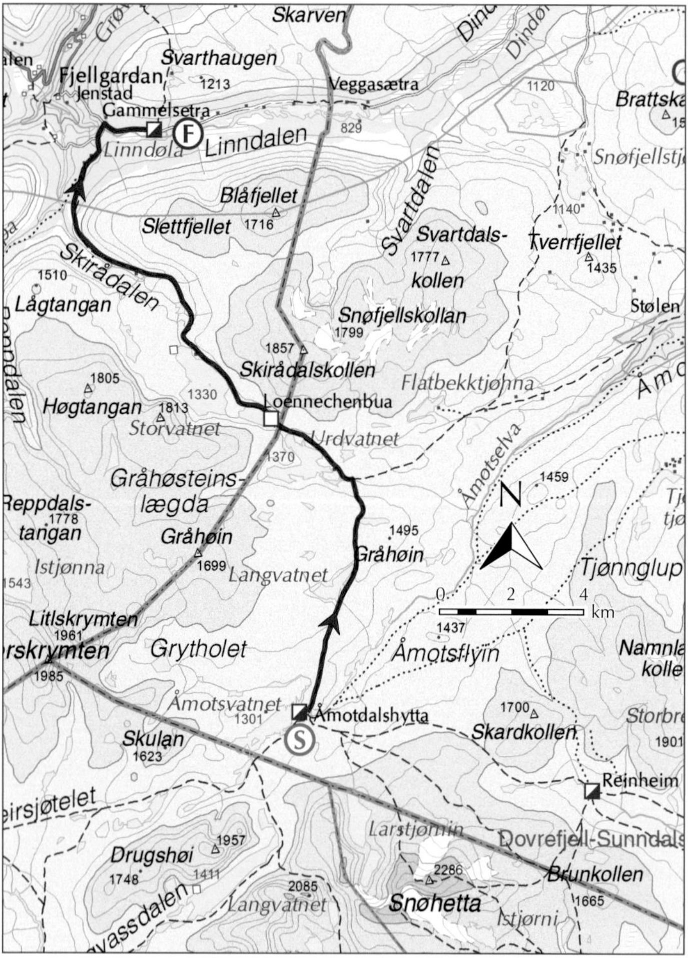

Turn left at this crossroad to Loennechenbua. Before reaching Loennechenbua you'll pass some other, private cabins, and there are beautiful views onto **Urdvatnet lake** with Storvasskollan (1811m) on the left. **Loennechenbua** is only visible once you've essentially reached it, at nearly 3km from the crossroad.

Loennechenbua is the DNT's smallest cabin with only two beds and three mattresses in a $10m^2$ room, but it has wood and basic cooking utensils like any other unserviced hut. Feel free to take a rest inside but do remember your dues.

From Loennechenbua continue towards Gammelsetra via the valleys of Flatskirådalen and Skirådalen. Follow the shore of the **Storvatnet** and Littvatnet lakes closely, negotiating the large rockfalls along the shore of both. It is slow going, picking a way across large boulders for some 3km. When most of Storvatnet is behind you, the path eases and becomes increasingly gravelly towards Flatskirådalen.

Continue to the top of the valley via some terraces with many small lakes. The views are beautiful and the clear and comfortable path meanders down into the birch forest of the lower **Skirådalen valley**. It then veers north and joins a dirt road; follow this for the last 2.5km to Gammelsetra. Markers are a bit scarce, but the trail is obvious and marked at crossroads.

Gammelsetra lies in a wonderful spot with views onto the Linndalen valley. It is a very historic mountain farm. The various buildings have been lovingly restored, keeping their unusual character and cultural heritage.

Gammelsetra is a truly charming and traditional summer farmstead

STAGE 4

Gammelsetra to Vangshaugen via Lundlia

Start	Gammelsetra mountain hut
Finish	Vangshaugen mountain hut
Distance	13km (8 miles)
Ascent	460m
Descent	525m
Difficulty	Challenging
Time	4½hr
Maximum altitude	807m
Map	Nordeca Trollheimen Sør 1:50,000 Nr 2828
Note	Outside the main season, a DNT key is needed to access the self-service hut at Vangshaugen.

It will be with some regret that you leave the special Gammelsetra mountain hut behind, but the scenery encountered on the first section of this stage will make up for it. A unique riverscape awaits. Waterways have incised deep valleys between the former summer farms that still sit at height, Lundlia being one of them.

The path is steep (or very steep) in and out of the Grøvn river valley, but otherwise of moderate difficulty only. The latter part of the stage towards Vangshaugen has some poorly marked sections.

Exit the gate of the **Gammelsetra mountain hut** and proceed on the dirt road due west until you come to the bridge over the **Linndøla river**. Follow the sign to Vangshaugen 'om Lundlia' and cross the bridge. Stay on the dirt road, and when it forks take the smaller right fork signposted towards Vangshaugen. Ignore a T-signed path that turns back sharply right into the woods. Stay on the wide path/dirt road as it continues to Nerhjelln (a former summer alm) and the Liabrua bridge over the **Reppa river** and then on towards the summer farm of **Lundlia**.

The **terraces** and **deep gorges** that are seen most prominently at Lundlia demonstrate how both gradual and rapid glacial processes have shaped the landscape here. The gravelly, sandy terraces at different elevations are the remains of sediment slowly deposited in lakes dammed between the mountainside

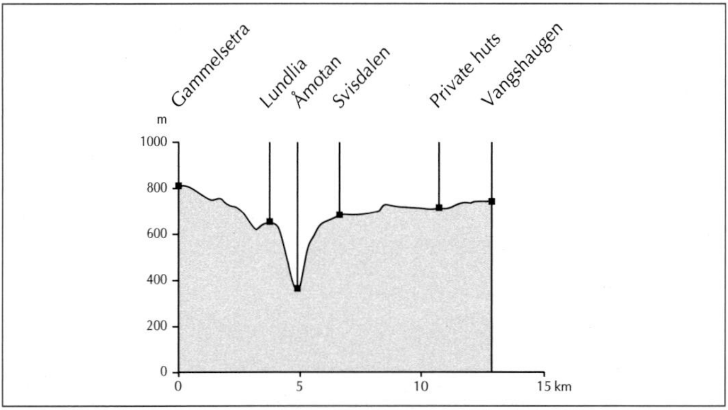

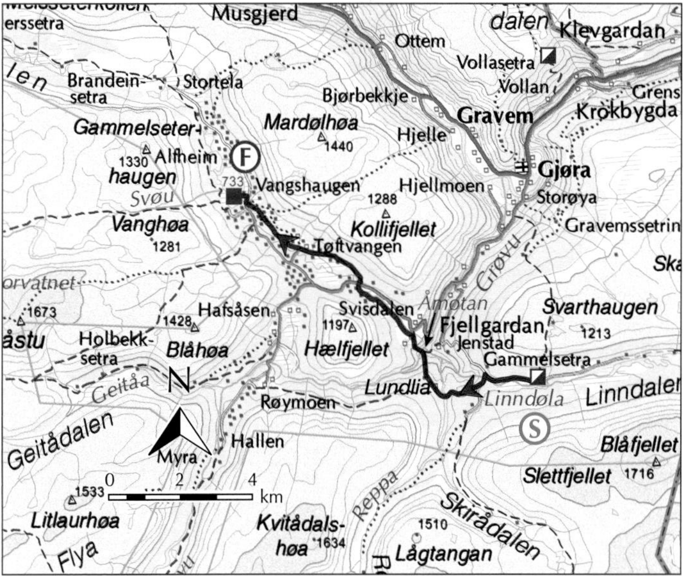

and the former glacier. During large-scale ice-melting and lake-drainage events, these were rapidly eroded by water, giving the area its almost canyon-like appearance.

Autumn sunset around Åmotan

At Lundlia, two different ways to Vangshaugen are signed. Take the one that goes over **Åmotan**, heading up the meadow past farmhouses. Beyond these, enter the forest and start a steep descent into the valley. You soon hear and see the thundery Svøufallet waterfall plunging down the mountainside.

The **confluence** of deep-cut river gorges and waterfalls in this valley is unique in Norway and will leave you awestruck and mesmerised. No fewer than six rivers and three waterfalls give rise to a thundery celebration of waterways on this stretch. The Linndøla and Skiråa, Reppa, Grødøla, Geitåa and Grøvu jointly drain into the Driva river. While the main tributaries of the Driva valley flow eastwards, the Driva itself has spectacularly changed course since the last ice age. In earlier times it flowed northwards at the town of Oppdal to join the Orkla river; today it changes course at the Allmannberget near Oppdal and then flows westwards until it reaches the fjord at the town of Sunndalsøra.

The path descends right to the river valley and crosses the Grøvu over a bridge. A very steep ascent through the forest follows, partly aided by chains. The path has eroded in sections of this ascent. At the top you'll reach the Svøu farm buildings, where you can catch your breath. There's a picnic table with superb views of the valley gorges and the settlement of Jenstad across the valley to the east.

The different **microclimates** you pass through on this stage are remarkable. The dense, wet forest on the north side and the pine forest on the south side of the Grøvn river valley feel markedly different.

Proceed up the grassy path towards and then along a tarmac road, but just before the bridge over the Grødøla river, turn left up a sign-posted and T-marked path that follows the Grødøla's southern bank for some 3km. This is a small but well-marked path through low shrub with plentiful bilberries in season, skirting the edge of the Svøumyran wetland in the Svisdalen valley.

The path approaches the tarmac road again at a bridge: double back over the bridge and take the signposted path left, now on the northern riverbank. It is well marked and easy to follow, until it enters an area with private cabins under development. Due to the recent building activity, the path becomes more difficult to find and less well marked. Fresh markings may well appear in the future.

At first it turns into a dirt road, with occasional waymarks visible. Keep heading in a westerly direction, following the T-signs where possible. Just before a ford over the river (with a parking lot on the opposite side of the footbridge), turn right into the forest, cross a small stream and take the initially vague path to the north-northeast, keeping the small stream to your right. Soon it becomes a good-quality forest trail going uphill and then then turning northwest again to follow the valley. It is poorly marked.

At a clear fork (rather a slanted crossing) take the smaller left path (the right goes on towards private cabins). Follow this until you arrive at a bridge over a stream. Cross the bridge, turn right and follow the occasional markings leading you uphill to a lovely viewpoint back east over the valley. The trail continues down from the little hill and crosses some cabin paths and tracks. Keep looking for marks. The path meets a dirt road once more; turn left (signed) and about 200 metres further on turn slightly right across an open space to find the forest trail again. From here the path is well and recently marked and it leads easily to **Vangshaugen mountain hut** at Storvatnet lake.

The name **Vangshaugen**, literally 'trap-hill' (trappershill/height), alludes to the fact that this location was used for thousands of years in the hunting of reindeer. People studied the migration patterns of the reindeer herds and used that knowledge to hunt and trap them. The herds needed to pass through a narrow section here and thus could be easily guided into traps and dead-ends.

The cabins at Vangshaugen as well as at Todalen in Trollheimen were built by the Englishman Ethelbert Lort Phillips around 1910 as hunting and fishing lodges for the English aristocracy.

STAGE 5

Vangshaugen to Eiriksvollen (Fale)

Start	Vangshaugen mountain hut
Finish	Eiriksvollen mountain hut
Distance	15.25km (9.5 miles)
Ascent	760m
Descent	1360m
Difficulty	Very challenging
Time	6hr
Maximum altitude	1221m
Map	Nordeca Trollheimen Sør 1:50,000 Nr 2828
Note	The DNT key is required for entry to the Eiriksvollen hut

This final stage of the Dovrefjell traverse connects Dovrefjell with Trollheimen. As the mountains of Dovrefjell recede from view, the spectacular vistas onto the hanging valleys over Sunndalen appear. The stage is graded as extra challenging due to the 1200m very steep descent into Sunndalen on sometimes muddy terrain. The path is generally well marked, but at the time of writing some sections were being redeveloped and marking was less obvious there.

From the **Vangshaugen mountain hut** walk to the parking area and follow the signpost to Eiriksvollen. ('Eiriksvollen' is a new name and is rarely seen on signposts. Older signs point to 'Fale'.) Follow the trail along the southern part of the Storvatn lake to its southern tip. At the signpost here, follow the 'T's of the marked path towards Fale-Grøa and Raubergshytta leading away from the lake shore. At the next fork follow the sign to Fale-Grøa (the path that goes west is to the Raubergshytta hut). As you proceed, a signpost for Grøa appears; turn left here (the Fale sign underneath is missing).

Continue on the lovely forest-and-meadow path, which is easy underfoot. T-markers are old and becoming sparse, and then disappear altogether as you continue towards a little dirt road. Turn left (northwest) at the dirt road and follow it for about 1.5km until you reach a parking area at **Stortela**. (At this point a poorly marked path back towards Vangshaugen is visible; it leads parallel to the road but has fallen into disuse and is hard to find from the other side.)

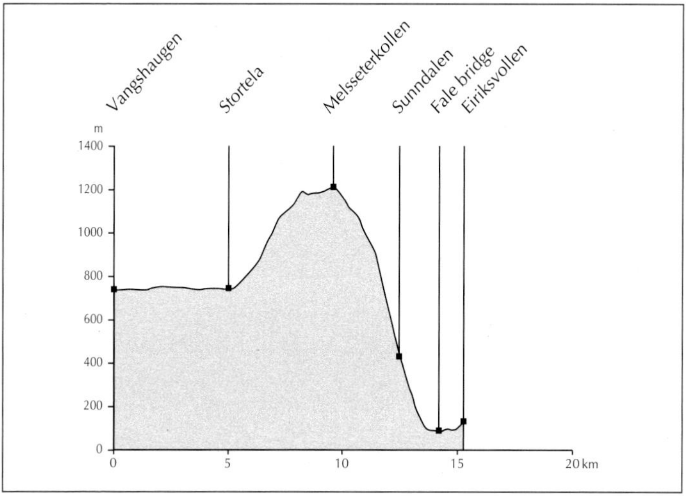
Vangshaugen
Stortela
Melsseterkollen
Sunndalen
Fale bridge
Eiriksvollen
m
1400
1200
1000
800
600
400
200
0
0
5
10
15
20 km

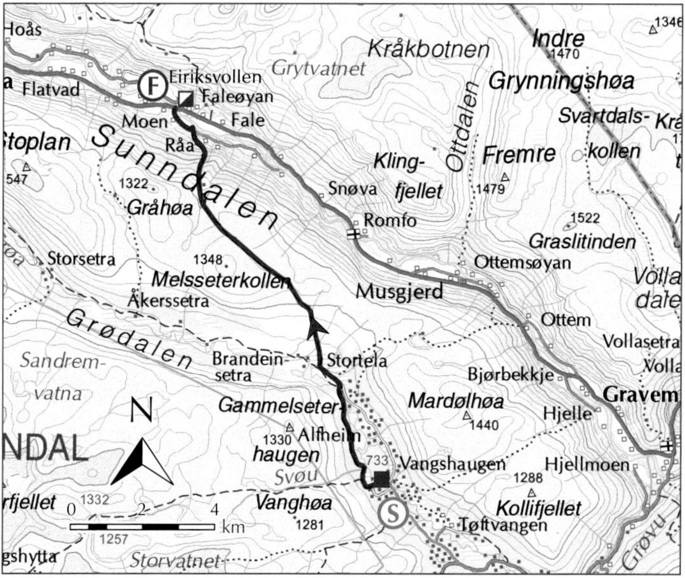
Hoås
Flatvad
Eiriksvollen
Faleøyan
Fale
Moen
Råa
Sunndalen
Grytvatnet
Kråkbotnen
Indre
1470
Grynningshøa
Svartdals-
kollen
Ottdalen
Fremre
1479
Kling-
fjellet
Snøva
Romfo
1522
Graslitinden
Ottemsøyan
Musgjerd
Ottem
Vollasetra
Bjørbekkje
Gravem
Hjelle
Mardølhøa
1440
Hjellmoen
1288
Kollifjellet
Tøftvangen
Vangshaugen
733
Stortela
Brandein-
setra
Gammelseter-
haugen
1330
Alfheim
Svøu
Vanghøa
1281
1322
Gråhøa
1348
Melsseterkollen
Storsetra
Åkerssetra
Grødalen
Sandrem-
vatna
N
1332
0
2
4
km
1257
Storvatnet
1346
547

About 100 metres beyond the parking lot, turn right (northeast) onto the signposted track to Fale. You now start to ascend on a well-marked trail towards Melsseterkollen. The path has several quite wet and marshy sections and an abundance of bilberry shrubs. It becomes drier and stonier underfoot as you get higher up the mountain. You are likely to cross a few snowfields as you proceed along the northern side of **Melsseterkollen** top.

The **view** that now slowly opens up is quite dramatic. You will see the incredibly steep walls of the Trollheimen massif plunge into Sunndalen valley some 1200m below. The walls are interspersed with a series of hanging valleys. This view will be prominent as you continue. The Dovrefjell mountains on the other side fade slowly away from view. This is clearly a transition zone between Dovrefjell and Trollheimen.

The path makes a pleasant start to the descent into Sunndalen valley after passing a series of lakes along the eastern side of the Røta stream. The first few hundred metres of altitude are towards a picturesque meadow with a cabin perched on it. Before reaching the cabin the path crosses to the other side of the Røta river and will soon become much steeper. Beware in wet conditions. The path is well marked throughout this part of the descent and there are some truly amazing views towards the cascades of the Røta river and across Sunndalen into Trollheimen.

Continue into a lightly forested area with mainly small birches. The path is very steep in sections, and as you lose altitude the woods become dense and here the trail will be a less defined and marked path zigzagging down. This section has been undergoing some redevelopment. As the path starts to level off the T-markers become more visible again and you reach a small clearing in the woods. Follow the path to the right, where a small farm shed appears. At the west end of the farm shed there is a gate; pass it and walk the last 100 metres over the grass towards the T-marked farmhouse and the road.

Turn left onto the road, signposted for the Innerdalshytta hut. The road takes you to the Fale bridge over the wide river. Cross the bridge, and immediately beyond it turn right down the bank to the side-road below. Cross right under the bridge, and after 100 metres follow the signs to Eiriksvollen through the gate, uphill. Follow the track as it zigzags uphill to reach the grassland. Stay on the left-hand side of the fields and walk uphill towards the red-topped poles. Here you will find another sign to Eiriksvollen nailed to a tree, indicating uphill to the left. Follow this, and some 50 metres later you'll reach the **cabin**. To get to the bus stop, continue for 100 metres straight east on the main tarmac road after crossing the Fale bridge.

TROLLHEIMEN

View onto Vinnufjellet from the top of Snekkerdalshalsen (Route 9, Stage 3)

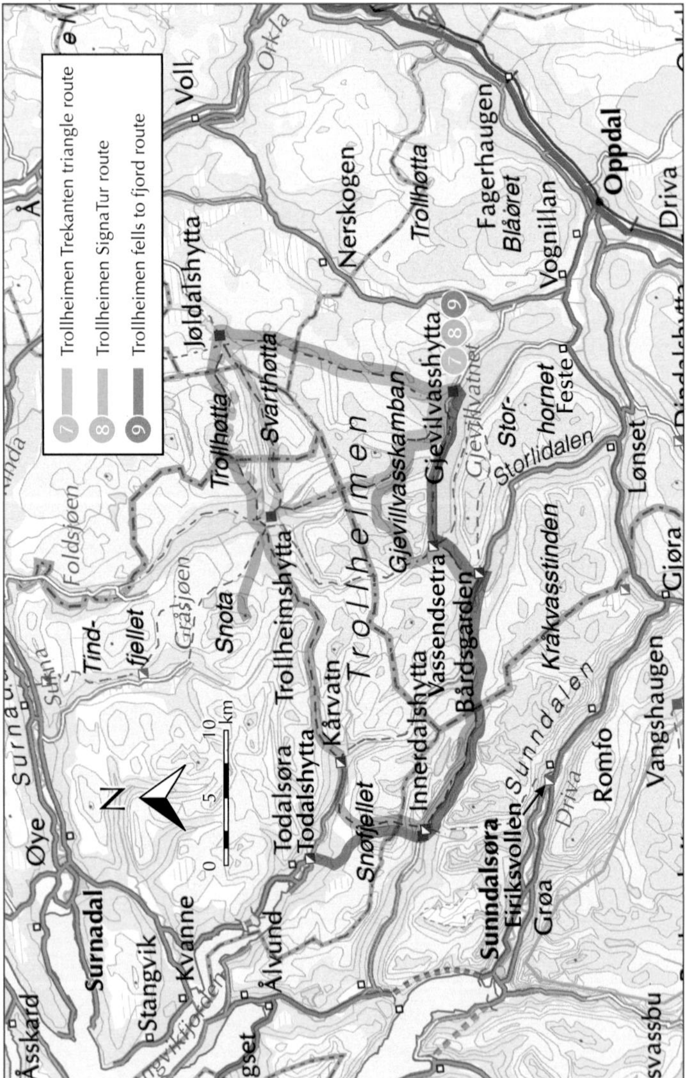
Trollheimen Trekanten triangle route
Trollheimen SignaTur route
Trollheimen fells to fjord route
7
8
9
N
0
5
10
km
Voll
Orkla
Jøldalshytta
Nerskogen
Trollhøtta
Fagerhaugen
Blåøret
Oppdal
Driva
Vognillan
Gjevilvasshytta
Gjevilvatnet
Svarthøtta
Trollhøtta
Stor-
hornet
Feste
Storlidalen
Lønset
Gjevillvasskamban
Trollheimen
Foldsjøen
Gråsjøen
Trollheimshytta
Snota
Tind-
fjellet
Surna
Gjøra
Kråkvasstinden
Vassendsetra
Bårdsgarden
Innerdalshytta
Kårvatn
Sunndalen
Romfo
Vangshaugen
Todalsøra
Todalshytta
Snøfjellet
Sunndalsøra
Eiriksvollen
Grøa
Øye
Surnadal
Kvanne
Stangvik
Ålvund
Åsskard
Stangvikfjorden

There are alpine tops and associated glaciers on the one hand and gentle broad valleys on the other. It is rugged, remote and challenging; and it has very comfortable, authentic mountain cabins that provide a lodging experience rich in history and hospitality. Such is the lure of Trollheimen – an enticing mix of natural and cultural heritage. And in contrast to other areas described in this guide, Trollheimen does not give away its beauty unless you put on your hiking boots and explore. The name Trollheimen ('home of the trolls') has been in use for the area since the 1880s as a way to attract hikers to these mountains. It is well known and loved by Norwegians, who form about 85% of visitors, and hiking here is a much more local experience than elsewhere in Norway.

Trollheimen's northern border is formed by the Surnadalen valley and the municipality of Rindal; to the west lie the fjords; in the east the Orkdalen valley and the train line towards Trondheim; and in the south it is bordered by the steep Sunndalen valley, where the Driva river flows from Oppdal to the fjord into the Norwegian Sea. Trollheimen lies in the counties of Møre og Romsdal and Trøndelag. The area contains a number of nature reserves, most prominently Trollheimen, Svartåmoen and Innerdalen.

As in the Dovrefjell and Jotunheimen national parks, the climate varies as you move eastwards, from an oceanic climate to a significantly drier, continental one. The landscape similarly changes markedly as you go west to east. The western valley of Innerdalen is said to be the most beautiful valley in Norway, but it is hidden well away. It is overlooked by the 'lighthouse' – the cone-shaped Innerdalstårnet (1452m). This iconic peak is believed to have been a nunatak (an isolated rocky peak that stands out in a glacier, on all sides surrounded by the ice but not covered by it) during the last ice age and it now hovers high above the valley. It is possible to scale the Innerdalstårnet without climbing gear – but only by those without a fear of heights! The other peaks in the west are the domain of climbers, including Kongskrona (1818m), Dronningkrona (1816m), and the local high of Store Trolla at 1842m. Towards the east lie Snota (1669m), whose glacier is rapidly disappearing, and the challenging triple-peaked Trollhøtta, at 1614m. Both of these mountains are included in the routes described in this guide. Blåhøa is at 1671m the highest peak in the east and can be reached by a detour from Gjevilvasshytta mountain hut, which is the start point for all three of the Trollheimen treks described here.

In the lower-lying valleys around 500–800m, large areas are forested. The valley around Trollheimshytta (visited on Routes 7 and 8) is covered with a beautiful ancient and undisturbed pine forest that has been declared a natural reserve, called Svartåmoen. It is

View onto Todalen and the fjord along the northern side of Snøfjellet (Route 9, Stage 3)

impressive and rare to see such a fertile and green valley untouched by human development, even though people have been present here for a long time. It is believed that Trollheimen was ice free at an early stage after the last ice age and that Stone Age people hunted here. Arrowheads as old as 4000 years have been found. People hunted the then-wild reindeer, and similar to Dovrefjell and Rondane many archaeological remains have been found of reindeer traps, estimated to be 500–1300 years old. The town of Oppdal, the main portal into Trollheimen, seems to have been of immense cultural importance in previous times. The largest agglomeration of burial mounds in Norway was discovered here. The approximately 750 burial sites date back to Viking times and earlier, as far as the Iron Age.

Moving through this landscape provides for a very varied experience, from smooth rounded tops with wide valleys that are carpeted by an ancient and pristine forest to the increasingly wild and more alpine environment.

PLANTS AND WILDLIFE

The lower mountains to the east, with their generally more rounded peaks, are now the home of a large herd of about 1300 reindeer. They belong to a small number of Sámi families that live off an old form of animal husbandry. The eastern part of Trollheimen, with its diversity in vegetation, forms part of their winter and early spring pasture, and is especially important as the herd disperses widely when the females spread out with their young.

ACCESS AND SERVICES

Oppdal, a town of about 7000 inhabitants, is a regional hub with well-established services. The train station is conveniently located a 5min walk from the main shopping mall, which offers a supermarket and a variety of shops. At the time of writing, two outdoor stores are also in close proximity, as well as one or two cafés in which to while the time away when waiting for a bus or train. Oppdal station has some large coin-operated lockers (large enough to store a backpack for a few hours while hunting a coffee; 3x20NOK coins needed).

Figure 2 shows a schematic overview of public transport options into Trollheimen. Oppdal is the portal for entry into Trollheimen. It lies on the Trondheim–Oslo train line. The bus station is right outside the train station, with connections to Gjevilvasshytta and Eiriksvollen huts.

Local transport

In July and August there is a twice-weekly (Sunday/Thursday) bus connection to and from Gjevilvasshytta (23km from Oppdal). There are also daily buses passing Feste, 12km west from Oppdal on the RV70, from where you can walk (11.5km, 2½hr) a dirt road up to Gjevilvasshytta.

The Oppdal–Kristiansund express bus also passes Fale Bru (Fale Bridge), a 15min walk from Eiriksvollen mountain hut and just under an hour's ride from Oppdal. Eiriksvollen to Innerdalshytta is an alternative entry into (or exit from) west Trollheimen. (Innerdalshytta is on Route 8, Stage 3–4 and Route 9, Stage 2–3.)

Another, less convenient but still viable option is to access Todalshytta (Route 9, Stage 3) and Kårvatn (Route 8, Stage 4–5) mountain huts through a combination of public transport and taxi. The regular express bus connection between Trondheim and Kristiansund passes Skei in Surnadalsøra, from where private transport to Todalen can be arranged. See Appendix C for further information on local transport.

Mountain huts

Access to the mountain huts that are relevant to the routes presented varies. Todalshytta, Kårvatn, Gjevilvasshytta and Bårdsgarden can be accessed by car. Eiriksvollen mountain hut is a 15min walk from the main road, while Innerdalshytta is about an hour away from a road. Jøldalshytta, Trollheimshytta and Vassendsetra can only be reached on foot.

The mountain huts belong to either the Trondhjems Turistforening (TT) or the Kristiansund og Nordmøre Turistforening (KNT). Both organisations are part of the DNT. Eiriksvollen, Innerdalshytta, Todalshytta, Bårdsgarden, Vassendsetra and Kårvatn are all self-service huts. All but Bårdsgarden require the DNT universal key for access. Gjevilvasshytta, Jøldalshytta and Trollheimshytta are fully serviced huts. In these huts you have the option for full board as well as individual meals, but you can't cater for yourself.

Figure 2: Rondane, Dovrefjell & Trollheimen access

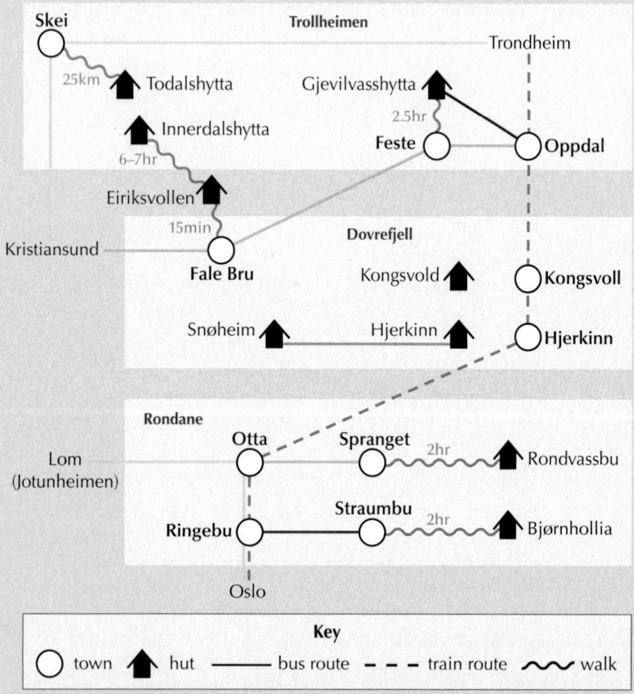

	Line	Connection
– – –	Oslo–Trondheim	Oslo–Gardermoen–Otta–Hjerkinn–Kongsvoll–Oppdal–Trondheim
———	205	Otta–Raphamn–Mysusæter–Spranget
———	206	Ringebu–Straumbu
———	FRAM Ekspress 901	Kristiansund–Fale Bru–Oppdal
———	summer shuttle bus	Hjerkinn–Snøheim (check https://snoheim.dnt.no/eng)
———	580	Oppdal–Gjevilvasshytta (Su, Th)
———	FRAM Ekspress 905	Kristiansund–Skei i Surnadal–Trondheim
———	Nordfjordekspressen VY146	Oslo–Gardermoen–Lillehammer–Otta–Lom

Hiking over Langfjellet towards Jøldalshytta mountain hut (Route 8, Stage 7)

THE ROUTES IN TROLLHEIMEN

The routes in Trollheimen are generally more challenging than in the other hiking areas covered in this guide. This is due to both the length of the stages and their elevations. Be sure to assess whether they are for you. Three Trollheimen routes are described in this chapter. Trekanten ('the triangle'; Route 7), which so many Norwegians have on their list, explores this majestic landscape by going into the heart of Trollheimen and the edge of a truly alpine landscape and then back out through reindeer country to Gjevilvasshytta. The 'SignaTur' (Route 8) is a recently developed tour that is fast becoming a classic. It is a challenging route that takes you around Trollheimen in a large circle and shows off both its alpine character and its glacial landforms as well as offering the chance to scale two challenging tops – Snota and Trollhøtta. Route 3 is one of only two routes in this guide that take you from fells to fjord. It comprises a traverse from the southeast to the northwest, starting at Gjevilvasshytta mountain hut and ending in Todalen.

Note that there are at least three mountaintops named Trollhøtta ('head of the Troll') in Trollheimen. In this guide the name refers to the 1614m peak near Trollheimshytta mountain hut.

ROUTE 7

Trollheimen Trekanten triangle route

Start/finish	Gjevilvasshytta mountain hut
Distance	59km (36.5 miles)
Ascent/descent	2295/2295m
Time	3 days
Variations	One-day extension: possible ascent/descent of Snota from Trollheimshytta mountain hut. For the second stage, there are two alternatives besides the main route: one more (Route 8, Stage 7) and one less (Stage 2A) challenging hike. This route cannot be meaningfully shortened as Trollheimshytta truly lies in the middle of troll country, very much away from civilisation.

For Norwegian hikers, this route is a classic. It goes into the heartland of Trollheimen with its high plateaus and deep valleys, the high tops providing either a backdrop or an additional challenge. At 57km in three stages it is a challenging route and requires reasonable fitness. On the other hand, the delightful Trollheimshytta mountain hut sits so idyllically in the middle of the ancient Scots pine forest of the Svartåmoen reserve that it is quite tempting to stay put and relax for a day or venture out to collect berries.

Stage 1 starts at Gjevilvasshytta and takes you over Riarskaret (1320m) near Blåhøa (1671m) and Riaren (1365m), and from there over Mellomfjellet to the Skallen escarpment (1227m) and down towards Trollheimshytta. Stage 2 goes along Geithøtta (1352m), which offers majestic views over the three 'heads' of the Trollhøtta (1614m) mountain. The lake in its cirque is called the 'troll's eye' and looks up to the hiker at the edge. This stage ends at Jøldalshytta mountain hut. The final stage goes through high fells terrain, along the foot of the Svarthøtta mountain range and through the Gjørdøldalen valley, where you might well encounter reindeer. Trekanten is a circular route and ends back at Gjevilvasshytta. Be sure to arrive in time to treat yourself to a freshly baked waffle in the afternoon.

This route can be extended by a day, with the option to scale Snota mountain (1669m) from Trollheimshytta. Refer to Route 8, Stage 6. Snota dominates the view from the hut; it is the second highest peak in eastern Trollheimen and there are wonderful vistas from the top. The hike should only be attempted in good weather. It is a long stage – 1300m up and down – and adds about 23km to the route.

There are effectively three options for the second stage. Firstly there's the common route over Geithøtta, as described in Stage 2. The second possibility is a valley hike, passing between Geithøtta and Trollhøtta, at first in a very narrow valley that slowly widens and takes you through the old summer pastures and farms towards Jøldalshytta (see Stage 2A). It is an enjoyable stage that is generally underrated as it literally stays in the shadow of the two other alternatives. A third option for the hike between Trollheimshytta and Jøldalshytta is the high traverse up and over the Trollhøtta top. This hike is much more challenging than the other two options but offers fantastic views over Trollheimen. As with the ascent to Snota, it should not be done in bad weather, and especially not in high winds. It is described in more detail in Route 8, Stage 7. The dedicated hiker could, of course, do all three by backtracking back and forth.

Although there is no mobile coverage at Trollheimshytta, staff at the hut have access to the weather forecast and can provide advice on current conditions on Snota and Trollhøtta.

If you plan to arrive by public transport, the author's advice would be to arrive on a Sunday afternoon (by bus from Oppdal) and hike the route clockwise, as described, starting Monday. As this is generally a route much loved by Norwegians, it is busier at weekends. The route is slightly less challenging when done anticlockwise (the 'normal' way), but the views are much more spectacular if done in a clockwise direction – especially in good weather.

STAGE 1

Gjevilvasshytta to Trollheimshytta

Start	Gjevilvasshytta mountain hut
Finish	Trollheimshytta mountain hut
Distance	21km (13 miles)
Ascent	860m
Descent	1030m
Difficulty	Very challenging
Time	6½hr
Maximum altitude	1319m
Map	Nordeca Trollheimen Nord 1:50,000 Nr 2827 and Nordeca Trollheimen Sør 1:50,000 Nr 2828
Note	A pair of trekking poles will come in handy when wading through streams on this stage.

The Trekanten triangle route starts with a truly memorable hike. The well-marked path showcases an amazing diversity of landscapes – up through a forest of pines and then birch and on to marshes as you proceed along the Gravbekken stream towards towering Blåhøa (1671m). The stage continues through a narrow pass between Blåhøa and Gjevillvasskamban and you'll find yourself in a desolate-looking moonscape until you reach the Riaskaret ridge and the vistas open towards Fossådalsvatnet lake. However, the view that will leave you speechless awaits at Skallen, where you can marvel at the expanse of an ancient Scots pine forest.

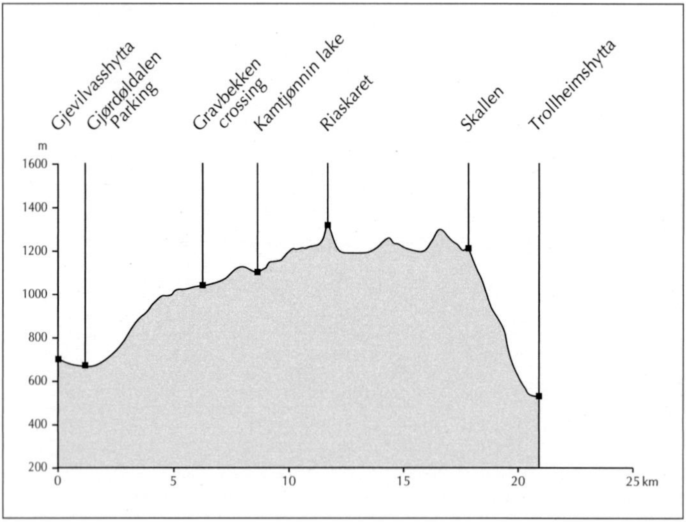

Starting from **Gjevilvasshytta**, leave the gate, cross the road and follow the sign down towards the lake to meet with a service road parallel to the lake. Follow the road right and after about 2km, cross a bridge (ignore the signpost towards Jøldalshytta). Shortly afterwards a parking area appears; this is where the trail starts. At the time of writing there was no charge for parking a car here.

A DNT sign marks the start of the trail towards Trollheimshytta at the edge of the parking area, leading immediately into the forest. Ascend gently up the Gjørdøldalen valley along the **Gravbekken stream** and its deep gully. Signs are

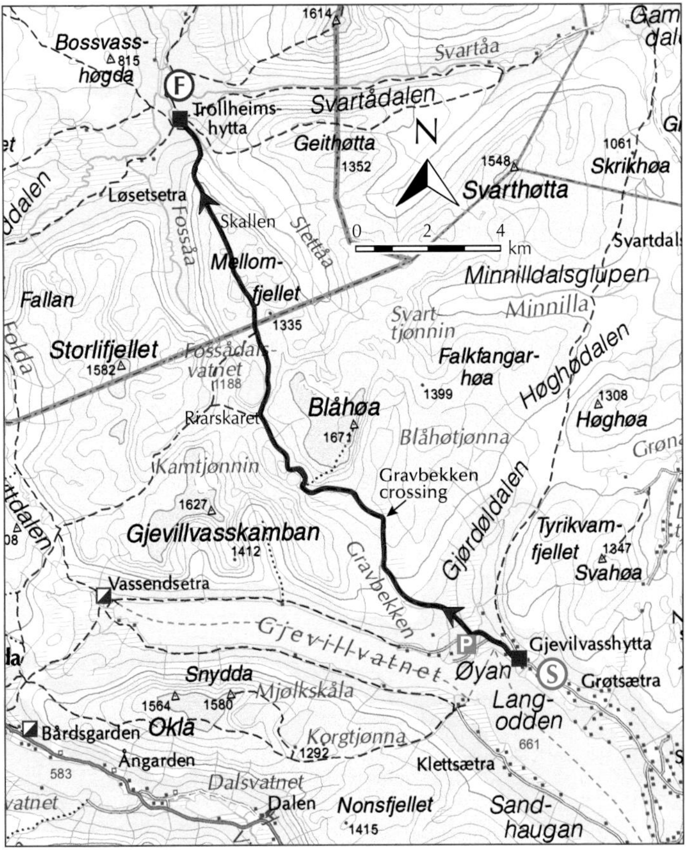

sparse here, but the path is evident in the dense forest. Once the birch/pine forest gives way to summer alms the path is marked with T-markers and red dots. Good marking continues throughout.

Ascend into an open, broad, gently undulating plateau where there may be sheep grazing during the summer months. The trail is at times wet in sections, and some small brooks need to be crossed as it continues along Gravbekken. Eastern Trollheimen's highest mountain, Blåhøa (1671m), appears in view with its steep walls on its western side.

Cross Gravbekken – this could be challenging in early spring or during rainy summers. On the other side of the stream, ascend gently among lovely wildflower meadows towards a saddle.

The area between Gjevillvasskamban and Kamtjønnin peaks is known for its diversity of alpine **wildflowers**. A particular species of alpine poppy appears to grow only here in this part of Trollheimen and was given the name *Papaver radicatum gjaerevollii,* after the world-renowned botanist Olav Gjærevoll, who dedicated much of his scientific career to Trollheimen's wildflowers.

At the saddle, completely new vistas open up into a narrow valley with the near-circular **Kamtjønnin lake** on the northwest side of Gjevillvasskamban. The wide valley gives away its glacial origin. It is a high alpine zone, with practically no vegetation apart from mosses and lichen. Just beyond the saddle you'll reach the halfway mark of the stage. The trail continues around and along the lakes and traverses the valley, ascending towards the highpoint of the day at **Riaskaret** (1319m).

Ignore the turnoff towards the Bårdsgarden and Vassendsetra mountain huts that goes left across Riaren (1365m). As you look over the ridge towards and over **Fossådalsvatnet lake** you get your first glimpse of Snota (1669m) and its glacier in the distance. It towers well above all other peaks, including Trollhøtta (1614m) and Geithøtta (1352m), and these three will be companions for the rest of the day.

Descend steeply to the lake, and after having walked along it, ascend gently towards a plateau dotted with more lakes. This is **Mellomfjellet**. Continue towards **Skallen** (1226m) at the edge of the plateau.

From **Skallen** the view towards the valleys below is nothing short of magnificent. The sheer scale of these valleys congregating at Svartåmoen is the most expansive in Trollheimen. Three rivers converge here into Gråsjøen lake. The woods below are dense. There is no farm, village or settlement in sight, and Trollheimshytta is well hidden from view.

Mobile coverage is patchy in Trollheimen, but highpoints such as Skallen and the mountaintops in view of Gråsjøen lake offer the best chances of mobile reception.

The descent is steep and short. The path is good and leads down a series of terraces and across botanic habitats from high, through medium and into low alpine zones of dense birch and pine forest. About 250 metres before reaching **Trollheimshytta**, close to the bridge over the Slettåa river, there are some very pleasant camping spots.

View from Skallen into the Svartåmoen valley, with Snota ahead

A warm and welcoming abode, **Trollheimshytta** was the first cabin built in Trollheimen by the Norwegian Trekking Association. It has always welcomed its guests with *god mat, lange senger, grei varding* – 'good food, long beds, great hospitality'.

STAGE 2

Geithøtta high traverse

Start	Trollheimshytta mountain hut
Finish	Jøldalshytta mountain hut
Distance	17km (10.5 miles)
Ascent	885m
Descent	685m
Difficulty	Challenging
Time	5hr
Maximum altitude	1325m
Map	Nordeca Trollheimen Nord 1:50,000 Nr 2827

The hike from Trollheimshytta over Geithøtta lets you appreciate the whole length of the Svartådalen valley and Trollhøtta mountain on the opposite side. In fact the triple-headed Trollhøtta is the defining feature of the hike for the first half, with the second half being a valley walk into the gently undulating fields towards Jølvatnet lake. Well marked throughout, it is a highly enjoyable stage and the shortest of this route.

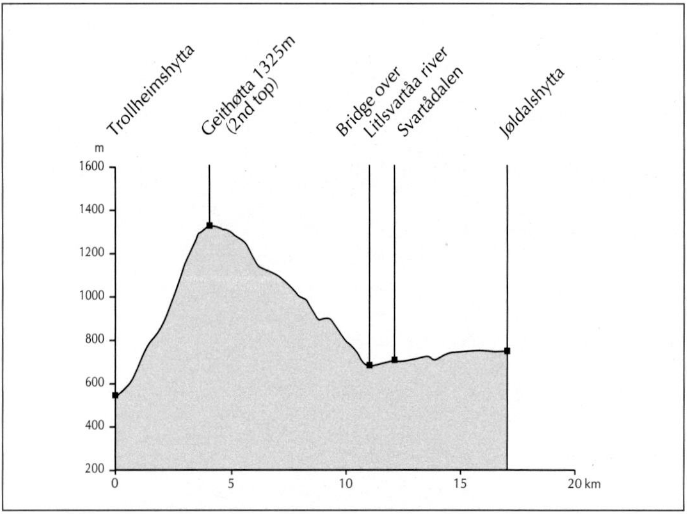

Turn right out of the **Trollheimshytta hut** and walk to the marked crossroads. Here the path forks, with the left-hand option going to Jøldalshytta mountain hut via Svartådalen (Stage 2A) and the right going past Geithøtta (1352m). Take the right-hand fork. The hike starts in earnest with a steady 150m ascent through the forest to a waterfall of the **Slettåa river**, which cascades down the Slettåadalen valley and eventually empties into Gråsjøen lake.

All of the large lakes and half of the water bodies in Trollheimen are regulated for use as reservoirs for **hydroelectric power generation**. This extensive appraisal and start of production took place in the 1960s and 70s and led to the protection of the remaining area from further exploitation. Trollheimen was declared a **nature reserve** in 1987.

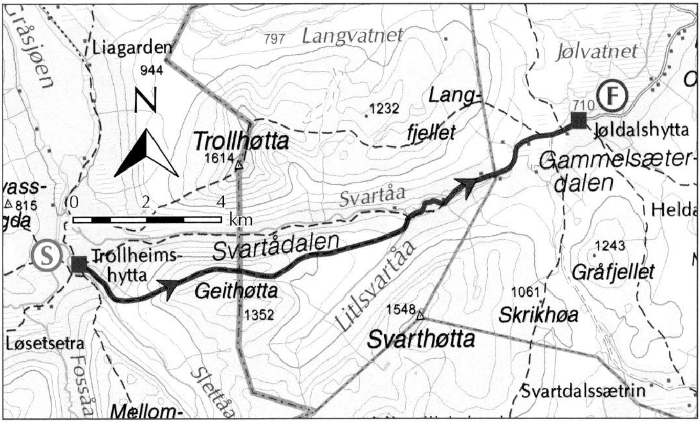

Shortly after the waterfall, follow the marking for a sudden 90° left turn and a steep uphill ahead. There are no switchbacks; the path goes straight up. It feels good underfoot though, with rocks rather than gravel – but watch out for patches of wetness or slippery stones. The trail is well marked, and navigation is no issue as long as you follow the markings. The ascent follows several gullies, crossing from one to the other until you reach the highpoint of the walk, north of the **Geithøtta** top and quite at the edge of Svartådalen. The view into the valley below is beautiful, with slopes falling away quite steeply. To the west, in good weather, you'll see Snota rising out of the large expanses of pine forest around Trollheimshytta.

View of the three Trollhøtta tops across the Svartådalen valley from Geithøtta

Spare a thought for the many ancient **pine trees** in the Svartåmoen nature reserve. As described in the Trondhjems Turistforening 1996 yearbook, many of them have been standing for hundreds of years, playing their part as home to countless rodents, birds and insects, showing the signs of age and weathering as their green branches slowly turn to dried-out monuments against the ever-changing sky. One day they will fall to the ground, but this could well be after many more of today's hikers have walked their final hike. So far, the oldest tree has been calculated to be 495 years old.

From the highpoint, continue for a few kilometres along the ridge at roughly the same height. The view is now dominated by Trollhøtta (1614m) to the north – at first its bulky top, but as you progress the whole of its cirque opens up. It truly is the defining feature of this walk. The descent starts with a gentle decline into the Litlsvartådalen valley and then into the **Svartådalen valley**. The path is generally excellent. It gets a bit muddy in places, but construction with planks is underway to prevent further erosion. Jøldalshytta is already visible from a long way off.

You'll pass the halfway point of the stage while you're on the descent, and not too long afterwards you'll reach the point where the path joins the valley walk out of Trollheimshytta, meeting at the bridge over the **Litlsvartåa river**. Cross the bridge, and on the other side the trail turns into a small service/tractor road which continues for about 6.5km to Jøldalshytta. You can either follow the road or take the marked trail that follows a slightly straighter path by cutting out some of the corners of the service road. Either way, it's an easy, gentle walk on flat terrain in a beautiful valley with wide-open views both in front and behind you until you reach **Jøldalshytta mountain hut**.

Rainbow over Jølvatnet lake and Jøldalshytta

STAGE 2A

Svartådalen (alternative route)

Start	Trollheimshytta mountain hut
Finish	Jøldalshytta mountain hut
Distance	16.25km (10 miles)
Ascent	440m
Descent	240m
Difficulty	Moderate
Time	5hr
Maximum altitude	740m
Map	Nordeca Trollheimen Nord 1:50,000 Nr 2827

Most hikers reading this guide will likely choose this route on a bad weather day, given the other options available, so be prepared for water from above and below. Still, the walk itself is through a charming valley, with lots of wildflowers growing in the shady and sheltered areas, making it a very attractive alternative also on sunny days.

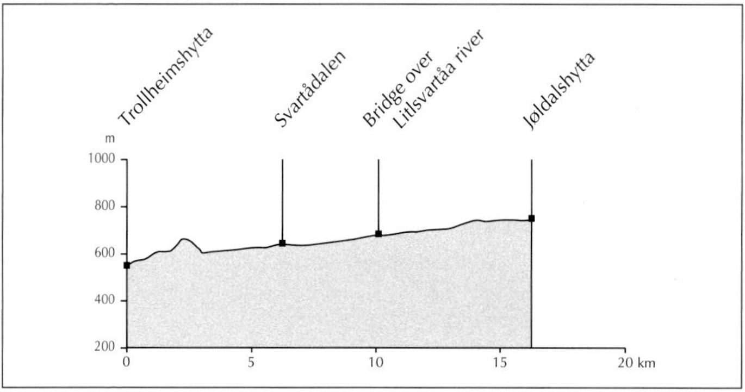

The path on this stage is well marked and especially easy to follow as it goes through a narrow river valley. At the start, turn towards the right around **Trollheimshytta** itself, past its ever-useful drying room (*tørkerom*). Soon the path

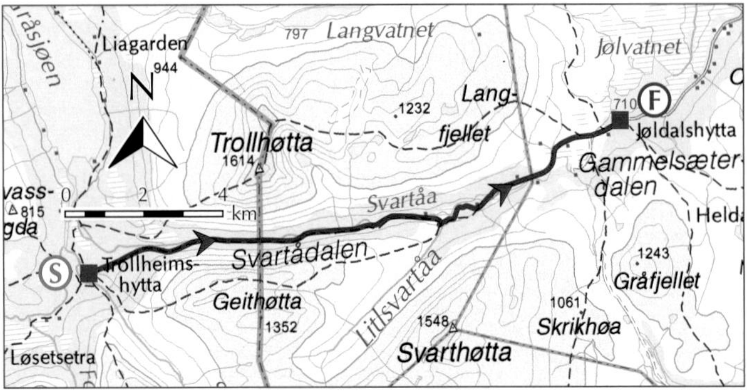

towards Jøldalshytta mountain hut splits: go left to follow the Svartådalen valley route into the moor and swampy areas.

For the first few kilometres the path will often feel wet underfoot, due to the swampy and boggy terrain. There are wooden planks laid out in some sections; be careful as these can become very slippery when wet.

Svartåmoen nature reserve lies adjacent to the southern end of Gråsjoen lake. Numerous rivers converge here in a delta of glaciofluvial gravel and sand deposits. The trained eye can observe kettle holes (depressions formed by big blocks of glacial ice that were left behind as the glacier retreated, and slowly melted in place) and eskers (sandy ridges, also left after the glacial ice retreated, initially deposited by the streams that flowed within and under glaciers). The ancient and virtually untouched Scots pine woods of the area are typical for the region.

Continuing upriver there is a slight ascent – albeit along an undulating path all the way towards Jøldalshytta – that is noticeable as you move along. Initially, you are quite high above the **Svartådalen** river, and it is difficult to see the gorge that the river has etched into the mountain. Continue to follow the path as it crosses a few streams and creeks – tributaries of Svartåa.

The valley that runs from east to west is narrow and so protects its **vegetation** from harsh winds and sunlight. Consequently, you will find many high towering perennials, with large leaves and high stems, such as wolfsbane and wild geraniums, but also many grasses such as wood millet and ferns, all of which would perish in more exposed areas.

The **Trollhøtta massif** towers on the opposite side of the river, with Geithøtta rising high above you. Many streams run down on the Trollhøtta side too, and even at the end of summer there are some waterfalls here.

After a few kilometres the trail levels with the river and passes a few delightful small beaches and bays that invite for a swim on a warm day. Moving upstream, the valley starts to dry up, and as you exit the narrow part of Svartådalen valley you'll pass by a number of summer pastures. A larger tributary of the Svartåa river comes down here and the trail over Geithøtta joins up with the valley walk.

Cross the bridge over the **Litlsvartåa river**. From here you can either follow the old tractor/service road for the final 6.5km to Jøldalshytta, or follow the T-marked path that weaves its way in a snake-like fashion, crossing the service road a few times. About a kilometre from **Jøldalshytta** there are a few very attractive camping spots that are relatively dry underfoot and offer some shelter in the otherwise open landscape.

Many of the pine trees found in Trollheimen are centuries old

STAGE 3

Jøldalshytta to Gjevilvasshytta

Start	Jøldalshytta mountain hut
Finish	Gjevilvasshytta mountain hut
Distance	21km (13 miles)
Ascent	550m
Descent	580m
Difficulty	Challenging
Time	6½hr
Maximum altitude	1072m
Map	Nordeca Trollheimen Nord 1:50,000 Nr 2827 and Nordeca Trollheimen Sør 1:50,000 Nr 2828

This pleasant stage features a moderate ascent and descent, and is long but otherwise not difficult. It completes the Trekanten triangle route by taking you out of the Gammelsæterdalen valley, up Skrikhøa (1061m) and past Kjølen (1292m), crossing the Minnilla river and eventually descending the Gjørdøldalen valley back to Gjevilvasshytta mountain hut. On the way, it passes alongside some of the higher peaks of eastern Trollheimen, such as Svarthøtta (1548m) and Blåhøa (1671m).

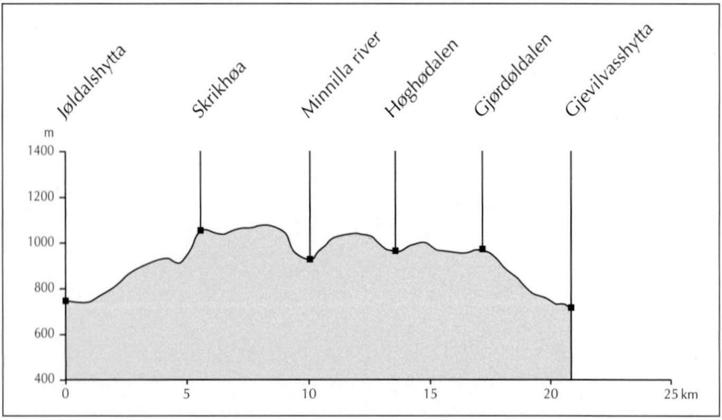

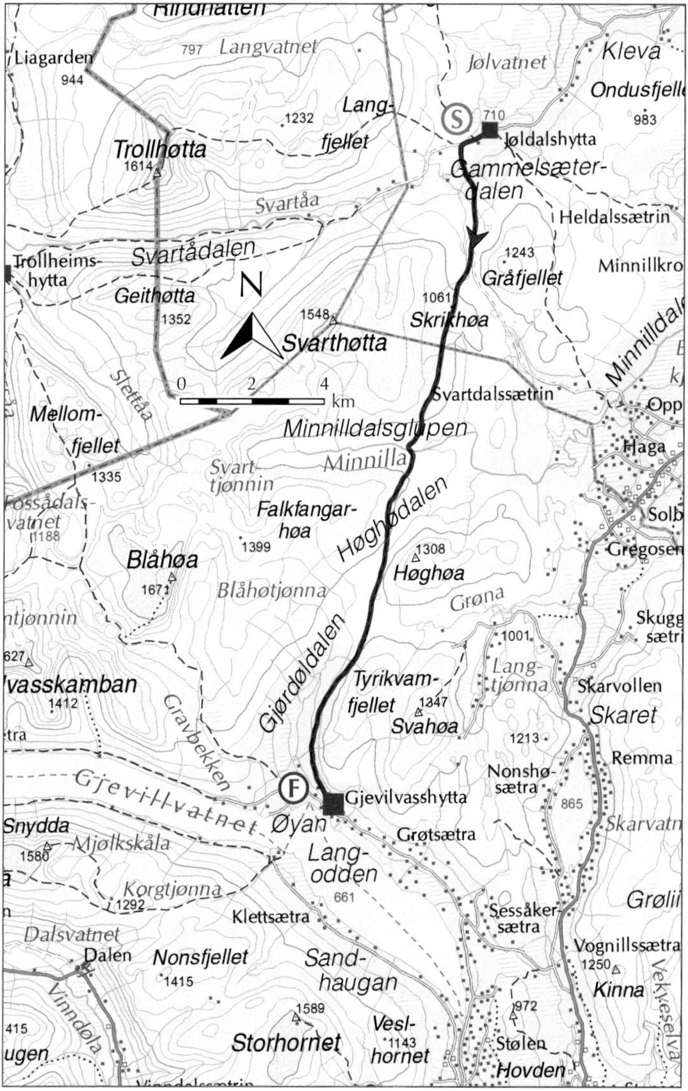
Liagarden
Langvatnet
Jølvatnet
Kleva
Ondusfjell
Langfjellet
Trollhøtta
Jøldalshytta
Gammelsæterdalen
Svartåa
Heldalssætrin
Trollheimshytta
Svartådalen
Gråfjellet
Minnillkro
Geithøtta
Skrikhøa
Svarthøtta
Minnilldal
Slettåa
Svartdalssætrin
Mellomfjellet
Minnilldalsglupen
Haga
Minnilla
Svarttjønnin
Falkfangarhøa
Høghødalen
Gregosen
Blåhøa
Høghøa
Blåhøtjønna
Grøna
Gjørdøldalen
Langtjønna
Skarvollen
Tyrikvamfjellet
Svahøa
Skaret
Gravbekken
Remma
Nonshøsætra
Gjevillvatnet
Gjevilvasshytta
Snydda
Øyan
Grøtsætra
Mjølkskåla
Langodden
Korgtjønna
Sessåkersætra
Klettsætra
Dalsvatnet
Vognillssætra
Dalen
Nonsfjellet
Sandhaugan
Kinna
Vinndøla
Vekveselva
Storhornet
Veslhornet
Stølen
Hovden
N
0 2 4 km

Crossing the bridge over the Minnilla river, with the Svarthamran tops as a backdrop

Leaving **Jøldalshytta mountain hut**, exit the gate and turn right onto the gravel road. Follow this road for about a kilometre, pass and ignore the sign to Trollheimshytta and turn left onto the path to Gjevilvasshytta. The path is well marked and easy underfoot – gravelly, sandy and only sometimes muddy. It leads through a wide, open landscape with only occasional small birch woods. (The nutrient-poor soil here only supports low-growing vegetation.) After crossing a small stream you'll come to the only significant ascent of the day: about 200m up **Skrikhøa** (1061m).

The next few kilometres are in the typical, open fells landscape that is so characteristic of this altitude, with a generally good path undulating at height over, along and beside hills. To your right the **Minnilldalsglupen valley** opens up and shortly afterwards the path descends towards the **Minnilla river** and crosses it over a permanent bridge.

This wide U-shaped Minnilldalsglupen **valley** is a picture-perfect example of a glacial valley. The cirque coming off the Svarthamran massif forms a half-circle, with the Minnilla flowing out and towards the lower-lying marshlands. These marshes and bogs form an important nature reserve for a large number of water birds and waders. The beautiful glacial valley and the river are at the halfway point of the stage and an excellent site for a lunch stop. The bridge construction is worth a look; it's made entirely of stones and wood, built to withstand the spring melts and tumbling waters.

From the bridge, ascend and continue into the **Høghødalen valley**, with the face of Høghøa (1308m) on your left.

There is a good chance of spotting **reindeer** in these valleys. They are shy but not wild. There are about 1300 animals in Trollheimen, and they are owned by a few families of Sámi origin. These families arrived in Trollheimen in the 1800s with their herds. Their disregard for previously established ownership rights led to a longstanding dispute with farmers that was only resolved in 1984. Today the reindeer herds and their management are part of the cultural heritage of the Trollheimen nature reserve.

Cross the saddle between Høghødalen and Gjørdøldalen. The path follows the left-hand side of the valley, slowly finding its way down towards Gjevillvatnet lake, with Blåhøa rising to your right. You'll soon enter the forest, and the path continues downhill until it reaches the road which takes you the final 500 metres to **Gjevilvasshytta hut** as well as to the turnoff to the parking area.

In season, Gjevilvasshytta offers a very Norwegian **afternoon tea** tradition, consisting of tea or coffee with freshly baked waffles, *rømme* (Norwegian cream) and *syltetøy* (jam).

Well worth finishing the route at Gjevilvasshytta

ROUTE 8

Trollheimen SignaTur route

Start/finish	Gjevilvasshytta mountain hut
Distance	152km (94.5 miles)
Ascent	6750m
Descent	6750m
Time	8 days
Variations	No extensions are described. The route can be shortened by skipping Stage 6, and it can be exited after Stages 2, 3 or 4 with private transportation arrangements. A lower-route alternative to Stage 7 – Trollheimshytta to Jøldalshytta – is provided by Route 7, Stages 2 or 2A.

This route is probably the most dramatic and also the most challenging in this guide. It takes the form of a large circle around Trollheimen, starting at the gentler profiles of the eastern ranges, continuing towards the wild and dramatic western areas and returning through glacier-shaped valleys. With the Trollheimen mountaintops as a magnificent backdrop, this route takes in some of what Norwegians consider to be their most beautiful summer pastoral valleys, such as Gjevilvassdalen, Storlidalen and Folldalen – and of course Innerdalen. The route includes two 'top tours': the day trip to Snota (1669m) from Trollheimshytta mountain hut (Stage 6) and the ascent over Trollhøtta (1614m) on the way to Jøldalshytta mountain hut (Stage 7). In contrast to similar routes in Jotunheimen, you will find far fewer people hiking in Trollheimen, making for a different experience altogether. A good level of fitness and stamina is needed to complete the long stages with their considerable ascents and descents on sometimes arduous terrain. It is for that very reason, of course, also a highly rewarding route. The two spectacular mountain climbs take you high into alpine territory from which views over many kilometres can be enjoyed – weather permitting.

The route starts and ends at the Gjevilvasshytta mountain hut, which is highly accessible by both public and private transport, making it an ideal entry point. Virtually all of the mountain huts on this route have a rich history and date back to the 1700s and 1800s. There is a sense of community in literally following the footsteps of hikers of centuries past, and something special in sharing these marvellous views across the ages.

The first stage goes over the Riaren escarpment, taking you straight into untouched landscapes. The path circles the Gjevillvasskamban massif as it heads towards Vassendsetra mountain hut. The next stage is a very short one, in comparison, ending in Bårdsgarden. While not described in this guide, a detour to the Okla tops with views over both Gjevilvassvatnet and Angardsvatnet lakes would be feasible. Stage 3 goes due west, leading out of the beautiful Storlidalen valley, over the ridge at Medskaret, along the old nunataks of Kringlehøa and Renndalskammen, and into the incredibly lush Innerdalen valley which is overlooked by the cone-shaped Innerdalstårnet. On the fourth stage there are ever more views over the Vinnufjellet massif as you ascend out of the Innerdalen valley towards the saddle at Bjøråskaret. The subsequent descent along a terrace-shaped landscape into Todalen valley ends at the charming Kårvatn mountain hut. Stage 5 treats you at the start to a glorious waterfall at Nauståfossen, and then leads due east through the length of the Naustådalen valley and the extensive wetlands at Stormyra to Trollheimshytta. At over 24km this is the longest stage of the route, although at the same time it is relatively gentle in terms of elevation differences. Stage 6 is an optional summit hike to Snota – a challenging but exceptionally beautiful round trip from Trollheimshytta. Stage 7 heads towards and over the triple tops of Trollhøtta, ending at the Jøldalshytta hut. It is a superbly dramatic stage that requires a head for heights. The final stage of the SignaTur route coincides with the third stage of the Trollheimen Trekanten triangle route (Route 7) and brings you back to Gjevilvasshytta.

The trek can be exited most easily at Bårdsgarden (after Stage 2), which is only a short taxi ride from Lønset, where public transport is available to Oppdal. Innerdalshytta (Stage 3) is about 4km by gravel road away from the nearest car park, and Kårvatn (after Stage 4) is accessible by road from Todalen. Kårvatn is about 30km away from the small township of Skei (in Surnadal), from which public transport is available to Kristiansund and Trondheim. While feasible, these exits are meant more in case of unforeseen circumstances rather than as attractive options.

Nauståfossen waterfall is Trollheimen's highest and cascades down a steep 110m cliff (Route 8, Stage 5)

In poor weather conditions, the summit hikes to Snota and over Trollhøtta should not be attempted. The latter has two safer alternatives in the form of Route 7, Stages 2 and 2A.

STAGE 1

Riaren high traverse

Start	Gjevilvasshytta mountain hut
Finish	Vassendsetra mountain hut
Distance	22km (13.75 miles)
Ascent	1055m
Descent	1085m
Difficulty	Very challenging
Time	7½hr
Maximum altitude	1380m
Map	Nordeca Trollheimen Sør 1:50,000 Nr 2828
Notes	A pair of walking poles will be handy for wading through streams on this stage.

This is a challenging high route that brings you to the other side of Gjevillvatnet lake over the Riaren ridge. The well-marked path goes through a wide diversity of landscapes – up through a forest of pines and then birch and on to marshes as you proceed along the Gravbekken stream towards towering Blåhøa (1671m). As you move through the narrow pass between Blåhøa and Gjevillvasskamban the landscape again changes dramatically, showcasing typical glacial lakes in three cirques. After ascending to the Riaskaret ridge you walk along it and then down on its western side. Green and flowering Hyttdalen valley and the charm of Vassendsetra await you at the end of the day.

Starting from **Gjevilvasshytta**, leave the gate, cross the road and follow the sign down towards the lake to meet with a service road parallel to the lake. Follow the road right and after about 2km, cross a bridge (ignore the signpost towards Jøldalshytta). Shortly afterwards a **parking area** appears; this is where the trail starts. At the time of writing there was no charge for parking a car here.

A DNT sign marks the start of the trail towards Trollheimshytta at the edge of the parking area, leading immediately into the forest. Ascend gently up the Gjørdøldalen valley along the **Gravbekken stream** and its deep gully. Signs are sparse here, but the path is evident in the dense forest. Once the birch/pine forest gives way to summer alms the path is marked with T-markers and red dots. Good marking continues throughout.

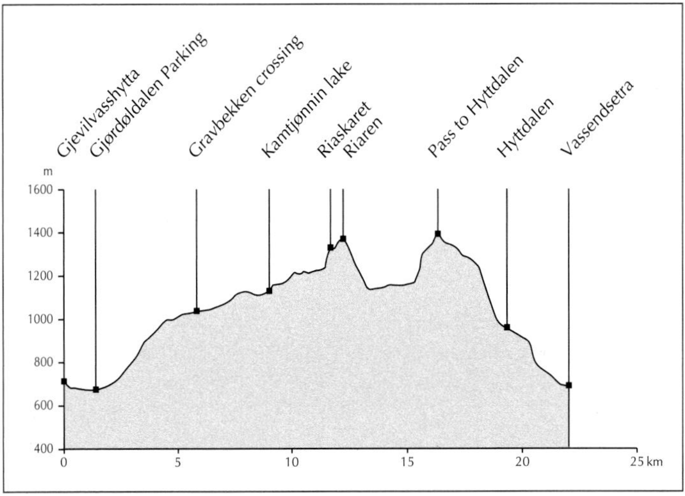
Gjevilvasshytta
Gjørdøldalen Parking
Gravbekken crossing
Kamtjønnin lake
Riaskaret
Riaren
Pass to Hyttdalen
Hyttdalen
Vassendsetra
m
1600
1400
1200
1000
800
600
400
0
5
10
15
20
25 km

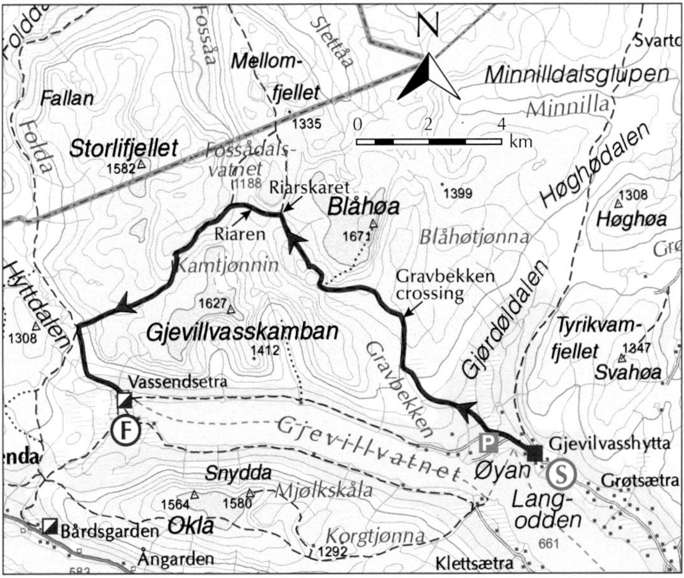
N
0
2
4
km
Mellom-
fjellet
1335
Slettåa
Fossåa
Fallan
Folda
Storlifjellet
1582
Fossådals-
vatnet
1188
Riarskaret
Blåhøa
1671
1399
Riaren
Minnilldalsglupen
Minnilla
Høghødalen
1308
Høghøa
Blåhøtjønna
Kamtjønnin
1627
Gjevillvasskamban
1412
Gravbekken
crossing
Gjørdøldalen
Tyrikvam-
fjellet
1347
Svahøa
Hyttdalen
1308
Vassendsetra
Gravbekken
Gjevillvatnet
Gjevilvasshytta
Øyan
Grøtsætra
Lang-
odden
661
Snydda
1564
1580
Mjølkskåla
Oklå
Bårdsgarden
Korgtjønna
1292
Ångarden
Klettsætra

Ascend into an open, broad, gently undulating plateau where there may be sheep grazing during the summer months. The trail is at times wet in sections, and some small brooks need to be crossed as it continues along Gravbekken. Eastern Trollheimen's highest mountain, Blåhøa (1671m), appears in view with its steep walls on its western side.

Cross Gravbekken – this could be challenging in early spring or during rainy summers. On the other side of the stream, ascend gently among lovely wildflower meadows towards a saddle.

The area between Gjevillvasskamban and Kamtjønnin peaks is known for its diversity of alpine **wildflowers**. A particular species of alpine poppy appears to grow only here in this part of Trollheimen and was given the name *Papaver radicatum gjaerevollii*, after the world-renowned botanist Olav Gjærevoll, who dedicated much of his scientific career to Trollheimen's wildflowers.

At the saddle, completely new vistas open up into a narrow valley with the near-circular **Kamtjønnin lake** on the northwest side of Gjevillvasskamban. The wide valley gives away its glacial origin. It is a high alpine zone, with practically no vegetation apart from mosses and lichen. The trail continues around and along the lakes and traverses the valley, ascending towards **Riaskaret**. Here, follow a sign pointing left (west) towards Vassendsetra and Bårdsgarden, making a short ascent onto the **Riaren** ridge (1365m).

Riaren is a high point of the stage and the views, 200m down into the valley around Fossådalsvatnet lake (1188m) and beyond, are impressive. It is a typical subglacial lake, although the glacier is now long gone.

The path continues with a 200m descent towards the lower of the two Fagerlitjønna lakes (1126m). Shortly before reaching the lake there is a junction; take the left path towards Vassendsetra/Bårdsgarden. The trail follows the lower lake's shore, moving gently up towards the higher lake, and then, after crossing the glacier stream, takes a sharp turn left up to the escarpment. After a 200m ascent towards the ridge (and the highest point of the stage at 1380m), be sure to turn around and savour the sight of the lakes behind you with Trollhøtta (1614m) in the far distance.

The next two kilometres are a traverse of the plateau towards the Hyttdalen valley. At first uninspiringly rocky and sandy (albeit relatively easy walking), the latter half is much greener with an abundance of very suitable and pleasant campsites, before you descend into **Hyttdalen** itself. (If you camp here, an easy (unmarked) stroll up to the top of Gjevillvasskamben (1627m) is worth

View northeast over the two Fagerlitjønna lakes, with Trollhøtta in the far distance

considering – but be aware of the steep 600m drop when you reach the edge of the cliff!)

Hyttdalen is a lovely green valley with several lakes and Neådalssnota (1621m) dominating the view to the north. The path becomes indistinct once you reach the valley floor, but red T-signs show the way to a four-way crossing ahead. Turn left here for Vassendsetra. The trail gently descends through bilberry bushes towards the Gjevillvatnet lake, which appears as you turn the corner around Hovmannshytten (1290m). Shortly before Vassendsetra, the path to Bårdsgarden (Stage 2) turns right. Keep left to arrive at the **Vassendsetra mountain hut**.

STAGE 2

Vassendsetra to Bårdsgarden

Start	Vassendsetra mountain hut
Finish	Bårdsgarden mountain hut
Distance	5.5km (3.5 miles)
Ascent	145m
Descent	200m
Difficulty	Easy
Time	2hr
Maximum altitude	828m
Map	Nordeca Trollheimen Sør 1:50,000 Nr 2828

After the long Stage 1, this is a short, easy hike. Enjoy a leisurely breakfast at the delightful Vassendsetra mountain hut before setting off towards Bårdsgarden. Alternatively, leave early and include the well-marked out-and-back detour to Okla mountain (1580m) – well worth it for the stunning views over Gjevillvatnet lake and the mountains beyond.

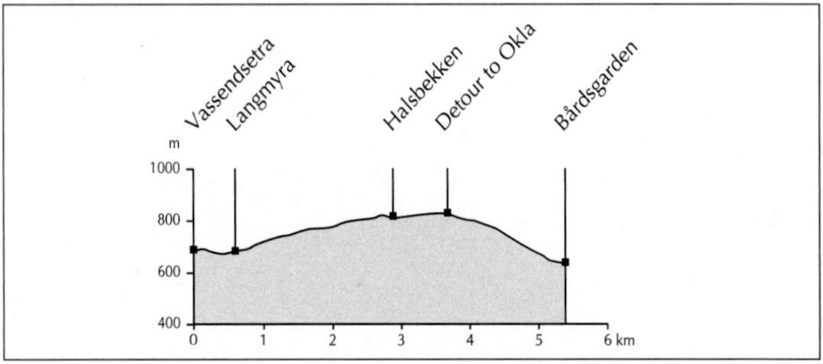

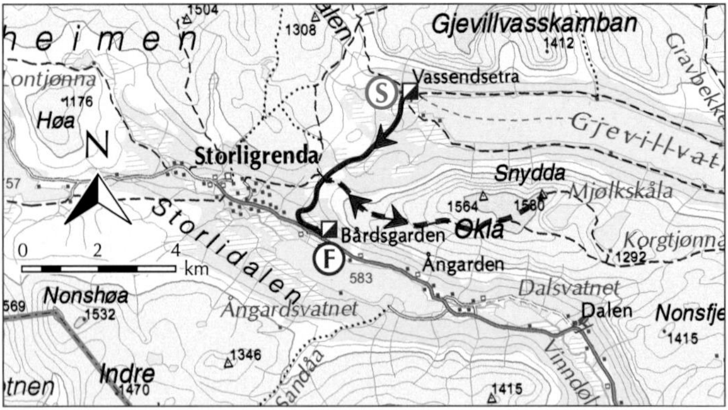

At Vassendsetra hut, turn towards the western gate, signposted to Bårdsgarden. Follow the well-marked path towards the bridge, cross the stream and continue left. Although you now proceed to cross the Langmyra wetlands and moor, the trail is not too wet due to the many stepping-stones available along the way. As you ascend along the Halsbekken river towards the highpoint of the stage, the path becomes drier underfoot.

The **views** start to open up along the ascent. Storlidalen valley becomes visible with the peaks of Nonshøa (1532m) and, further west, Storsomrungnebba (1798m) rising in stark contrast to the vibrant green of the valley below. As this route moves further westwards the nature of the mountain peaks gradually changes from the rounded tops of Okla (to the east, 1580m) towards the more pointy and rugged tops of western Trollheimen, making this route interesting and varied.

Just before the saddle there's a right fork signposted to Storlia. Keep left here and soon reach a four-way crossing. Left at the crossing is an extension up towards Okla-Snydda (1580m; it's approximately a 7km, 650m ascent to the top, from where you return the same way – see https://ut.no for further details; search for 'Okla Snydda'. On a good day the views over the lake below and the mountains behind are stunning), while right goes via an alternative path to Trollheimshytta. For Bårdsgarden go straight ahead, cross a bridge and descend further, keeping the stream on your left. The path has been re-marked here recently, and the signposts are relatively frequent throughout the descent towards Bårdsgarden. The last kilometre is mostly on a tractor service road, until shortly before the hut the route reaches the main road, running parallel along it for the last 200 metres to **Bårdsgarden**.

Fresh eggs are a special treat at the Bårdsgarden farm

Bårdsgarden is part of a working dairy farm and overlooks Ångardsvatnet lake. It is a DNT hut, but it is managed by the farmer's family (who live next door) on behalf of the Trondhjems Turistforening. Slightly different procedures apply; look out for the information signs near the entrance. Mobile coverage is available. Besides the usual pantry items found in self-service mountain huts, the farmer will sell you delicious homemade bread and fresh eggs if you wish.

In good weather the dark tops of Nonshøa (1532m), Storsomrungnebba (1798m) and others are lit up by the afternoon sun. The memorable panorama can be enjoyed from a large bench on the hut's front veranda.

STAGE 3

Bårdsgarden to Innerdalen

Start	Bårdsgarden mountain hut
Finish	Innerdalshytta (Gammelhytta) mountain hut
Distance	23.75km (14.75 miles)
Ascent	675m
Descent	900m
Difficulty	Very challenging
Time	8hr
Maximum altitude	1123m
Map	Nordeca Trollheimen Sør 1:50,000 Nr 2828
Note	Walking poles will come in handy on the very steep final descent to Innerdalen.

The conical shapes of the Kringlehøa peaks (1466m and 1493m) are the defining features of this stage as you ascend through the Tovhaugan plateau towards the Medskaret saddle. Given the barrenness around Langvatnet and Renndalsvatnet lakes, it is difficult to imagine that soon you will arrive in a very green valley that has a long history of human habitation. Before you reach Innerdalen, however, a particularly steep descent through the forested Renndalen valley on a heavily eroded path will test your knees.

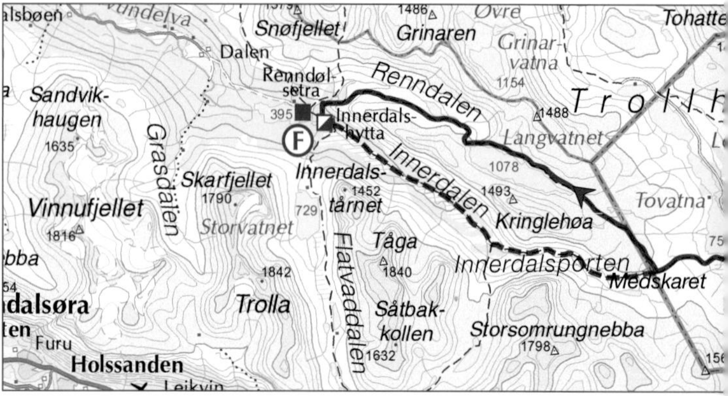

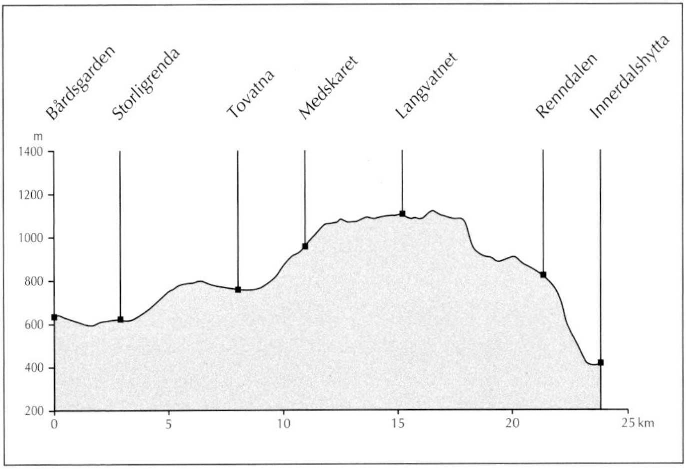

Exit the **Bårdsgarden hut**, turn right and continue on the grass path, following the signs to Innerdalen. Walk parallel to the road towards **Storligrenda** for about 750 metres, past the signposted turnoff to Gjevilvasshytta/Trollheimshytta. You then join the tarmac for another good 2km, until the trail to Innerdalen/Vollasetra is signposted to the left. Turn left here, cross the stream and at the T-junction shortly afterwards turn right towards Innerdalen. The path is good and steady underfoot and ascends gently over a fairly open, lightly wooded area towards Tovhaugen.

The twin lakes of **Tovatna** come into view, and the path runs parallel to the southern shore for a while before rising towards the **Medskaret** saddle.

At **Medskaret** you can enjoy the view back towards the Storlidalen valley, with the peak of Nonshøa (1532m) rising on your right, Bårdsgarden in the distance at the foot of Bårdsgardskamben (1150m) and views towards Vassendsetra. Ahead you see the twin tops of Kringlehøa (1466m and 1493m) dropping steeply on the northern side into Lạngvatnet lake, and opening the entry into the Innerdalen valley on Kringlehøa's left-hand (southern) side.

At the signpost on Medskaret you have the option between a lower route into the valley aptly named Innerdalsporten (literally 'gate into Innerdalen'), or the higher route past Langvatnet lake. Take the lower route in inclement weather; it is more direct, slightly shorter and less exposed, but significantly wetter underfoot as it runs all along the river on the valley floor. For the high route (described here), turn right and continue further up from Medskaret and closer to Kringlehøa until you reach the level of **Langvatnet lake**. The path takes you along the right, northern side of the lake. The trail is generally good underfoot, save for a bouldery section across an extended rockfall of a few hundred metres. At the far end of the lake there is a small dam and a control station for hydropower.

Hydropower provides for more than 90% of Norway's electricity needs. A large part of Trollheimen's waterways are used for hydroelectric power generation.

Cross the dam on the southern side and zigzag down the spectacular natural barrier that holds the lake, descending into **Renndalen** for about 150 vertical metres. Once at the valley floor it's an easy walk gently downhill past the two Renndalsvatnet lakes. Before reaching Innerdalen, though, you will have to negotiate a very steep descent on a highly eroded gravel path through the forest into the valley below. Care is required.

The scenery becomes increasingly spectacular, with the Renndøla river and waterfall plummeting nearby and a waterfall from the Fluo river on the opposite side of Innerdalen coming into view as well. A panorama of the Vinnufjellet massif and glaciers as well as the Trolla (1842m) and Tåga (1840m) mountaintops will gradually reveal itself in glimpses through the woods.

The path levels off a few hundred metres from the **Innerdalshytta mountain hut**. In fact, in season you have a choice of three cabins: there are two privately run, fully serviced huts – Renndølsetra and Innerdal Turisthytte – where you can indulge in traditional Norwegian fare and relax by a log fire; or there's the self-service option in the historic 'old hut' where you can make your own fire and dinner. The DNT Innerdalshytta hut is called Gammelhytta (lit. 'old hut').

Norwegians claim **Innerdalen** to be one of the most beautiful valleys in the country. As you arrive, you can be your own judge. The valley is dominated by Innerdalstårnet's (1452m) conical peak, often called 'Innerdalen's cathedral'. Small glacial streams empty through countless cascades and waterfalls into the lake below. The valley has a rich cultural history, having been used for summer farming for many years.

STAGE 4

Innerdalen to Kårvatn

Start	Innerdalshytta mountain hut
Finish	Kårvatn mountain hut
Distance	13.25km (8.25 miles)
Ascent	810m
Descent	1000m
Difficulty	Challenging
Time	5½hr
Maximum altitude	1175m
Map	Nordeca Trollheimen Sør 1:50,000 Nr 2828 and Nordeca Trollheimen Nord 1:50,000 Nr 2827

You might find yourself reluctant to leave beautiful Innerdalen. The peaks of the Vinnufjellet massif are the highest in Trollheimen and the glaciers only add to the otherworldly feeling of being in the middle of fairy-tale country. But leave you must, and this stage to Kårvatn promises many views as you hike up and out of the narrow Innerdalen valley to the Bjøraskaret escarpment. Be sure to look back! Once beyond the pass, you're treated to wide-open views towards Todalen and the fjord, making up for any regret about leaving Innerdalen.

The **summer alms** in valleys such as Innerdalen and Sunndalen were established by Iron Age people and expanded by the Vikings, who in addition hunted for the furs of bear, fox and reindeer, as these were highly marketable in Northern Europe.

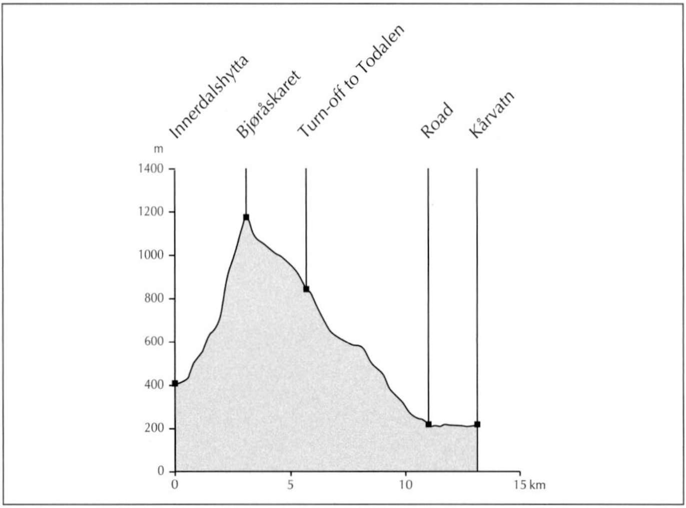
Innerdalshytta
Bjøråskaret
Turn-off to Todalen
Road
Kårvatn
m
1400
1200
1000
800
600
400
200
0
0
5
10
15 km

Todalshytta
Bruset
Todalen
Taløyan
Kårvatn
Naustådalen
1127
Neådalsvatna
728
Neådal
Neådalen
Gammelseter-
1140
1078
fjellet
Toåa
Bjøråskaret
Stor-
botnen
1579
1486
Øvre
Snøfjellet
Grinaren
Grinar-
vatna
Tohatten
1444
Dalen
Renndøl-
setra
1154
Renndalen
395
Innerdals-
hytta
1488
Trollheim
Langvatnet
Lontjønna
Grasdalen
Skarfjellet
1790
Innerdals-
1452
tårnet
1078
1493
Innerdalen
1176
Høa
N
Tovatna
Storvatnet
729
Kringlehøa
Tåga
757
Flatvad
1840
1842
Trolla
Såtbak-
0
2
4
km

Innerdalstårnet towers above the Innerdalen valley; the waterfall drains Storvatnet lake

To start, leave **Innerdalshytta** (Gammelhytta) to the right and take the downhill path towards Renndølsetra. Pass the gate and cross the bridge. The trail to Kårvatn is signposted; take this path up. It leads along the gorge of the Rennbekken river as it moves steeply up the forest. The numerous cascades and the river will be your companion for the next hour or so as you walk in parallel along the forest and uphill. The path is eroded at times and wet, but it is well marked and trodden. On good weather days remember to look behind, as the best views during the ascent are back towards Innerdalen. More and more of the high Vinnufjellet peaks will become visible.

Around halfway up the hill there's a signpost for Todalen. Turn left here for both Todalen and Karvåtn. The second part of the ascent begins to take you in a northerly direction away from the Renndalen valley. It is a steep, gravelly path and you need to watch your footing at times. At the end of the ascent the **Bjørå** saddle comes into view just beyond the high summer meadow where you might encounter a few sheep.

The saddle at **Bjøråskaret** is a great place to enjoy a break in good weather conditions. Vindufjellet peaks such as Kongskrona (1818m) and Dronningkrona (1816m) and their respective glaciers, Store Trolla (1842m), Tåga (1840m) and Innerdalstårnet (1452m) and other tops will all be in view, creating a sensational display.

As you move down on the other side of the Bjøråskaret saddle the change in vegetation is remarkable. Only mosses grow here on these exposed northern slopes where scattered snowfields remain during summer. The descent from the pass is less steep than the ascent, but you need to pick your way through boulders down towards Bjøråvatnet lake.

Continue on the right-hand side of the lake, and soon enough the terrain flattens out into a pleasant meadow and moor with expansive views along Todalen from the fjord towards Tverråbotnfjellet – quite a contrast to the narrow valley views encountered earlier around Innerdalen.

At Midtryggen (a small ridge between streams) the path forks, with the trail to Todalen going off to the left. Keep straight ahead here. Continue slowly downhill through gently undulating terrain. Although it passes moors on both sides, the path generally avoids these and so is mostly dry underfoot. Descend a gentle slope towards the road into Todalen valley. The trail meets the road with 2.5km to go to the hut. Turn right onto the road and follow the red-dotted stones that lead up to **Kårvatn mountain hut** in the Dalahaugen hamlet.

Kårvatn mountain hut, with rain clouds lifting in the early morning

The **Kårvatn** farm sits at the end of Todalen valley, with the summer farm valleys of Gammelseterdalen and Naustådalen leading to the north and south belonging to the farm. While its first official mention is in 1645, as part of a taxation list of the Danish King Christian IV, there have been archaeological finds from the Iron Age and Viking age. Since 1978 it has been part of a long-time study mapping changes in climate and pollution. Due to its very clean air and water, and almost no exposure to pollutants, measurements from Kårvatn are used nationally and internationally to study the long-term swings in natural processes as well as being a baseline for comparison.

STAGE 5

Kårvatn to Trollheimshytta

Start	Kårvatn mountain hut
Finish	Trollheimshytta mountain hut
Distance	24km (15 miles)
Ascent	880m
Descent	550m
Difficulty	Very challenging
Time	8hr
Maximum altitude	973m
Map	Nordeca Trollheimen Nord 1:50,000 Nr 2827

The stage between Kårvatn and Trollheimshytta is the longest of the SignaTur route and a test of stamina. There is an emergency shelter around halfway that could be used in adverse weather conditions. The overall ascent is not huge, though, and there is something utterly compelling about hiking along these deserted landscapes. They may have been touched by humankind, but this is not visible to the naked eye and they remain as engaging as ever.

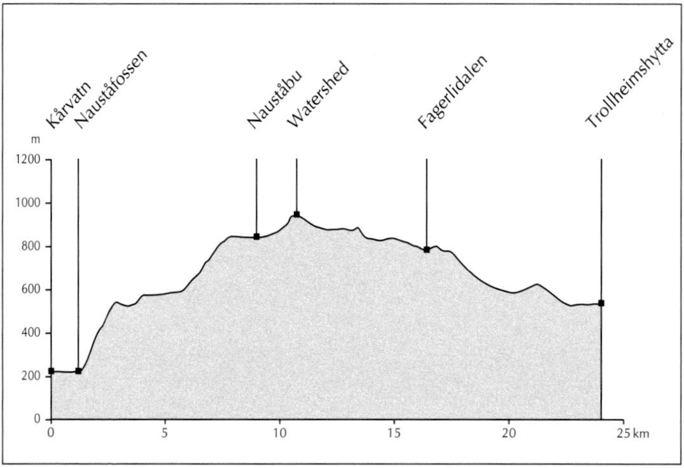

Leave the **Kårvatn mountain hut**, turn right and follow the sign across the bridge over the Nauståa river towards Trollheimshytta. Shortly afterwards, at a T-junction, there is the choice of a slightly easier path signposted to Trollheimshytta going left (it rejoins the main route beyond the Nauståfossen waterfall), or the more scenic route past **Nauståfossen waterfall** going right. Take the right, and follow the red dotted path to the base of the waterfall.

> **Nauståfossen** cascades down 110m and is thereby Trollheimen's highest waterfall. The thundering water plunges into a pool that is deep enough for a swim, and it is even possible to walk through towards its back and into a cove behind the waterfall – all at one's own risk, of course.

Onwards, the path takes you steeply up into the forest, with the sound of the falls slowly receding. At a fork where the left-hand option goes across the Bronnabekken stream, don't cross but keep to the right-hand path uphill. Soon the easier variant of the trail rejoins the main path. Keep following the trail of red dots, bands and T-signs up to the **Naustådalen valley**.

This section is essentially a valley walk connecting Todalen and Svartåmoen, and is thought to have been of high importance as a transport route for hunters and trappers in years gone by. The path is generally dry underfoot, with a few stream crossings and some remarkably flat sections. At the time of writing the bridge over the Tveråa river (3.8km from Kårvatn) was fine but a second bridge

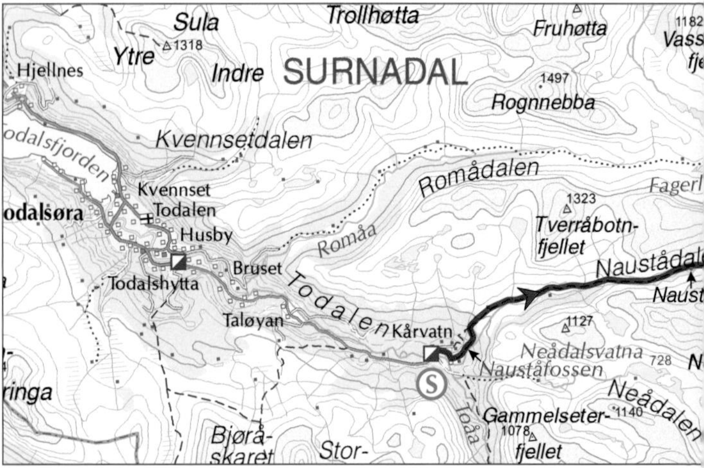

crossing a small gorge at Strankåbotn (6.6km from Kårvatn) had partly collapsed and was unsafe. Do not use it; instead go downstream where within 100 metres there are a few safe options to ford the river.

Continue on a gentle rise towards Naustådalsvatnet lake and the small emergency cabin, Nauståbu – a very basic **emergency shelter** which sleeps three and can be used if the weather turns foul on this long hike. It's about 10km from Kårvatn to this point, and 15km to Trollheimshytta.

On the approach to Trollheimshytta, along Stormyra moors, the tops of Trollhøtta and Geithøtta form an attractive backdrop

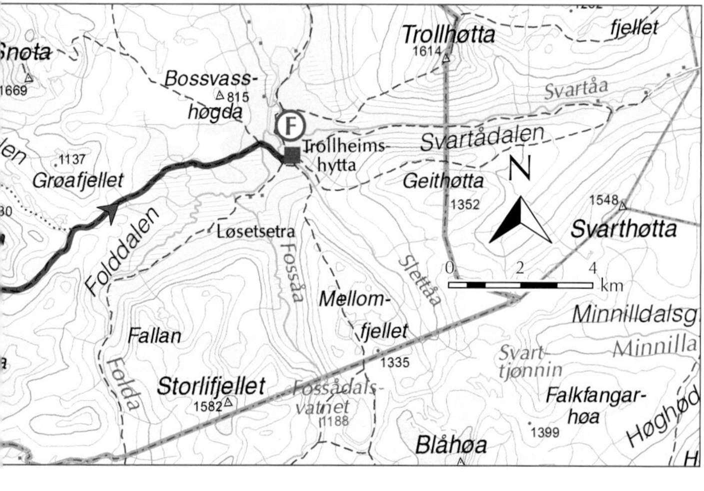

The path continues comfortably underfoot to a watershed at 973m which is the highest point of the day. From here the peak of Neådalssnota (1621m) is in view to your right, and shortly afterwards Trollhøtta (1614m) appears at the end of the valley, once you pass Øvre Salsvatnet lake.

The descent is gentle and good underfoot and the beautiful **Fagerlidalen valley** opens up to your left, with the top of Snota (1669m) behind it. The last few kilometres to Trollheimshytta mountain hut lead through Stormyra – beautiful meadows, forest and moor. The path can be very wet, depending on the season, but it is clear and the descent is gentle. After passing an old summer farmhouse, now a summer house, you will soon reach a bridge over the Folda river, and shortly afterwards a bridge over the Slettåa river. **Trollheimshytta mountain hut** is some 250 metres beyond, welcoming and warm.

STAGE 6

Snota summit

Start/finish	Trollheimshytta mountain hut
Distance	23.5km (14.5 miles)
Ascent/descent	1280m
Difficulty	Very challenging
Time	9hr
Maximum altitude	1669m
Map	Nordeca Trollheimen Nord 1:50,000 Nr 2827

This stage is truly what Norwegians refer to as *topptur* – a hike to the top of a mountain. Starting and ending at Trollheimshytta mountain hut, it is indeed quite a hike: nearly 12km up and then down again, with an elevation difference of 1280m. It is also one of the highest tops to hike to in Trollheimen, and very visible from the Trollheimshytta front porch. It will beckon. This outing should only be undertaken in good weather conditions; the staff at Trollheimshytta will be able to give you information about the trail, the state of the glaciers and an actual weather forecast. Note that some scrambling is required on the steeper sections towards the top, and care must be taken to locate the correct path around the first glacier.

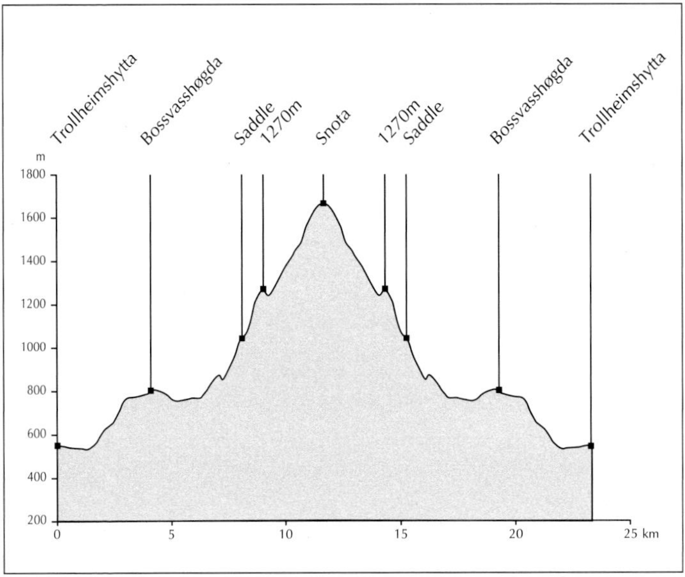

The hike starts off nice and gentle. Leave **Trollheimshytta**, take a left past the large signpost, then after 250 metres cross the bridge over the Slettåa river and turn right in the direction of Kårvatn and Snota. Cross a second, hanging bridge over the Folda river, and 150 metres later reach a signposted turnoff towards Snota. Follow this path uphill; it is an easy, gentle ascent among the Scots pines and birch trees, and there are bushes dense with berries in season. When the path reaches another fork, take the left towards Snota and hike up towards **Bossvasshøgda** (815m). The trail runs just under the actual top.

Once over this height, **views** towards the beautiful lake and wetlands of Bossvatnet open up beneath, while the view ahead to Snota provides a firm reminder of your objective.

The path becomes stonier and wetter underfoot, as there is a lot of water around here. The valley and saddle that need to be climbed are visible ahead, and the way is well marked. It is a direct climb over a relatively rocky path – not the easiest underfoot.

> At the top of the saddle there are lovely **views** over Gråsjøen lake, Trollhøtta (1614m) and Geithøtta (1352m), with Svartådalen cutting deeply in-between the two mountains.

Turn left at the saddle and continue towards a secondary top at **1270m**, with a steady ascent over flat inclined rocks that may be quite slippery when wet. From here proceed to a ridge around the secondary peak, and then the remainder of the Snota massif and some of its glaciers open up in front of you.

From around 1300m upwards the path consists of only rocks, stones and gravel, and there is no vegetation around. Some sections are steep and require the use of hands and feet. As you approach the first glacier, keep an eye out for the T-marks to locate the correct path. It is marked, but not very well, which could be a challenge in low visibility. Be aware that the old path used to go over the glacier, but the ice has now retreated considerably and going over it is no longer feasible due to cracks and movement of the glacier. Plus, the old ascent on the far

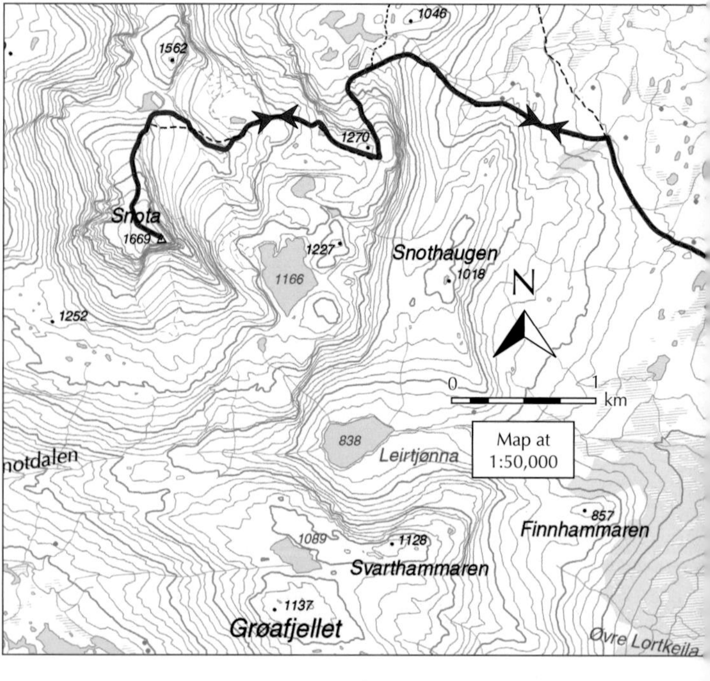

end of the glacier has become too steep, with no footholds anymore. Some of the T-markings have therefore become obsolete.

The approach is to the left around this lower glacier as you look at it. Make sure to follow red dots that go off to the left. The markings are old but visible and the ascent continues over a ledge that runs at around four-fifths of the way up the rock face that is seen ahead. It doesn't look like there could be a path, but there is, and it's walkable although airy in a few spots. To find the ledge, go higher than you might think. Beware of markings that take you lower, closer to the current top edge of the glacier. (The GPS track does not have sufficient lateral resolution to distinguish between the two different paths on the steep rock face.)

As you move up, the ledge becomes quite clearly visible. Many people have used it. It is between one and four metres wide, ascending and leading to the second glacier that soon appears in view. At this glacier you can walk over the rocks at its eastern side – although at the time of writing it was still safe to ascend over the snow, parallel to the rocks, as a shortcut for an easier traverse. Once you reach the

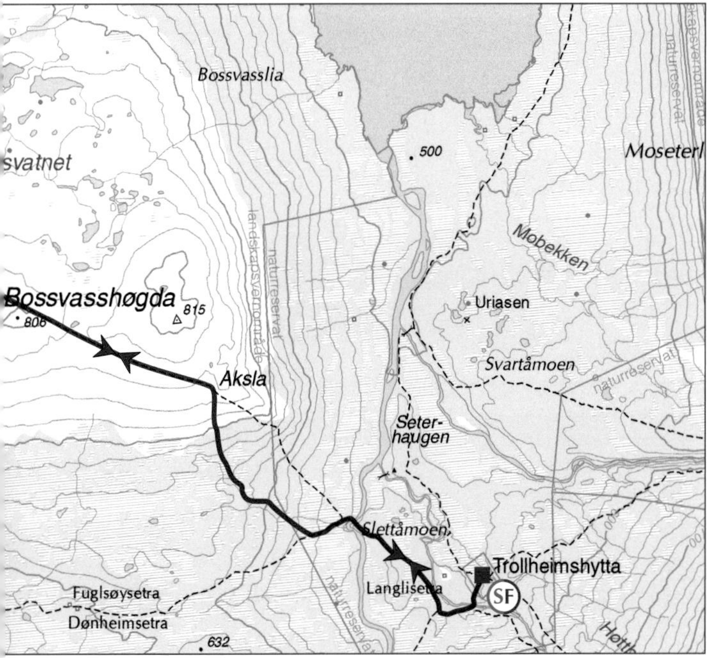

other side of glacier the well-marked path turns in a wide half-circle around the glacier and back up towards the south and the final slope and ascent of **Snota** (1669m).

On a good day the views from **Snota** will be nothing short of spectacular. You will be able to spot all the lesser tops, near and far. Towards the southeast are Blåhøa and Hembre Gjevilvasskamban, and in the west is Store Trolla, as well as the highest peaks of Vinnufjellet, Dronningkrona and Kongskrona.

From the summit, retrace your steps all the way back to **Trollheimshytta**.

STAGE 7

Trollhøtta high traverse

Start	Trollheimshytta mountain hut
Finish	Jøldalshytta mountain hut
Distance	19.75km (12.25 miles)
Ascent	1350m
Descent	1150m
Difficulty	Very challenging
Time	9hr
Maximum altitude	1614m
Map	Nordeca Trollheimen Nord 1:50,000 Nr 2827
Note	This stage includes some very steep and exposed sections; do not attempt it if you suffer from vertigo.

This stage is, without doubt, the most dramatic and majestic of all the stages in Trollheimen. It requires surefootedness and a good head for heights: the Besseggen ridge in Jotunheimen is wide in comparison to some of the traverse awaiting here. In poor weather conditions, or if you suffer from vertigo, consider Stage 2 or 2A of the Trollheimen Trekanten triangle route (Route 7) as an alternative.

Start by going left from the **Trollheimshytta** entrance towards the northeast, with the towering outline of Snota (1669m) ahead. At the beginning it is an easy stroll through meadows and moors and through the light pine forest of the Svartåmoen nature reserve. A new bridge has been constructed over the Svartåa river, and

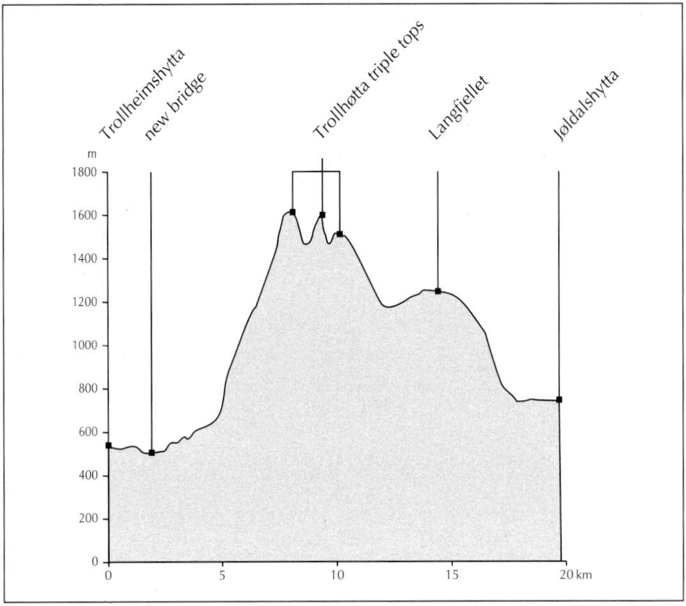

the new route is T-marked. After crossing the bridge, follow the trail to the right, signed for Trollhøtta (1614m). It closely follows the riverbanks of the Folda and Svartåa and picks up the original route. (Do fill up your water bottle in one of the streams, as Trollhøtta's three tops are dry.)

Continue on the trail as it again moves through open meadows before once more entering a forest of gnarled Scots pine trees.

Some of the **Scots pine trees** in the Svartåmoen nature reserve, whose age has been determined by scientists, were found to be well in excess of 450 years old and in a healthy state. The preservation of this unique old-age forest is one of the main reasons for the establishment of the reserve. It serves as a baseline against which the state of similar woods in Scandinavia can be compared.

After about 4km, what was a gradual ascent becomes steeper, and the path turns straight uphill through the forest and then beyond the tree line. The next 800m of vertical ascent are a mostly steep, rocky climb, usually well picked by the T-markers but often requiring the use of hands for support and balance.

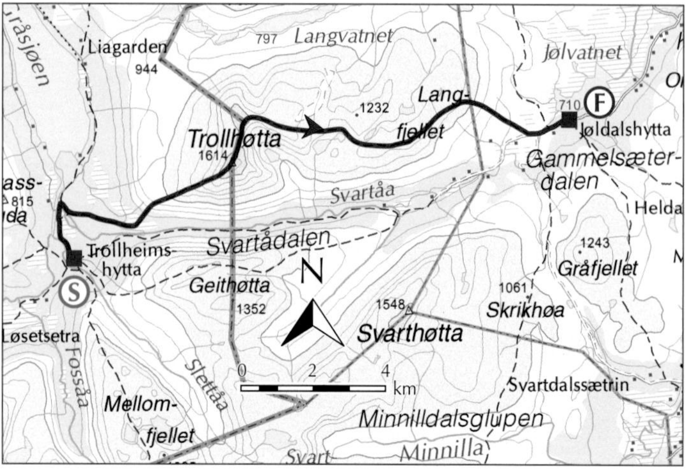

Geithøtta's top (1352m), across the Svartådalen valley, is a useful measure of progress towards Trollhøtta's greater height. Remember to catch your breath and turn around to enjoy the fabulous views that start to open up from the north to the southeast, with Snota dominant in the west and Geithøtta to the south.

The path over the top is very well marked, with T-markers at regular, short intervals; a reminder of how disorientating the featureless top would be when covered in clouds of fog.

> **Trollhøtta**, with its three tops and beautiful lake at the bottom of its cirque, is referred to as the 'one-eyed three-headed troll' in local folklore. The highest of the three Trollhøtta tops is peculiarly stony, flat and extended. This means that the best views are enjoyed from the edges and not at the cairn that marks its actual top; in good weather you can enjoy the complete panorama of Trollheimen – clockwise from Blåhøa, Gjevillvasskamben towards Storlifjellet, Neadalssnota, Vinnufjellet in the far distance, and Snota – a unique sight of all the tops and mountains that have been companions throughout your hiking week.

The path continues straight ahead in northeasterly direction, and the two other minor tops of Trollhøtta appear, as well as the cirque to the southeast with its 'troll's eye' – the lake below (Trollauget). The descent from the first peak and the ascent to second (1596m) are short but steep, across and over boulders. The

View from the cirque of Trollhøtta to the Trollauget lake and Svartådalen below

saddle between is wide and easily navigated. Once more you find yourself on a flat top, but with a sheer cliff on one side.

The descent into the next saddle is really very steep, and while it is well marked it calls for careful footing and hand support. The saddle is narrow – just a few metres wide. The ascent to the third and final top is very exposed, but the path is well chosen. Unless you are susceptible to vertigo, it is quite easily traversed in good conditions. However, it becomes dangerous in poor weather, or in high winds, especially when carrying a heavy backpack.

Once you've reached the last cairn (1522m) and conquered the three-headed and one-eyed troll, the descent to Jøldalshytta is lengthy but straightforward. The trail down from the third peak is very well and regularly marked. You pass two lakes where you can refill your water bottle. Continue from there along the aptly named **Langfjellet** ('long fells') for a few kilometres. The route is easy to follow but rocky and uneven underfoot. It stays at height well after you first spot Jøldalshytta and the valley below.

Eventually, the path turns into the valley for approximately 350m of vertical descent. Continue along the reasonably flat and easy-going final stretch to the hut, first through moorland and then on a gravel road for the final kilometre.

Jøldalshytta has lovely views towards the similarly named lake and a few healthy-looking cows roaming around the hut – the source of some tasty milk, yoghurt and cheese for the next morning's breakfast.

STAGE 8

Jøldalshytta to Gjevilvasshytta

Start	Jøldalshytta mountain hut
Finish	Gjevilvasshytta mountain hut
Distance	21km (13 miles)
Ascent	550m
Descent	580m
Difficulty	Challenging
Time	6½hr
Maximum altitude	1072m
Map	Nordeca Trollheimen Nord 1:50,000 Nr 2827 and Nordeca Trollheimen Sør 1:50,000 Nr 2828

The hardest work of route is behind you. The SignaTur trek ends with a somewhat long but not technically difficult stage. The best views are around the midway point when the Minnilldalen valley opens up on your right, ending in the steep, perfectly formed cirque of the Svarthamran. It is worth making time for a stop shortly after crossing the impressive bridge over the Minnilla river, to enjoy these panoramas.

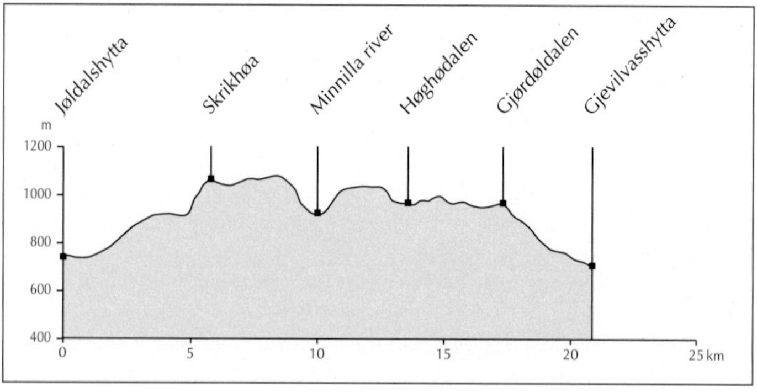

Leaving **Jøldalshytta mountain hut**, exit the gate and turn right onto the gravel road. Follow this road for about a kilometre, pass and ignore the sign to

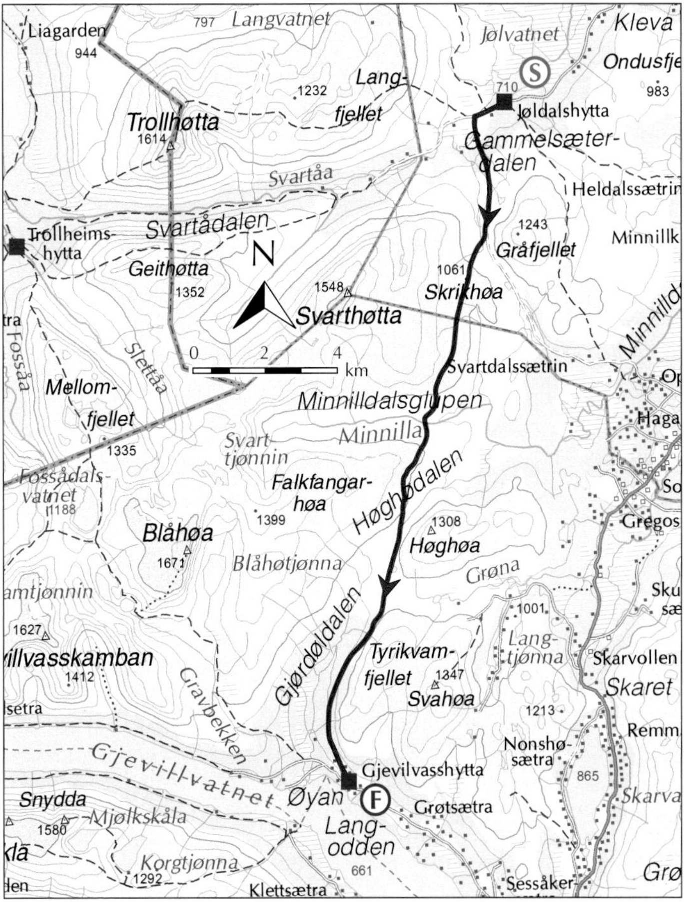

Trollheimshytta and turn left onto the path to Gjevilvasshytta. The path is well marked and easy underfoot – gravelly, sandy and only sometimes muddy. It leads through a wide, open landscape with only occasional small birch woods. (The nutrient-poor soil here only supports low-growing vegetation.) After crossing a small stream you'll come to the only significant ascent of the day: about 200m up **Skrikhøa** (1061m).

The next few kilometres are in the typical, open fells landscape that is so characteristic of this altitude, with a generally good path undulating at height over, along and beside hills. To your right the **Minnilldalsglupen valley** opens up and shortly afterwards the path descend towards the **Minnilla river** and crosses it over a permanent bridge.

This wide U-shaped Minnilldalsglupen **valley** is a picture-perfect example of a glacial valley. The cirque coming off the Svarthamran massif forms a half-circle, with the Minnilla flowing out and towards the lower-lying marshlands. These marshes and bogs form an important nature reserve for a large number of water birds and waders. The beautiful glacial valley and the river are at the halfway point of the stage and an excellent site for a lunch stop. The bridge construction is worth a look; it's made entirely of stones and wood, built to withstand the spring melts and tumbling waters.

From the bridge, ascend and continue into the **Høghødalen valley**, with the face of Høghøa (1308m) on your left.

There is a good chance of spotting **reindeer** in these valleys. They are shy but not wild. There are about 1300 animals in Trollheimen, and they are owned by a few families of Sámi origin. These families arrived in Trollheimen in the 1800s with their herds. Their disregard for previously established ownership rights led to a longstanding dispute with farmers that was only resolved in 1984. Today the reindeer herds and their management are part of the cultural heritage of the Trollheimen nature reserve.

Cross the saddle between Høghødalen and Gjørdøldalen. The path follows the left-hand side of the valley, slowly finding its way down towards Gjevillvatnet lake, with Blåhøa rising to your right. You'll soon enter the forest, and the path continues downhill until it reaches the road which takes you the final 500 metres to **Gjevilvasshytta hut** as well as to the turnoff to the parking area.

In season, Gjevilvasshytta offers a very Norwegian **afternoon tea** tradition, consisting of tea or coffee with freshly baked waffles, *rømme* (Norwegian cream) and *syltetøy* (jam).

ROUTE 9

Trollheimen fells to fjord route

Start	Gjevilvasshytta mountain hut
Finish	Todalshytta mountain hut
Distance	55km (34 miles)
Ascent	1855m
Descent	2525m
Time	3 days
Variations	An additional overnight stay at Vassendsetra is possible. The tour could be exited at Bårdsgarden and Innerdalen mountain huts if needed.
Note	There is no public transport at the end of this route.

It doesn't get much more Norwegian than this. With its combination of high fells and fjord, shaped by the humongous forces of glaciers and ice, the route comprises fascinating and beautiful landscapes, history and cultural heritage, forming a true example of what Norwegians call *friluftsliv* – life outdoors.

Gjevilvasshytta, in its idyllic location and with its long history, is the route's starting point. Access to Gjevilvasshytta is by bus from Oppdal. As you walk along the lakeshore and experience the Mediterranean-like smell of the pine forest, it won't be long before you find yourself imagining what it would have been like to live and work in the summer pastures around Vassendsetra. You might indeed decide to live that dream and extend this route by a day with an overnight stay at Vassendsetra. Otherwise you'll end the day at Bårdsgarden, which is adjacent to a working dairy farm. Out of Bårdsgarden the route takes you along and up out of the Storlidalen valley – make sure to enjoy the views you are leaving behind. Typical Norwegian fells awaits on your way to the Medskaret saddle, and from there the route takes you along Langvatnet lake towards a very steep descent out of Renndalen and into Innerdalen. This enchantingly beautiful valley was once under threat of being dammed for hydroelectric power generation, but thanks to the efforts of the families living there it became a protected area. It used to be a *husmannsplass* – farmland that was deemed of too poor quality for the farmer that owned it to work it themselves. The land was therefore leased out to so-called *husmannen*, who generally barely managed to eke out a living for their families. Innerdalen is now the centre for rock climbing in the Trollheimen area, which is not surprising when you look around onto the scraggy tops surrounding this narrow valley. Innerdalshytta mountain hut often hosts climbers and climbing training courses in season. The third and final stage of the route takes you out of

Innerdalen over the Bjøråskaret pass. After a steep ascent out of the valley, with all the views you could wish for, it is a wonderful hike down towards the Todalshytta hut in its lovely historic setting near the fjord at Todalen.

Note that you'll need to take the universal DNT key for access to the Vassendsetra, Innerdalshytta and Todalshytta huts.

You could leave the trek at Bårdsgarden (after Stage 1), which is only a short taxi ride from Lønset, where public transport is available to Oppdal. Innerdalshytta (Stage 2) is about 4km by gravel road away from the nearest car park. You will need to arrange transport from Todalen at the end of the trek. The nearest public transport is in Surnadal (Skei), some 25km away. Consider hiking or hitch-hiking, or arrange a taxi through Surnadal Taxisentral, tel +47 71 66 37 00 or +47 90 90 82 77.

STAGE 1

Gjevilvasshytta to Bårdsgarden via Vassendsetra

Start	Gjevilvasshytta mountain hut
Finish	Bårdsgarden mountain hut
Distance	18km (11.25 miles); 12.5km (7.75 miles) to Vassendsetra
Ascent	280m; 135m to Vassendsetra
Descent	365m; 165m to Vassendsetra
Difficulty	Moderate
Time	6hr; 4hr to Vassendsetra
Maximum altitude	828m
Map	Nordeca Trollheimen Sør 1:50,000 Nr 2828

The fells to fjord route begins with a pleasant hike parallel to the shore of Gjevillvatnet lake. On a warm, sunny day you might well imagine yourself to be hiking in the Mediterranean. The microclimate on this side of the lake makes for a thriving pine forest that releases its distinctive refreshing smell in sunny conditions.

The second part of the stage, from Vassendsetra, could be taken separately, allowing for a night at this lovely location. In that case, the stage from Vassendsetra to Bårdsgarden could be extended with an out-and-back diversion up the ridge to Okla Snydda (1580m) on the way to Bårdsgarden.

As the stage moves westwards, the nature of the mountain peaks gradually changes from the rounded tops of Okla to the more pointy and rugged tops of western Trollheimen, making this route interesting and varied.

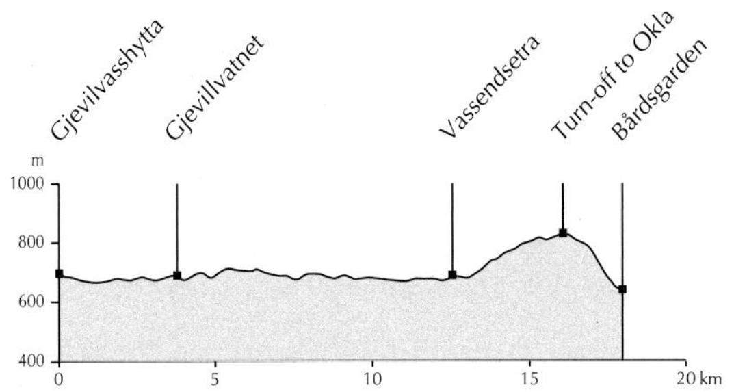

Exit the gate at **Gjevilvasshytta mountain hut**, cross the road and descend along the grass path to reach the road below. Turn right and walk for 3.8km along the road, at first on tarmac and later gravel. Cross a bridge and pass by a parking area. The hike to Trollheimshytta (Route 7, Stage 1) departs here, but continue straight towards a second parking area, belonging to the private cabins nearby.

Continue to a second bridge and a gate. Cross the bridge and go through the gate and continue straight until you reach a private cabin called Håmmårsetra. The trail is not marked until you reach Håmmårsetra, but from there onwards T-markers appear regularly along the way. On your right the cirques of Gjevillvasskamban (1627m) dominate the view most of the way, while on the other side of the lake Okla (1580m) is your steady companion.

The path is an old connection between the **summer mountain farms** (*sætra*) situated along the lake, namely Håmmårsætra, Rensbekksætra and Vassendsætra. Håmmår refers to the 'steep cliff side' you just passed. Rensbekk means 'clean stream' while Vassend means 'end of the lake' – all very aptly named.

The distinctive **pine tree smell** is caused by chemical compounds called terpenes. Pine trees produce these especially when the temperature rises. Terpenes stimulate cloud formation in the sky (by acting as condensation nuclei), causing temperatures to drop. In this way, pine trees play a neat role in temperature regulation in the forest.

Close to the Rensbekksætra farmhouse the path crosses, as the name implies, the sparkling Rensbekken stream coming down from Gjevillvasskamban. Underfoot around here is mostly dry forest trail, but the last 2.5km to Vassendsetra can be quite wet as you walk through marshes. **Vassendsetra** is a beautifully located self-service hut on the edge of the lake. It does invite to stay at least for a while. (Numerous books and websites still refer to a boat that sails over the lake in summer. This service was terminated in 2014.)

From **Vassendsetra hut**, turn towards the western gate, signposted to Bårdsgarden. Follow the well-marked path towards the bridge, cross the stream and continue left. Although you now proceed to cross the Langmyra wetlands and moor, the trail is not too wet due to the many stepping-stones available along the way. As you ascend along the Halsbekken river towards the highpoint of the stage, the path becomes drier underfoot.

> The **views** start to open up along the ascent. Storlidalen valley becomes visible with the peaks of Nonshøa (1532m) and, further west, Storsumrungnebba (1798m) rising in stark contrast to the vibrant green of the valley below.

Just before the saddle there's a right fork signposted to Storlia. Keep left here and soon reach a four-way crossing. Left at the crossing is an extension up towards Okla-Snydda (1580m; it's approximately a 7km, 650m ascent to the top, from where you return the same way – see https://ut.no for further details; search for 'Okla Snydda'. On a good day the views over the lake below and the mountains behind are stunning), while right goes via an alternative path to Trollheimshytta. For Bårdsgarden go straight ahead, cross a bridge and descend further, keeping the stream on your left. The path has been re-marked here recently, and the signposts are relatively frequent throughout the descent towards Bårdsgarden. The last kilometre is mostly on a tractor service road, until shortly before the hut the route reaches the main road, running parallel along it for the last 200 metres to **Bårdsgarden**.

Bårdsgarden is part of a working dairy farm and overlooks Ångardsvatnet lake. It is a DNT hut, but it is managed by the farmer's family (who live next door) on behalf of the Trondhjems Turistforening. Slightly different procedures apply; look out for the information signs near the entrance. Mobile coverage is available. Besides the usual pantry items found in self-service mountain huts, the farmer will sell you delicious homemade bread and fresh eggs if you wish.

In good weather the dark tops of Nonshøa (1532m), Storsomrungnebba (1798m) and others are lit up by the afternoon sun. The memorable panorama can be enjoyed from a large bench on the hut's front veranda.

Okla-Snydda rising from the shores of Gjevillvatnet lake, as seen from the path to Vassendsetra

STAGE 2

Bårdsgarden to Innerdalen

Start	Bårdsgarden mountain hut
Finish	Innerdalshytta (Gammelhytta) mountain hut
Distance	23.75km (14.75 miles)
Ascent	675m
Descent	900m
Difficulty	Very challenging
Time	8hr
Maximum altitude	1123m
Map	Nordeca Trollheimen Sør 1:50,000 Nr 2828
Note	Walking poles will come in handy on the very steep final descent to Innerdalen.

This stage goes deep into Trollheimen's western parts, where the mountaintops are at their most rugged and the valleys at their greenest. It is a long but beautiful hike, with a short, challenging descent through forest towards the end. The comfortable Innerdalshytta, in one of Norway's most beautiful valleys, is a lovely mountain hut to rest for the night – or indeed for a day should you wish to explore the valley at leisure.

Exit the **Bårdsgarden hut**, turn right and continue on the grass path, following the signs to Innerdalen. Walk parallel to the road towards **Storligrenda** for about 750 metres, past the signposted turnoff to Gjevilvasshytta/Trollheimshytta. You then join the tarmac for another good 2km, until the trail to Innerdalen/Vollasetra is signposted to the left. Turn left here, cross the stream and at the T-junction shortly afterwards turn right towards Innerdalen. The path is good and steady underfoot and ascends gently over a fairly open, lightly wooded area towards Tovhaugen. The twin lakes of **Tovatna** come into view, and the path runs parallel to the southern shore for a while before rising towards **Medskaret** saddle.

At **Medskaret** you can enjoy the view back towards the Storlidalen valley, with the peak of Nonshøa (1532m) rising on your right, Bårdsgarden in the distance at the foot of Bårdsgardskamben (1150m) and views towards Vassendsetra. Ahead you see the twin tops of Kringlehøa (1465m and 1493m)

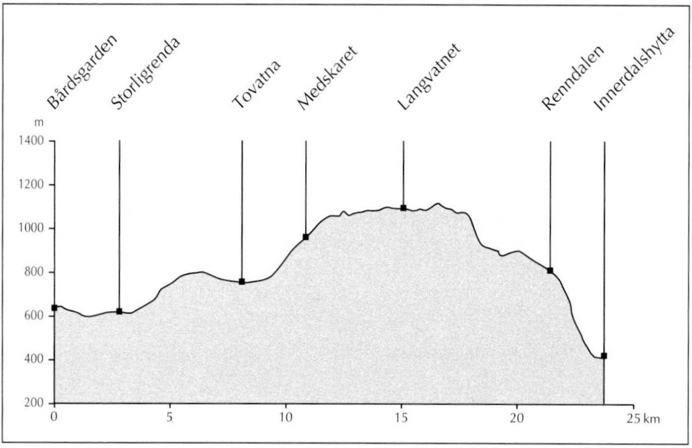

dropping steeply on the northern side into Langvatnet lake, and opening the entry into the Innerdalen valley on Kringlehøa's left-hand (southern) side.

At the signpost on Medskaret you have the option between a lower route into the valley aptly named Innerdalsporten (literally 'gate into Innerdalen'), or the higher route past Langvatnet lake. Take the lower route in inclement weather; it is more direct, slightly shorter and less exposed, but significantly wetter underfoot as it runs all along the river on the valley floor. For the high route (described here), turn right and continue further up from Medskaret and closer to Kringlehøa until you reach the level of **Langvatnet lake**. The path takes you along the right, northern side of the lake. The trail is generally good underfoot, save for a bouldery section across an extended rockfall of a few hundred metres. At the far end of the lake there is a small dam and a control station for hydropower.

Hydropower provides for more than 90% of Norway's electricity needs. A large part of Trollheimen's waterways are used for hydroelectric power generation.

Cross the dam on the southern side and zigzag down the spectacular natural barrier that holds the lake, descending into **Renndalen** for about 150 vertical metres. Once at the valley floor it's an easy walk gently downhill past the two Renndalsvatnet lakes. Before reaching Innerdalen, though, you will have to negotiate a very steep descent on a highly eroded gravel path through the forest into the valley below. Care is required.

The scenery becomes increasingly spectacular, with the Renndøla river and waterfall plummeting nearby and a waterfall from the Fluo river on the opposite side of Innerdalen coming into view as well. A panorama of the Vinnufjellet massif and glaciers as well as the Trolla (1842m) and Tåga (1840m) mountain-tops will gradually reveal itself in glimpses through the woods.

The path levels off a few hundred metres from the **Innerdalshytta mountain hut**. In fact, in season you have a choice of three cabins: there are two privately run, fully serviced huts – Renndølsetra and Innerdal Turisthytte – where you can indulge in traditional Norwegian fare and relax by a log fire; or there's the self-service option in the historic 'old hut' where you can make your own fire and dinner. The DNT Innerdalshytta hut is called Gammelhytta (lit. 'old hut').

> Norwegians claim **Innerdalen** to be one of the most beautiful valleys in the country. As you arrive, you can be your own judge. The valley is dominated by Innerdalstårnet's (1452m) conical peak, often called 'Innerdalen's cathedral'. Small glacial streams empty through countless cascades and waterfalls into the lake below. The valley has a rich cultural history, having been used for summer farming for many years.

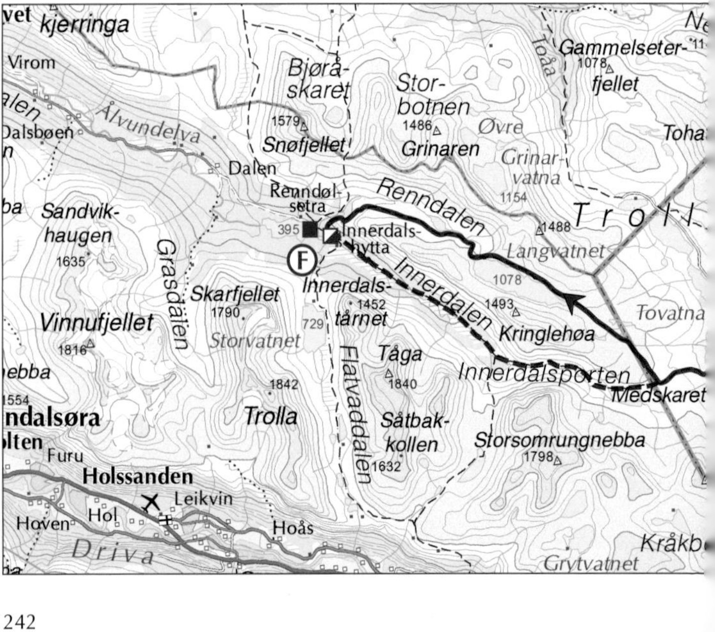

Innerdalstårnet, often shrouded in mist, towers above the Innerdalen valley

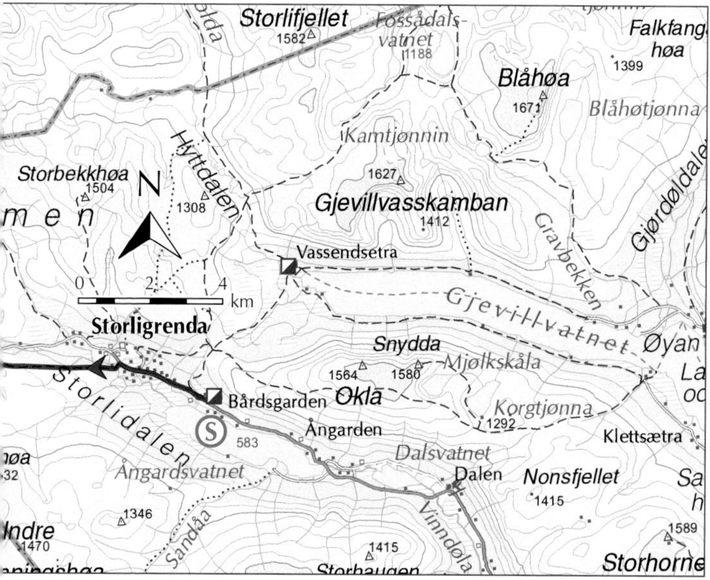

STAGE 3

Innerdalen to Todalen

Start	Innerdalshytta mountain hut
Finish	Todalshytta mountain hut
Distance	13km (8 miles)
Ascent	900m
Descent	1260m
Difficulty	Challenging
Time	6hr
Maximum altitude	1175m
Map	Nordeca Trollheimen Sør 1:50,000 Nr 2828 and Nordeca Trollheimen Nord 1:50,000 Nr 2827

This stage showcases like no other the diverse landscapes of Trollheimen. Waterfalls and cascades, fast-running streams and rivers, hanging valleys that have transformed into lush meadows and fairy-tale forests. You might get views onto glacier-covered rugged peaks as well as those that have seen their rough edges smoothed by eons of ice scraping away at their bedrock, and those that stayed above the ice fields all along.

The final descent into Todalen is steep and often tricky underfoot.

The **summer alms** in valleys such as Innerdalen were established by Iron Age people and expanded by the Vikings, who in addition hunted for the furs of bear, fox and reindeer, as these were highly marketable in Northern Europe.

To start, leave **Innerdalshytta** (Gammelhytta) to the right and take the downhill path towards Renndølsetra. Pass the gate and cross the bridge. Take the trail signposted to Kårvatn; it leads up along the gorge of the Rennbekken river as it moves steeply up the forest. The numerous cascades and the river will be your companion for the next hour or so as you walk in parallel along the forest and uphill. The path is eroded at times and wet, but it is well marked and trodden. On good weather days remember to look behind, as the best views during the ascent are back towards Innerdalen. More and more of the high Vinnufjellet peaks will become visible.

Around halfway up the hill there's a signpost for Todalen. Turn left here. The second part of the ascent begins to take you in a northerly direction away from the

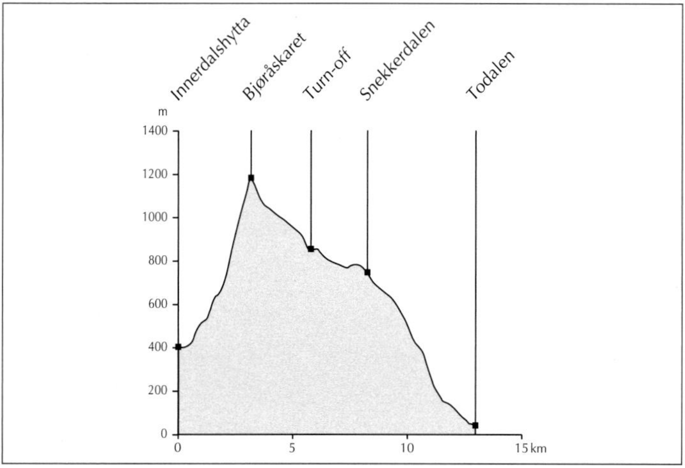
Innerdalshytta
Bjøråskaret
Turn-off
Snekkerdalen
Todalen
m
1400
1200
1000
800
600
400
200
0
0
5
10
15 km

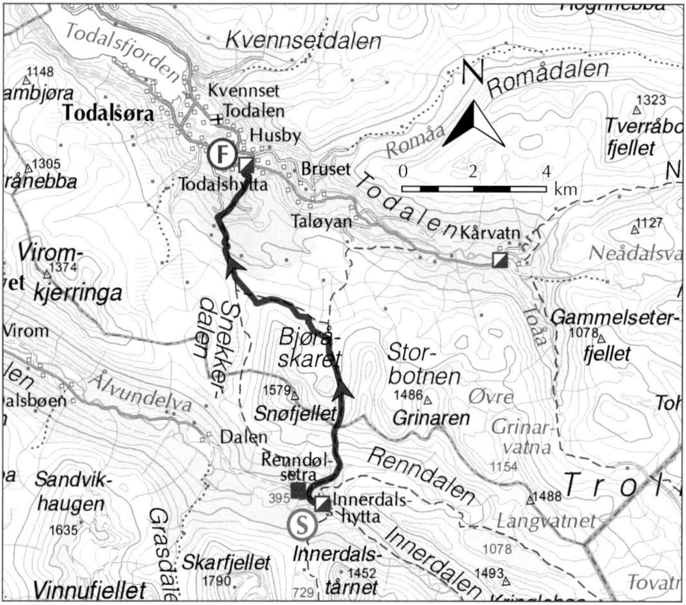
Todalsfjorden
Kvennsetdalen
Kvennset
Todalen
Husby
Todalsøra
F
Todalshytta
Bruset
Romådalen
Romåa
N
0
2
4
km
Todalen
Taløyan
Kårvatn
Tverråbo
fjellet
1323
1127
Neådalsva
1148
ambjøra
1305
rånebba
Virom-
1374
kjerringa
Virom
Snekker-
dalen
Bjøråskaret
Stor-
botnen
Toåa
Gammelseter-
1078
fjellet
Ålvundelva
1579
Snøfjellet
1486
Grinaren
Øvre
Grinar-
vatna
Dalen
Renndøl-
setra
Renndalen
1154
1488
395
Innerdals-
hytta
S
Langvatnet
Sandvik-
haugen
1635
Grasdale
Skarfjellet
1790
Innerdals-
tårnet
1452
729
Innerdalen
1078
1493
Vinnufjellet
Tovatn

Renndalen valley. It is a steep, gravelly path and you need to watch your footing at times. At the end of the ascent the **Bjørå** saddle comes into view just beyond the high summer meadow where you might encounter a few sheep.

The saddle at **Bjøråskaret** is a superb place to enjoy a break in good weather conditions. Vindufjellet peaks such as Kongskrona (1818m) and Dronningkrona (1816m) and their respective glaciers, Store Trolla (1842m), Tåga (1840m) and Innerdalstårnet (1452m) and other tops will all be in view, creating a sensational display.

As you move down on the other side of the Bjøråskaret saddle the change in vegetation is remarkable. Only mosses grow here on these exposed northern slopes where scattered snowfields remain during summer. The descent from the pass is less steep than the ascent, but you need to pick your way through boulders down towards Bjøråvatnet lake.

Continue on the right-hand side of the lake, and soon enough the terrain flattens out into a pleasant meadow and moor with expansive views along Todalen from the fjord towards Tverråbotnfjellet. The trail comes to a fork; go left here (straight ahead leads to Kårvatn mountain hut). Staying more or less at height, walk parallel to the northern side of Snøfjellet (1330m), crossing streams as the trail leads through heather and berry meadows. Occasionally the path is quite wet and muddy.

Shortly before reaching the Snekkardalen valley the **view** opens again towards Vinnufjellet and other major tops, allowing you to see from Trollheimen's highest peaks down to the fjord at sea level. This makes the stage unique.

The trail continues into Snekkardalshalsen and soon reaches a forest. The descent into Todalen starts here. The path is very steep at times, muddy, wet and loose, so care is needed. It leads through forests and meadows and along streams, with views straight out of a fairy-tale. There are plenty of opportunities for berry or mushroom picking in season (for those who know what they're doing – especially with regard to mushrooms).

After the difficult descent the path merges with a service road; continue ahead onto this and follow it for about 1km. Soon new T-signs appear, leading you left across a field through a small wooded area to the **Todalshytta mountain hut**. The larger Todalen mountain hut is only available for hire as a whole, but two smaller self-service huts can be accessed using the DNT key. They share washroom facilities with the main hut.

RYFYLKE

Classic view of Lysefjord from Lysebotn (Route 10, Stage 5)

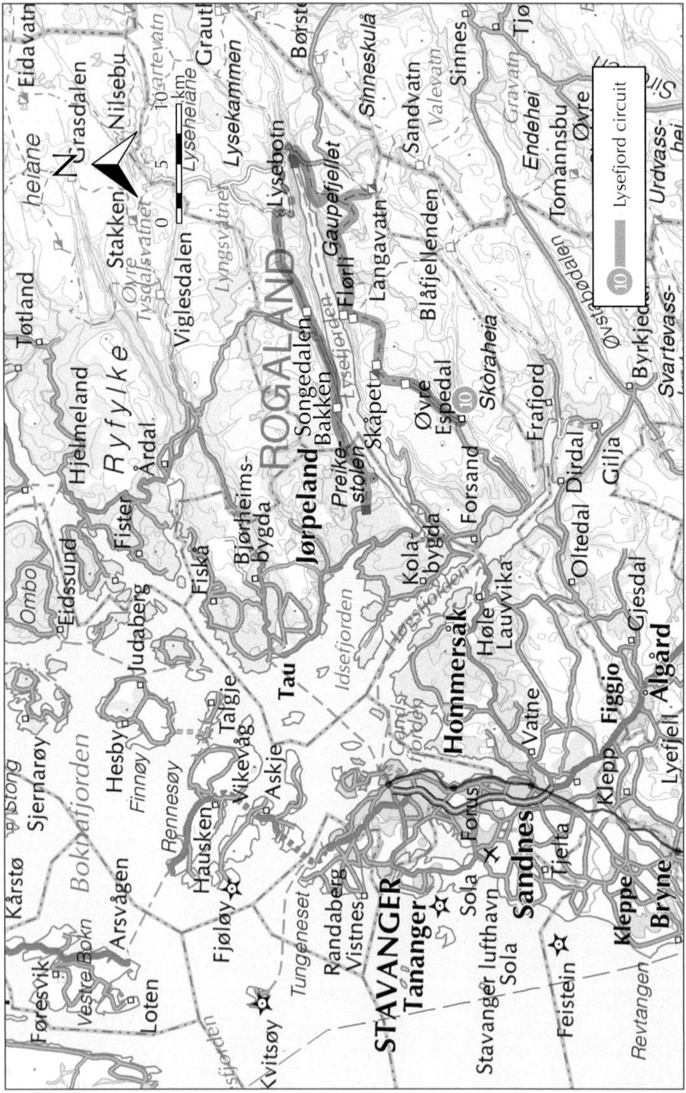
Lysefjord circuit
ROGALAND
Ryfylke
STAVANGER
Sandnes
Jørpeland
Preikestolen
Lysebotn
Lysefjorden
Forsand
Øvre Espedal
Skåpet
Langavatn
Songedalen
Bakken
Florli
Gaupefjellet
Tau
Hommersåk
Ålgård
Figgjo
Bryne
Kleppe
Tananger
Sola
Stavanger lufthavn Sola
Randaberg
Vistnes
Hjelmeland
Årdal
Fister
Judaberg
Hesby
Finnøy
Rennesøy
Boknafjorden
Kvitsøy
Dirdal
Frafjord
Gilja
Oltedal
Gjesdal
Viglesdalen
Stakken
Nilsebu
Grasdalen
Tøtland
Eidavatn
Lysekammen
Sinneskulå
Sandvatn
Sinnes
Blåfjellenden
Skòraheia
Tomannsbu
Endehei
Byrkjedal
Øvstabødalen
Høgsfjorden
Idsefjorden
Gandsfjorden
Lauvvika
Høle
Kolabygda
Bjørheimsbygda
Fiskå
Eidssund
Ombo
Sjernarøy
Talgje
Vikevåg
Askje
Hausken
Fjøløy
Tungeneset
Kårstø
Arsvågen
Føresvik
Vestre Bokn
Loten
Forus
Tjelta
Klepp
Vatne
Lyefjell
Feistein
Revtangen
km

Hiking along the Lysefjord (Route 10, Stage 6)

No hiking guide to Southern Norway could be considered complete without a route along its western fjords. The Ryfylke region of Rogaland County is formed by an archipelago of islands and skerries at the mouth of an extensive system of fjords. Among them is the Lysefjord – literally the 'fjord of light' as it glimmers and reflects both its beautiful, deep waters and the spectacular steep cliffs that surround it. Between those cliffs are lush and fertile valleys that used to be the homesteads of many farms, and a high mountain plateau rises above 1000m. The cliffs around the deep fjord hold many spectacular sights and unique experiences, such as the 'vertigo hikes' at Preikestolen (Stage 7) and Kjeragbolten (Stage 4) or the longest wooden staircase in the world at Flørli (Stage 3).

At the coast, Ryfylke is bordered by the cities of Egersund in the south and Haugesund in the north. Further inland the Folgefonna glacier and the Hardangervidda plateau are natural borders towards the northeast. The area is approximately 4500km^2 in size, with short distances between mountains and fjords. Ryfylke experiences an Atlantic, maritime climate. Low-pressure systems in the summer can bring abundant rain, but temperatures at that time of year are generally more moderate than in the east of the country. The chance of snowfall in summer is quite negligible compared to the other mountain areas described in this guide, and paths generally become reasonably free of snow over the course of June. Regular weather changes are frequent, though, since low-pressure systems can move away as fast as they arrive.

Ryfylke's landscape bears traces of human influence dating back to the end of the last ice age 11,000 years ago. When the ice cap over Norway

Views before the last steep descent into Flørli (Route 10, Stage 2)

retreated, the coast of Rogaland was one of the first parts of the country to become ice free. Reindeer moved northwards from Northern Europe, and so did the first Stone Age people that populated Southern Norway. Arrowheads, flints, harpoons and fishhooks have been found, but also pieces of exquisite beauty that would have had a spiritual meaning rather than being purely utilitarian. Near the hamlet of Flørli, today a witness to industrial heritage with the first hydroelectric power station in the Lysefjord, a Bronze Age settlement has been reconstructed at Forsand. Both sites demonstrate the importance of the land and its productive capacity for humans past and present.

Hiking around the Lysefjord enables a unique perspective on the interplay between humans and nature. The area is a significant contributor to Norway's hydropower-based electricity generation, and its history is in front of your eyes at Flørli and Lysebotn. At the same time, you can marvel at the engineering ingenuity that hides the modern developments from sight behind the sheer cliff faces. One day you can walk through a landscape without any sign of human interference; the next you can follow a trail below a string of silent but powerful giant masts – as much a part of this hike as the spectacular views into the deep blue water of the fjord.

LANDSCAPE AND GEOLOGY

The landscape was first formed by the incredible forces of nature over hundreds of millions of years. There were vast ice sheets on top of the high fells, slowly grinding away any difference in height and so today the area presents itself as a high plateau, showing its bare bedrock in many places. This bedrock is generally more than 1000 million years old; it is very hard and acidic and consists mostly of variations of gneiss and granite. Generally speaking, granite bedrock leads to rounder forms in the landscape, while gneiss bedrock gives rise to longer forms and sharper-edged scenery. Superb examples of both can be seen around the Lysefjord. With its wide U-shaped form, parallel symmetry and steep walls, Lysefjord is the prototype of a draining glacier forming a fjord as it was filled up when the ice melted and the ocean level rose. On days when low clouds shroud the fjord below in mystery, it's not difficult to imagine them being at the height of former glacial ice.

ACCESS AND SERVICES

Ryfylke is just a short ferry, bus or car ride from the cities of Stavanger and Sandnes in southwest Norway. Combined, Stavanger and Sandnes form Norway's third largest urban area, with a full selection of services and shops. They are about a 5hr car or bus ride from Bergen in the north and about 8hr by train, car or bus from Oslo, and just under 1hr by plane from either city. Travelling by bus or train is not necessarily cheaper than flying. Sola airport, just outside Stavanger, has multiple daily domestic air connections to all other major cities in Norway, such as Oslo, Bergen or Trondheim, and about two-dozen international connections to European airports such as London, Amsterdam and Copenhagen. Both express shuttle and local transport is available from the airport to city centres.

Local transport

The local bus and ferry services are slightly cumbersome to navigate, due to being spread across three different municipalities (Stavanger, Sandnes and Sand) and being serviced by different operators, both public and private. A certain amount of puzzling over timetables and locations may be necessary, but doing so makes it entirely possible to move around without a car. See Figure 3 for an overview and Appendix C for local transport information and details of timetables.

Mountain huts

Access to the different mountain huts relevant to the route presented varies. Lysebotn Turisthytte and Flørli Turisthytte can be reached by ferry, with only a short walk from the quay. Songedalen fjellgard and Bakken Gard are serviced by ferry as well but require a lengthy walk (from Songesand quay) or steep climb (from Bakken quay) to the hut respectively.

Figure 3: Ryfylke access

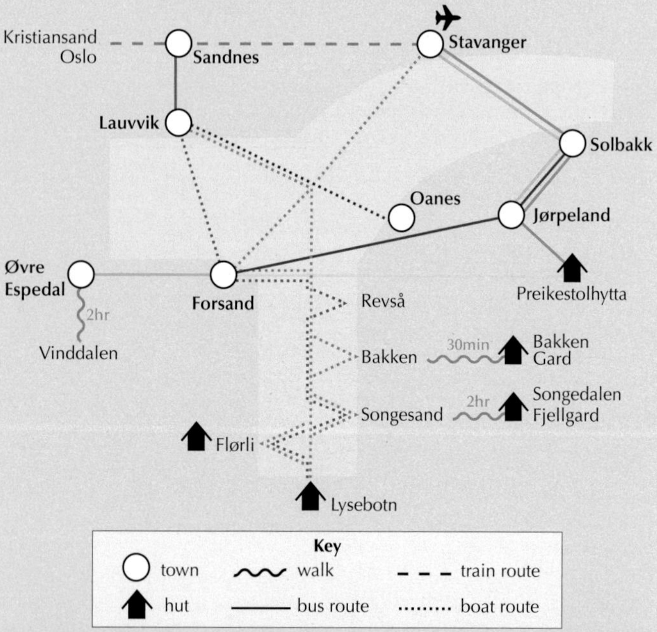

	Line	Connection
– – –	Oslo–Stavanger	Oslo–Kristiansand–Sandnes–Stavanger
········	passenger ferry 560	Stavanger (Fiskepiren)–Forsand–Lysebotn (both express and regular)
········	car ferry Boreal 1024	Lauvvik–Oanes; no public transport from Oanes
———	120	Forsand–Jørpeland–Solbakk.
———	122	Forsand–Øvre Espedal (Mo–Fr; on request during school holidays)
———	100	Stavanger–Solbakk–Jørpeland
———	Tide/Boreal	Stavanger–Solbakk–Jørpeland–Preikestolhytta
———	47	Sandnes–Lauvvik
———	Pelles Reiser	Forsand–Preikestolhytta
········	Summer ferry	Lauvvik–Forsand–Revså–Songesand–Flørli–Lysebotn

Magical view into Lysefjord from Hoppet (Route 10, Stage 7)

Preikestolen Fjellstue is reachable by car and is serviced by several tour operators such as Pelles Reiser, Boreal and Tide with transfers to Stavanger and Forsand. Langavatn mountain hut and Skåpet mountain hut are only accessible on foot. Lysebotn can be reached by car during summer (note the road opens sometime in May, depending on the amount of snow), but this is a lengthy drive from the coast around mountains and fjords.

The mountain huts visited are all very different. Skåpet and Langavatn are self-service huts. Lysebotn Turisthytte is a fully serviced hut, as is Preikestolen Fjellstue, although both offer self-catering facilities. (Note that you would have to bring your own supplies, since there is only minimal kiosk-like shopping in both locations.) Preikestolen Fjellstue is privately owned. It is advisable to book ahead since they are not bound by the DNT rule to offer accommodation to all arriving hikers. Flørli Turisthytte, Songedalen fjellgard and Bakken Gard are unserviced huts (see this book's main introduction for more details on the differences between the types of hut). With a bit of advance planning, shopping for supplies is easy. Shop in Stavanger (above the central train/bus terminal), Forsand (at the quay) or Sandnes (next to the bus/train terminal) upon arrival. At the time of writing, none of the huts require a DNT key for access.

THE ROUTE IN RYFYLKE

The Lysefjord circuit presented here is bound to become a classic ('SignaTur') in years to come. Easily accessible, but quite challenging, it offers world-class 'vertigo hikes', with remote stretches in wide-open, high plateau landscapes hiked by few. In-between, the former farming valleys and early industrial heritage remind us of human endeavours and enterprise. And all of this with one of the most quintessentially beautiful fjords as a backdrop.

ROUTE 10

Lysefjord circuit

Start	Øvre Espedal or Vinddalen parking area
Finish	Preikestolhytta
Distance	84km (52 miles)
Ascent	5785m
Descent	5655m
Time	6–7
Variations	The route is very flexible and can be entered, exited, altered and shortened at all 'ports', such as Flørli, Lysebotn, Songesand and Bakken. Stages 1 and 2 could be done in one day and Stages 5 and 6 can be altered to suit transport options and preferences.

'Lysefjord' translates literally as 'fjord of light', and its granite cliff faces seem to reflect the sunlight much more than the surrounding mountains, giving it a characteristic glowing appearance. It is considered to be one of the most beautiful fjords in southwest Norway and is home to a few outstanding and world-renowned destinations that are visited on this route: Flørli (Stage 2), Kjerag(bolten) (Stage 4) and Preikestolen (Stage 7). Over the course of this hike all around the Lysefjord you not only experience these magnificent locations but you also hike over the high mountain fells, witnessing both the result of millions of years of ice sheets grinding at the bedrock and the weathering that has occurred since the last ice age. You come across former farmhouses that bear witness to a lively community that existed around the fjord in centuries past. Today, many of these houses have been revitalised by the Stavanger Trekking Association (a regional member of the DNT) and are now mountain huts. All this is against the unique and stunning backdrop of the fjord.

Despite its apparent lack of tops, this route is not to be underestimated. The topography holds challenges as you often move over very hilly or steep sections. The route's total ascent and descent holds its own against the likes of Trollheimen and Jotunheimen, and over a much shorter distance. The high fells are completely exposed to the elements, be it 12 hours of sunshine or 12 hours of rain. It is therefore not surprising that you could meet only few hikers on some of the stages, in contrast to the people-magnets of the Kjeragbolten and Preikestolen.

The route's diverse mountain huts offer a very Norwegian experience. You'll stay in all three types of hut: the fully catered ones in Lysebotn Turisthytte and Preikestolen Fjellstue; the self-serviced mountain cabins of Skåpet and Langavatn; and the unserviced mountain huts of Flørli Turisthytte, Bakken Gard and Songedalen fjellgard. Therefore, this route is slightly easier on the budget compared to others in this guide as you could stock up on supplies in Stavanger, Sandnes or Forsand before heading out. Camping along the route is a little more difficult in the high fells landscape, but it is possible around Kvernavatnet lake between Skåpet and Flørli. Small commercial campsites are located in Flørli, Lysebotn, Songesand and near Preikestolen Fjellstue. Beautiful spots can be had around Skogavatnet between Bakken Gard and Preikestolen.

For details of how to access the route's starting point, see Appendix C. The trek starts with an easy climb from Øvre Espedal/Vinddalen to the mountain hut of Skåpet – a set of box cabins on the mountaintops that offer a unique type of accommodation among the DNT's huts. Stage 2 brings you over the high fells and down to Flørli, where the old hydroelectric power plant and adjacent buildings have been redeveloped into a small hamlet that welcomes hikers and other outdoor enthusiasts during summer. Stage 3 starts with the hard and spectacular ascent of the Flørli staircase: 4444 steps make a breathtaking climb up the world's longest wooden staircase. You climb them adjacent to an impossibly steep rail line and steel pipeline – a fascinating piece of industrial heritage that will leave you marvelling at human audacity. From here you continue to Langavatn mountain hut, making this a long but rewarding day. Stage 4 is no less spectacular, nor less challenging, as you walk towards the Kjeragbolten – an impressive gigantic boulder that is wedged into a mountain crevasse at 1084m above the Lysefjord: a vertigo sight for sure. Stage 4 ends in Lysebotn at the end of the fjord and marks the halfway mark of this route. From here Stages 5 and 6 continue on the northern side of the fjord and take you among the old farms, where hardy folk used to eke out a living. The fjord and its steep walls are never far away, and you could hike down at several points to enjoy views, take a swim or even catch the ferry. Stage 7 completes the route with what is arguably the most loved 'vertigo hike' in the whole of Norway: Preikestolen ('pulpit rock'). Approaching it from Bakken Gard at the end of Stage 6 is no mean feat. Chances are you'll be surrounded by many day hikers and tourists on the pulpit itself, all enjoying the magnificent views. You will no doubt descend towards Preikestolen Fjellstue with a sense of satisfaction and achievement.

While the route cannot be readily extended, it can be altered and shortened to suit individual needs and capability. In that sense, it is the most flexible of all the routes presented in this guide. Smart use of the ferry timetable is key in this, with ferry access to Lysebotn, Flørli, Songesand quay (7.5km from Songedalen) and Bakken quay (a short, steep hike down from Bakken Gard) – see Appendix C. Exit and entry to the route is possible at all these locations. The huts at Skåpet and Langavatn can only be reached on foot.

It is perfectly possible to do the route in the opposite direction, starting from Preikestolen Fjellstue and hiking clockwise. A very early start is recommended for this, in order to be on the pulpit at sunrise for a wonderful and less crowded experience. Note that in this case, transport arrangements would have to be made for the end of the route at Vinddalen/Øvre Espedal as there is quite limited public transport available from there to Forsand quay. Also, if you were to walk clockwise, be aware that walking down the Flørli steps is not safe; they are too steep and unsecure for that. There is an alternative, longer trail over the Rallarstien (a century-old service path) and down through Flørlistølen towards Flørli; from there continue the route by going up the steps, and at the top turn right over the Rallarstien and continue to Skåpet.

When planning your visit, be aware that there are a number of festivals and sports events in and around Lysefjord during the summer, such as RockMan, The Hiking Festival, The Lysefjord Run and the Tripp Trapp Triathlon, which might impact accommodation availability. See www.regionstavanger-ryfylke.com for details – but bear in mind that these festivals do not automatically mean there will be no accommodation available, and also remember that no DNT member will be turned away from a DNT hut.

STAGE 1

Øvre Espedal to Skåpet

Start	Øvre Espedal (or Vinddalen parking area)
Finish	Skåpet mountain hut
Distance	10.5km (6.5 miles)
Ascent	585m
Descent	95m
Difficulty	Moderate
Time	3½hr
Maximum altitude	610m
Map	Nordeca Lysefjorden 1:50,000 Turkart 2681

The first couple of stages of the Lysefjord circuit are a gentle leg-warmer for the more challenging routes ahead. Stages 1 and 2 could be done in a single day, ending at Flørli – certainly if transport to Vinddalen is not an issue. Øvre Espedal is the furthest public transport can take you.

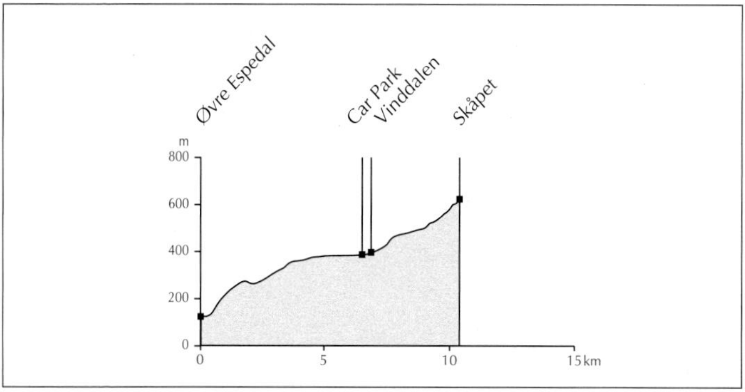

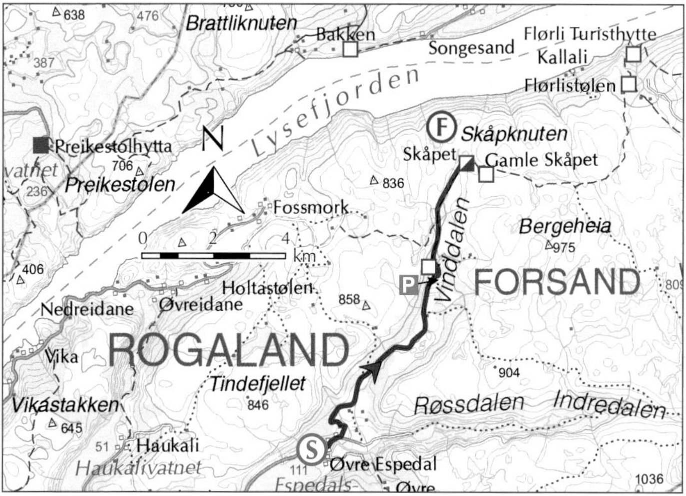

It is a pleasant walk on tarmac from the quiet farming community at Øvre Espedal to the Vinddalen parking area. At the eastern end of the village of **Øvre Espedal** go left at a Y-junction. A small road takes you steadily up the Vinddalen valley, first ascending 250m through a series of hairpins, before reaching the fertile summer meadows of the Vinddøla river. This road was only opened in 1975 and brought a welcome resource of fertile grasslands to the valley's farming communities. You will pass big bales of hay wrapped up to use as fodder in the winter.

At the end of the summer meadows, 7km from Øvre Espedal, you'll reach the parking area. The actual T-marked trail starts here. Cross the bridge left of the parking area and follow the river up to the valley. The trail is very easy to follow. After a few minutes you'll pass the red **'Vinddalen' hut** that now belongs to the Norwegian Trekking Association. It is locked, though, and not in common use.

The **track** is essentially an old service path, known locally as the Svenskevegane. It was built by Swedish workers hired by the hydroelectric power companies working at Flørli in the early 1900s. If you look carefully you can see that many of the rocks bear the signs of having been blasted away with explosives, with a characteristic radial pattern in the remaining rock.

You ascend slowly, at first through the narrow river valley along a pine forest, and later along large meadows. The trail crosses streams whose volume will vary depending on the season and recent rainfalls. Several brooks and smaller streams converge at Tyrejuvet, where a permanent bridge crosses the largest of them. (An alternative approach to Skåpet from the parking area of Skrøyla, near Fossmork, joins at Tyrejuvet for the last ascent towards the mountain hut at Skåpet.)

Continue along the stream, skirting Krylryggen (697m) through birch forest before reaching the treeline and making the final approach to the delightful mountain cabin of **Skåpet** at the edge of the Soddatjørna lake. You can choose to stay at Skåpet or continue to Flørli (Stage 2).

The self-service mountain hut of **Skåpet** follows a new concept introduced by the Stavanger Trekking Association (STF). There are six individual huts

Breakfast at Skåpet mountain hut

that are booked as a whole and each sleep up to six, providing for a higher level of privacy in the sleeping quarters, while the cooking and communal areas and wood-fired sauna are located in separate buildings. The main hut also has an attic for hikers who do not wish to book a cabin ahead of time. This new concept has been very well received by families and groups of friends, and the cabins are very popular.

STAGE 2

Skåpet to Flørli

Start	Skåpet mountain hut
Finish	Flørli Turisthytte
Distance	8.75km (5.5 miles)
Ascent	340m
Descent	865m
Difficulty	Moderate
Time	4hr
Maximum altitude	810m
Map	Nordeca Lysefjorden 1:50,000 Turkart 2681
Note	Flørli Turisthytte is an unserviced hut and you'll need to bring all your food along or buy at the kiosk or café in the hamlet. In the busy summer months a hut warden might be present.

This delightful hike continues along the old 'Svenskevegane' over the pass at Skåpknuten and alongside Kvernavatnet lake before proceeding through high meadows (with views down towards the steep walls of the Lysefjord) prior to the increasingly steep descent towards Flørlistølen and Flørli. The end of the stage is essentially at sea level, and the fjord's first industrial heritage site – the hydroelectric plant built in the early 1900s – makes a fascinating destination.

Leave the main communal hut at **Skåpet** and turn left towards the wood-fired sauna building. Ahead, across the stream, you'll see the first T-markers that guide you up to the valley and towards the pass between **Skåpknuten** (953m) and Sandvassknutane (889m). Follow these, and by the time you reach the pass you have once again left the treeline behind. The trail is mostly smooth and dry underfoot.

> In the typically low-nutrient, slightly acidic soil of the **Ryfylkeheiane** (the mountains and hills of the Ryfylke region), bare rocks are often interspersed with wet areas where various sedge plants species thrive and form the main type of vegetation in marshes and swamps and along the many waterways and lakes.

From the pass, descend towards Kvernavatnet lake. A large, flat area appears with meadows and marshes. The path crosses the meandering stream several times.

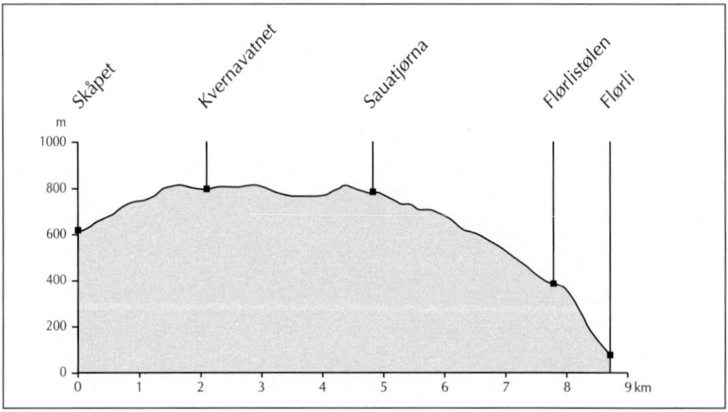

The ruins of an old dwelling in the extensive meadow could well belong to one of the many **summer farms** so prevalent in this country. Here milk was used to make the butter and cheese that were transported down to the local villages once a week over the course of the summer months. Here in Ryfylke the names referring to *støle* mark these summer farms, where further north *seter, sætre* and many other similar spellings are used. The area also makes for a lovely camping spot.

At the third crossing, before climbing the ridge, several paths across the river are T-marked. All ultimately converge on the other side. Continue on the trail in a gradual ascent up the ridge towards the highpoint of the day at 810m, before turning north around Sauafjellet (892m) and passing Sauatjørna lake (750m).

At this point the first **views** into the Lysefjord well below and Søra Dalafjellet opposite open up along the delightful valley formed by the Rindalsbekken stream and its subsidiaries. On top of the high fell plateaus of Stegafjellet (758m) and Hellefjellet (955m), large erratics can be spotted. These huge boulders were moved along by the glaciers and randomly deposited as the ice disappeared.

The descent starts very gently at first, but as you move past Stegafjellet the path becomes wet underfoot and also steeper. When you reach the treeline again, pines are prevalent; later birch mixes in until the pine trees disappear

Hiking along Stegafjellet with views into Lysefjord

altogether. About a kilometre from Flørlistølen the path becomes steep and then very steep once you pass the **hut** itself. (Flørlistølen mountain hut belongs to the Stavanger Trekking Association and can be rented out – see https://booking.visbook.com/no/5498 or https://ut.no.)

The path on the final descent is mainly rock and gravel, and very steep. Progress could be slow in wet conditions. **Flørli Turisthytte** is domiciled in a farm building that is well over 200 years old. Its prominent position as the highest building in the small hamlet of Flørli gives it extraordinary views over the fjord and beyond towards the Dalafjellet and Steinfjellet opposite.

Flørli has a small kiosk and café that serves simple but tasty fare in the summer months. Several accommodation options are linked to the café and the current owner is making a real effort to develop this attractive industrial heritage space.

Conditions for **hydropower** generation are perfect in Flørli, and the first hydroelectric plant here was finished in 1918 and replaced in 1999 by a modern, all-underground version. The small hamlet by the fjord boasts the old industrial buildings, school and workers' accommodation. A small exhibition tells the story of human ingenuity and audacity in harnessing this resource. The old control room is intact, and the analogue technology would probably still work today.

STAGE 3

Flørli to Langavatn via Kjerag plateau

Start	Flørli Turisthytte
Finish	Langavatn mountain hut
Distance	18.25km (11.5 miles)
Ascent	1620m
Descent	760m
Difficulty	Very challenging
Time	8hr
Maximum altitude	1104m
Map	Nordeca Lysefjorden 1:50,000 Turkart 2681

The day starts with the unique thrill of 4444 steps up the longest wooden staircase in the world. Cardiovascular health will be tested, and this is not for those with vertigo. The stairs are unsecured (although there is usually a handrail/cable of sorts) and steep to very steep in sections, but the views invariably make up for any toil and sweat. The subsequent hike is a long one over the Kvernafjellet high plateau (965m) and winds in a series of significant ups and downs towards the Kjerag plateau before descending to Langavatn mountain hut. Note that the total ascent for the stage is double that of the steps themselves. The views are ever-changing, even after the stairs, as you proceed through the glacial landscape and around countless small lakes in this high fells region. The trail is generally well marked and the terrain is varied, with wood, bedrock, marsh and bog all featuring throughout the stage.

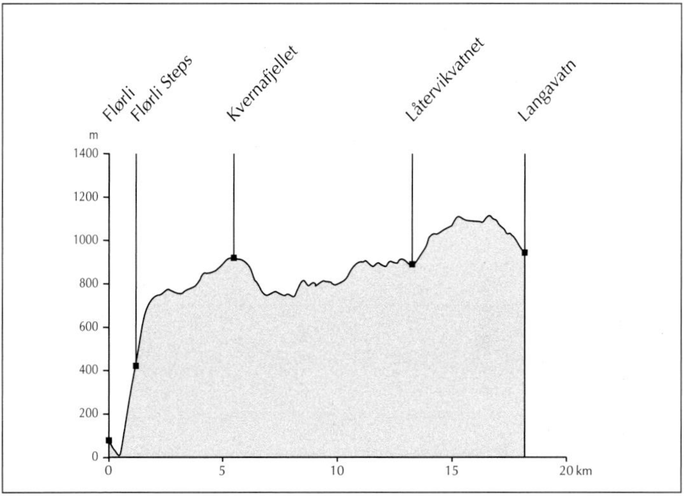

Fill your waterbottle at the hut as there will be no flowing water until you are past Kvernafjellet. Leave the main door of **Flørli Turisthytte**, turn right and follow the gravel path 500 metres down towards the fjord and past the old power production and control station. The start of the steps is signposted. The first few steps are easy; then it goes pretty much straight up. Every 500 steps there is a progress marker and there are regular points along the way where you can step aside and catch your breath. The views as you move up the staircase are truly breathtaking – both literally and figuratively!

The **stairs** were built to aid in the construction of the steep transport railway line as well as the dam and steel pipeline, for which materials needed to be lugged up. Men were hired and paid by the kilogramme that they could bring up towards Ternevatnet (738m). Loads were weighed both at the start and high up to prevent any 'falling by the wayside'.

The Flørli steps in morning light

At the top of the stairs, follow the service road first around the dam of Ternevatnet lake and then towards Klubbatjørna lake and beyond to the northern edge of the large **Stora Flørvatnet lake**. Here turn left at the signpost and go past the small building, where the road ends and the hiking trail resumes.

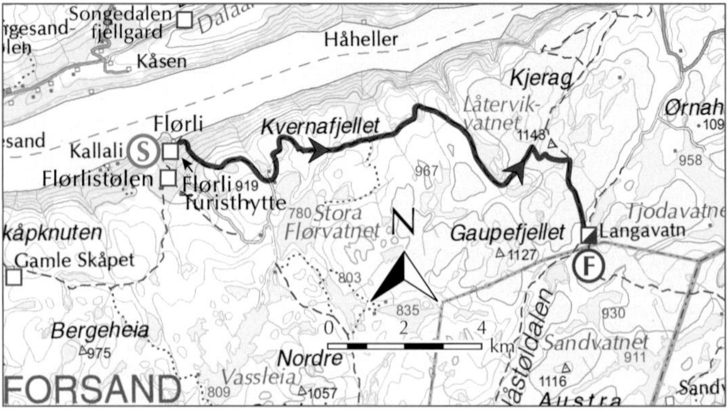

At first the markers run more or less parallel to the power line, winding between numerous small lakes before approaching the top of **Kvernafjellet** (965m).

> Note the many **stones**, small and large, as well as big boulders that were left behind after the last ice age, resting on the smooth bedrock that has been ground away over the millions of years of the Quaternary period.

The trail now moves east, descending towards the Skansen area, continually moving up and down and passing many a small lake as it brings you closer to the steep ridge of the Kjerag plateau. The marshes around Skansen are full of cloudberries; if you come at the right time you'll be able to collect them for a delicate dessert at the hut.

At the top of a short, steep ascent, views towards the south open up onto **Låtervikvatnet lake**. Stay at height above the lake, and then descend to reach its southern tip. Turn east here and follow the T-markers closely up the steep slope to the **Kjerag plateau**. Shortly afterwards, at a signposted crossroads, turn right to Langavatn. A kilometre further on, close to the highest point of the day at 1104m, you'll arrive at a second signed junction. Turn right again. From here it is 2.4km to Langavatn mountain hut, crossing a number of gullies before the final descent to the cabin. **Langavatn** is beautifully situated on the south point of a lake that invites for a dip on a sunny summer's day.

On top of Kvernafjellet, in a landscape shaped by ice and glaciers

STAGE 4

Langavatn to Øygardsstølen and Lysebotn via Kjeragbolten

Start	Langavatn mountain hut
Finish	Øygardsstølen parking area/Lysefjorden Turisthytte
Distance	12.5km (7.75 miles)
Ascent	580m
Descent	880m
Difficulty	Challenging
Time	6hr
Maximum altitude	1143m
Map	Nordeca Lysefjorden 1:50,000 Turkart 2681

This stage visits another unique, world-famous site which is certainly a spectacular feature of the route. The Kjeragbolten is an erratic boulder that is sandwiched between two mountainsides and suspended 1000m above the fjord. The Kjerag cliff was put on the map in 1994 when it hosted its first base jump, stealing the show from the actual Kjerag mountaintop (1143m), which nevertheless offers expansive views over the whole Ryfylke plateau for many kilometres. Note that trail markings around here can be quite sparse and may be difficult to locate in poor visibility. The descent into Øygardsstølen is at times very steep but there are commanding, lofty views down to Lysefjord and Lysebotn.

From Øygardsstølen it is a 7km, steeply winding tarmac road down to Lysebotn. It is fairly busy in season and so not recommended for walking. The Stavanger Base Jump Club (SBK) runs regular transfer services from/to Øygardsstølen/Lysebotn to supplement their business. Booking is highly recommended – tel +47 984 44 159. Alternatively, you could hitchhike. If you decide to walk (not recommended), take a headlamp – the road passes through a long tunnel.

Leave **Langavatn mountain hut**, turn left towards the stile and then take the signposted path out of the valley towards Kjerag and Flørli. Retrace your steps from the previous stage for about 2.4km until you reach the Y-junction. Left is back to Flørli, so turn right towards Kjerag and Lysebotn. (The km readings on the signposts are slightly wrong – up to 0.5km understated.)

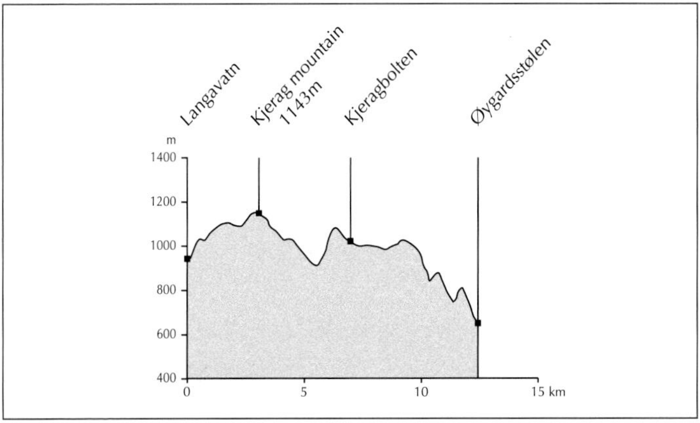

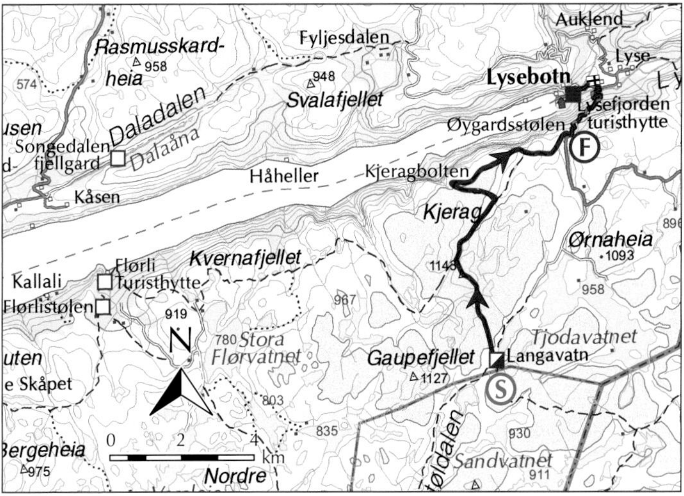

Follow the trail to a sizeable cairn at the 1143m highpoint of the **Kjerag plateau**. This is also the highest point of the stage with views to match. From here, hike steeply down into the valley and towards the lake (at 1016m) and then along the terraced glacial valley of Storedalen until, 1.4km from the lake, you reach the signposted turnoff for the Kjeragbolten. Turn left here.

The path basically goes straight up the slope for about 200 altitude metres. Watch out for the T-markers as they are often old and faded. Once you reach the plateau again, the steep valley that contains the Kjeragbolten becomes visible straight ahead. Trail markings here are scattered; finding them in foggy weather could be a challenge. Otherwise, the terrain is wide and open with expansive views, and the general direction of travel is reasonably obvious, just north of due west.

As you proceed over the plateau here, notice the many **calcified fractures** that stick out of the surrounding bedrock, sometimes many metres long. This calcified material is much less prone to weathering than the surrounding rock, so you are looking essentially at the chemical weathering that has occurred on the bedrock since the end of the last ice age, approximately 11,000 years ago.

Intrepid hiker on the Kjeragbolten

Kjeragbolten is at the end of a narrow rocky gully, with a stream that empties into the fjord just below the boulder itself. It hangs suspended some 1000m above the fjord and is quite spectacular and vertigo inducing. Many people queue for a photo opportunity on the rock. Should you decide to step onto it, proceed with care and do not attempt it in high winds.

There are eight **base jump** exits near and around Kjeragbolten, and about 2000–3000 jumps are performed every year. Base jumpers must complete over 250 skydives before they can sign up for a base-jumping course. Despite these measures, it remains a seriously dangerous activity.

To continue towards Øygardsstølen, retrace your steps up the gully and at the signpost turn left (north) towards the large cairn. There turn right (east) and follow the well-trodden path along the hillside, over the high fells terrain. As the path veers close to the cliff, Lysebotn can be seen deep down in the valley, some 1000m below. It is an awe-inspiring sight in good weather.

The path crosses another two valleys with associated ups and downs, before finally descending to the car park area at Øygardsstølen. The descents are steep and partly secured with chains on the bare rock. No climbing equipment is required, but a good grip is essential. Parts of the trail have been improved by Nepali Sherpas to prevent further erosion. You'll see a stone emergency shelter that has been built in the old Norwegian tradition of such buildings; the many thousands of day-trip visitors each year regularly include unprepared walkers who require assistance and rescue.

At **Øygardsstølen** there is a small restaurant and café perched high above the fjord with outstanding views. It is worth taking a break here before heading down the 7km to Lysebotn. In season the SBK bus is recommended for this section of the stage. Once at Lysebotn, **Lysefjorden Turisthytte** is located a two-minute walk from the ferry quay on the main road.

STAGE 5

Lysebotn to Songedalen

Start	Fyljesdalen or Lysefjorden Turisthytte mountain hut
Finish	Songedalen fjellgard mountain hut
Distance	10km (6.25 miles) or 25km (15.5 miles)
Ascent	385m or 1065m
Descent	645m or 675m
Difficulty	Moderate
Time	3hr or 6½hr
Maximum altitude	670m
Map	Nordeca Lysefjorden 1:50,000 Turkart 2681
Note	Stavanger Base Jump Club offers transport from Lysefjord to Fyljesdalen, on request and capacity permitting.

This stage offers two possible starting points: you can either begin at Lysebotn and walk for 15km (680m total ascent, 3½hr) up a narrow service road to Fyljesdalen; or you can skip this tarmac road and instead start at Fyljesdalen proper. If you start at Fyljesdalen the stage is essentially a very pleasant valley walk, giving the legs a bit of rest after the challenges of the past two stages. It moves through old farming communities and along the hydroelectric power lines that are so important for Norwegian society, powering homes and industry with a renewable resource.

The M/S Lysebotn ferry, run by Kolumbus, is small enough to be able to dock at Håheller, so it would be an alternative to come up the steep (and unmarked) path that joins in with this stage close to Håhellervatnet lake. Note the ferry timings, if you decide to take this option.

If you start at Fyljesdalen you could consider combining this stage with Stage 6, but be aware that the last stretch of Stage 6 is the most challenging. The route would then be 20km long, with the sting in the last 2km.

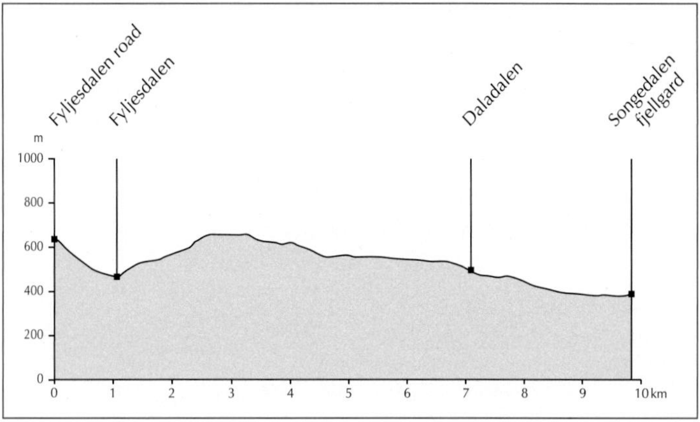

If you're starting from **Lysebotn**, leave the Lysefjorden Turisthytte and go left up the main road out of the village. After 1.2km leave the main road and continue straight, signposted to Stakken/Nilsebu/Grautheller. The road steadily winds up the mountain, and after 8.5km you pass Storatjørna lake, clearly showing the signs of varying water levels. Shortly afterwards, views onto Lysefjord itself open up. The road then turns north, and the near-perfect cup-shaped valley of Fyljesdalen becomes visible. At 14.9km there's a small parking area on the right and a small transformer station on the left. Red dots mark the start of the hiking trail opposite the parking area, next to the transformer station.

From here, follow the path straight downhill and into the **Fyljesdalen** valley, and then straight up on the other side towards the Fyljesdalsskardet pass. The trail is very variable underfoot; gravelly and rocky at times, wet and marshy at others.

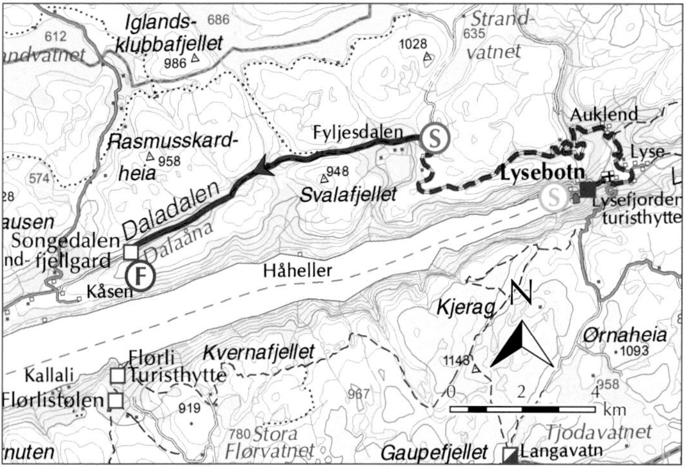

Fyljesdalen seems to have its own microclimate and is full of flowering meadow plants and bilberry bushes.

You'll pass two memorial plaques commemorating events that took place here in **World War 2**. Four planes – among them two gliders – set off from Scotland on 20 November 1942, to attempt a sabotage action on the heavy water plant run by the Germans at Rjukan in the Telemark region. The idea was to have the gliders penetrate the enemy's airspace without giving themselves away with the noise of normal aircraft. The pilots were aided by the Norwegian resistance, who set out lights near the landing spots, but heavy fog made it impossible to land and one of the gliders crashed here into Fyljesdalen with 17 soldiers on board. Most of them died either during the crash or shortly after, and the remaining were found by German soldiers, despite the efforts of the local population to help.

The pass, at around 2.7km from the road, is the highest point of the stage. As you leave Fyljesdalen, Daladalen comes into view. Continue down **Daladalen** towards Håhellervatnet lake, where an unmarked path coming up from Håheller joins from the left.

For the remainder of the stage you hike parallel to the river, crossing it a few times. (One of these crossings has a rope strung across the shallow river; better to ignore the rope and cross in the usual rock-hopping way, since the slack in

the rope makes for quite an unstable hold.) The path is well marked all the way to the unserviced hut of Songedalen fjellgard, and you'll enjoy new views over the Lysefjord and towards Preikestolen. The **hut** has its water source down the meadow by the river, where there is also a lovely natural pool.

STAGE 6

Songedalen to Bakken

Start	Songedalen fjellgard mountain hut
Finish	Bakken Gard mountain hut
Distance	9.5km (6 miles)
Ascent	730m
Descent	945m
Difficulty	Challenging
Time	4hr
Maximum altitude	390m
Map	Nordeca Lysefjorden 1:50,000 Turkart 2681

Initially this stage is straightforward, leading from Songedalen fjellgard towards the Songesand quay. The last 2km from there to Bakken are quite adventurous and will likely take as much time as the preceding 8km. Picking your way along the cliffs of the fjord, progress here is slow due to the steep terrain, the rocks and scree, and the many ups and downs. In heavy rain or snowmelting season there could be rock slides. In this case, hike from Songedalen fjellgard to Songesand quay (8km, 2hr), take the boat from there to Bakken quay and then hike up the steep path to the mountain hut. Markings are generally good, but you need to look out for them during the traverse along the fjord cliff.

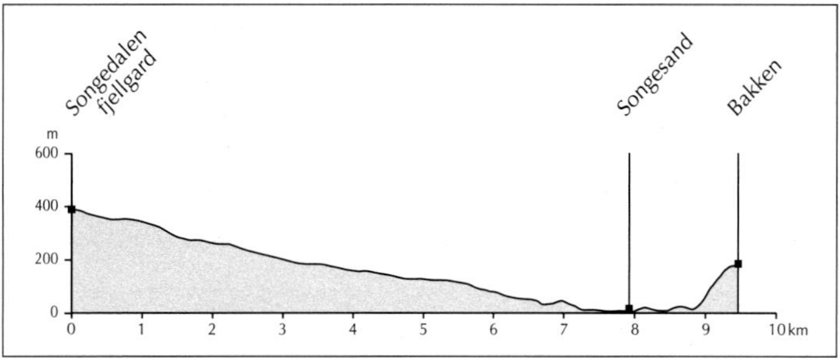

Leave the **Songedalen fjellgard hut** by walking towards the path, then turn right and proceed down the valley on the tractor road. You soon arrive at the west gate of the property. Continue moving gently downhill, parallel to the river. At 1.7km the hike markings continue on the river's right, before the tractor road crosses a bridge. Both the tractor road and hiking path will join the main road 900 metres further on, so you can choose to take either.

The **Dalaåna river** flows fairly slowly at first in a rather flat riverbed but empties into the fjord at Songedalen in a small, steep ravine – a reminder that its water levels must have been much higher before the introduction of hydro-electric power generation at its feeder lakes high on the plateau.

Fill your water bottle often around here, as there are not many opportunities to do so further along this stage. Reach the main Fv661 road and follow it along the valley towards Songesand, passing a few farms on the way. (Songedalen Camping, on the Fv661, provides an option for campers along this stretch of the route: otherwise, suitable camping spots are difficult to find.)

Continue down along the tarmac for about 5km until you are almost at the **Songesand** quay. The T-markers towards Bakken appear at the first bend of the road upwards from the pier. Here you have to first climb a stilt ladder over a fence. Watch out for the T-markers as you proceed along the coastline. The path is highly uneven and challenging, sometimes marshy and across wet tree roots; at other times rocky and requiring hands and feet or the use of the chains provided to cross over some rockfalls.

Steep sections on the way to Bakken require some care

Shortly before reaching Bakken mountain hut, follow the path as it turns uphill. Continue past the sign towards 'Bakken kai', along what is now clearly a man-made path with stone steps to ease the ascent, ensuring access from the quay to the hut in all weather. The best views of the stage are at this end of it, from the small promontories up at this centuries-old farmstead. You are at the bend of the Lysefjord and the panoramas are phenomenal.

Bakken Gard started as a so-called *husmannsplass* – a piece of land that was leased out by the landowning farmer, usually due to its lesser quality. *Husmannen* could hardly make these farms work for their large families, and many hundreds of thousands left for North America between 1825 and 1910. Bakken Gard was an exception, in that the last inhabitants – a brother and sister called Johannes and Gjertrud Bakken – welcomed visitors and created different streams of income through their entrepreneurship and ingenuity. The farm was left to the municipality of Forsand in 1973, and the municipality gifted it to the Stavanger Trekking Association in 2018. It is a little gem on the fjord, and the STF completed a full renovation for the 2020 season.

STAGE 7

Bakken to Preikestolhytta

Start	Bakken Gard mountain hut
Finish	Preikestolen Fjellstue/Preikestolhytta mountain hut
Distance	15km (9.5 miles)
Ascent	1545m
Descent	1445m
Difficulty	Very challenging
Time	7hr
Maximum altitude	630m
Map	Nordeca Lysefjorden 1:50,000 Turkart 2681

This stage completes the Lysefjord circuit and is unquestionably the most spectacular in terms of the views it offers. This is especially true during the 'airy' sections between Hoppet and Hengjande, and of course on top of Preikestolen itself. There is a short (15-metre) section around Hoppet that is challenging – especially if you need to control your vertigo – but it is well secured with chains. The surprising sting lies in the elevation. The path undulates heavily, reaching a total vertical distance of almost 3000m over only 15km horizontal, which is more and steeper than any of the other stages in this book. It is often a very narrow trail while in the woods, and features a wide range of terrain, and it is easy for the last few kilometres as you descend from Preikestolen. On the way down the mountain there are fine views towards Stavanger and the Ryfylke islands, lying in the fjords around Stavanger.

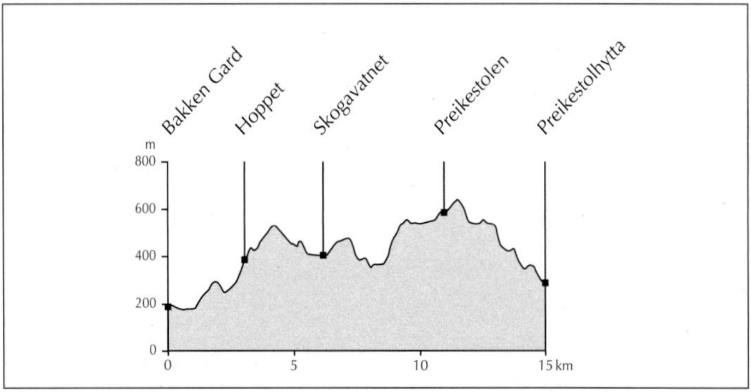

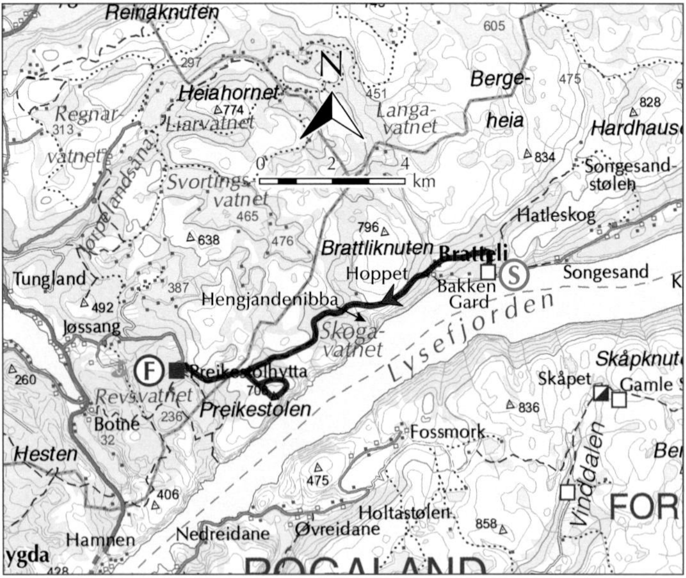

Leave **Bakken** and turn north, following the path up the valley, past the gate. Keep left at the signpost and after 450 metres you'll reach the bridge over the Brattliåna stream. Cross and proceed westwards to reach Øvre Bratteli at about 2km. Continue below the house and cross a creek. Shortly after there's an unmarked T-junction; the left path leads down to Bratteli quay, so take the right and continue uphill.

At around 3.3km the path finds its way around the **Hoppet** cliffs. This is a short, steep section, secured by chains. It comprises a traverse of around 15 metres along a smooth, steep rockface. You don't need special skills, but you do need to be fit and preferably have no fear of heights. Some sections are airy, but they're not difficult to traverse.

After rounding Hoppet the trail leads past two lakes. Just after leaving the first lake there's an unmarked detour to Hengjandenibba – another 'vertigo viewpoint' over the Lysefjord with associated photo opportunities (and no queues). The second **Skogavatnet lake** has a very nice camping spot at its west end: a rare find on this route. The path varies underfoot, with rocks, roots, dry and wet, muddy, steep and slippery sections alternating rapidly. If you are not used to this type of path, progress might be slower than expected.

From the western end of Skogavatnet lake it's another 3km to the Preikestolen path. The trail is as varied as before, although being inland from the fjord there are no airy sections. After a last steady climb you'll reach the path to Preikestolen. The crossroads at Neverdalsskaret is a good spot for a break and some people-watching. (You will likely see more people here in five minutes than on your whole route to date.) You could leave your pack near the junction at Neverdalsskaret if you plan to come back the same way after visiting Preikestolen.

From the junction, turn left and ascend towards the plateau and the Neverdalstjønna lakes. Continue to the far end of the lakes, where there's a small emergency shelter; from here to Preikestolen the path is well above the treeline on bare bedrock. The pulpit rock itself can only be seen just before the final approach, and there are some exposed, lofty (but short) sections of the path just before reaching it. Access to the pulpit rock could be dangerous at any time of year in high winds and gusts.

Preikestolen has been a people-magnet since it was 'discovered' in the late 1890s. It then took two days to reach. Today it is easily the most visited day-hike destination in Norway, with around 300,000 people making the trek each year in the short summer season. Despite the human traffic, the views remain magical and Preikestolen is the most recognisable of all the Norwegian 'vertigo hikes' and well worth the effort.

Preikestolen is one of Norway's favourite 'vertigo' points, at 600m above Lysefjord

Note the many **glacial striae** on the rocks on your final ascent towards the pulpit rock. The mountains of the Ryfylkeheiane have been covered by ice many times; these grooves are the result of rocks being dragged along, etching into the bedrock beneath.

For the descent you have two options. The first is to retrace your steps to the Neverdalsskaret junction. An alternative route takes you above Preikestolen around the 'back' of the mountain and rejoins the main route at the emergency shelter. If you choose the latter, walk back some 30 metres from the pulpit rock and follow the T-markers steeply up the mountainside to your left. You will likely see other hikers on top, and the T-markers are clear, so it is easy to figure out where to go. Be aware that this steep section is a bit of a scramble and would be particularly challenging with heavy bags or in wet or windy conditions. Continue on top of the plateau, moving across it towards the west, and go down a small valley until you reach the emergency shelter on the main path. From here follow the main path back towards Neverdalsskaret.

It is just over 2km down from Neverdalsskaret to the Preikestolen Fjellstue, on a wide, stony path built by Nepali Sherpas in 2014–18 to accommodate the growth in visitor numbers and prevent uncontrolled erosion. A remarkable piece of work. This final section has beautiful views towards Stavanger and the islands around and beyond.

Preikestolen Fjellstue ('mountain lodge') is a modern-style, comfortable lodge built in 2008. The old cabin, **Preikestolhytta**, dates from 1949 and is now in use as a hostel by the same owner as the lodge.

APPENDIX A

Overview of routes and daily stages

Stage	Length (km)	Duration (hr)	Difficulty	Start alt (m)	Max alt (m)	Finish alt (m)	Ascent (m)	Descent (m)	Page no.
Jotunheimen									
Route 1: Jotunheimen Besseggen route									43
1 Besseggen ridge	14	6	Challenging	994	1743	1008	980	965	44
2 Memurubu to Gjendebu	10.75	4	Challenging	1008	1484	990	640	660	47
3 Gjendebu to Fondsbu	15.75	5	Challenging	990	1374	1065	440	365	50
Route 2: Jotunheimen classic route									54
1 Besseggen ridge	14	6	Challenging	994	1743	1008	980	965	55
2 Memurubu to Glitterheim	20.75	8	Very challenging	1008	1685	1390	1080	700	58
Extension Glittertinden summit	11.75	5	Challenging	1390	2457	1390	1140	1140	62
3 Glittertinden high traverse	15.75	9	Very challenging	1390	2457	1106	1145	1430	66
3A Glitterheim low traverse	16.5	6	Challenging	1390	1680	1106	340	625	69
4 Galdhøpiggen summit	12.5	8	Very challenging	1106	2469	1106	1390	1390	72
5 Spiterstulen to Leirvassbu	15.75	5½	Moderate	1106	1487	1400	425	130	76
6 Leirvassbu to Gjendebu	19.25	7	Challenging	1400	1541	990	200	610	79
Route 3: Jotunheimen traverse route									83
1 Fondsbu to Olavsbu	14	5½	Challenging	1065	1601	1440	750	375	84

Stage	Length (km)	Duration (hr)	Difficulty	Start alt (m)	Max alt (m)	Finish alt (m)	Ascent (m)	Descent (m)	Page no.
2 Olavsbu to Skogadalsbøen	17.75	6½	Challenging	1440	1617	833	350	960	87
3 Skogadalsbøen to Fannaråki	11	5	Challenging	833	2068	2068	1335	100	90
4 Fannaråki to Turtagrø	8	3½	Moderate	2068	2068	884	15	1200	94
Rondane									
Route 4: Rondane summits									104
1 Entry to Rondvassbu	7	2	Easy	1084	1242	1173	180	90	105
2 Rondslottet high traverse	17.75	10	Very challenging	1173	2178	914	1350	1610	108
3 Langglupdalen	21	7½	Very challenging	914	1429	1070	900	750	111
4 Høgronden high traverse	20	9	Very challenging	1070	2115	914	1280	1430	115
5 Illmanndalen	19	6	Challenging	914	1301	1084	490	320	119
Route 5: Rondane traverse route									123
1 Spranget to Bjørnhollia	19	6	Challenging	1084	1301	914	320	490	124
2 Langglupdalen	21	7½	Very challenging	914	1429	1070	900	750	128
3 Dørålseter to Grimsdalshytta	16	6	Challenging	1070	1388	1000	730	800	132
4 Grimsdalshytta to Hjerkinn	17.75	5½	Challenging	1000	1340	1017	490	470	135
Extension 1 Rondslottet and Vinjeronden summits	13.5	8	Challenging	1173	2178	1173	1100	1100	138
Extension 2 Veslesmeden summit	12.5	4½	Challenging	1173	2015	1173	850	850	142
Extension 3 Storronden summit	8.5	3½	Challenging	1173	2138	1173	900	900	146

Stage	Length (km)	Duration (hr)	Difficulty	Start alt (m)	Max alt (m)	Finish alt (m)	Ascent (m)	Descent (m)	Page no.
Dovrefjell									
Route 6: Dovrefjell traverse route									156
1 Kongsvold Fjellstue to Reinheim	15.25	4	Moderate	900	1351	1340	520	80	158
2 Snøhetta high traverse	12.75	6	Very challenging	1340	2286	1304	900	935	161
2A Reinheim to Snøheim over Snøhetta	12.25	6	Challenging	1340	2286	1474	950	815	165
2B Snøheim to Åmotdalshytta low route	12.25	5	Moderate	1474	1725	1304	365	535	169
3 Åmotdalshytta to Gammelsetra	24	7½	Challenging	1304	1465	807	350	850	172
4 Gammelsetra to Vangshaugen	13	4½	Challenging	807	807	740	460	525	176
5 Vangshaugen to Eiriksvollen	15.25	6	Very challenging	740	1221	140	760	1360	180
Trollheimen									
Route 7: Trollheimen Trekanten triangle route									190
1 Gjevilvasshytta to Trollheimshytta	21	6½	Very challenging	710	1319	540	860	1030	191
2 Geithøtta high traverse	17	5	Challenging	540	1325	740	885	685	195
2A Svartådalen alternative valley route	16.25	5	Moderate	540	740	740	440	240	199
3 Jøldalshytta to Gjevilvasshytta	21	6½	Challenging	740	1072	710	550	580	202
Route 8: Trollheimen SignaTur route									206
1 Riaren high traverse	22	7½	Very challenging	710	1380	680	1055	1085	208
2 Vassendsetra to Bårdsgarden	5.5	2	Easy	680	828	625	145	200	211

Stage	Length (km)	Duration (hr)	Difficulty	Start alt (m)	Max alt (m)	Finish alt (m)	Ascent (m)	Descent (m)	Page no.
3 Bårdsgarden to Innerdalen	23.75	8	Very challenging	625	1123	400	675	900	214
4 Innerdalen to Kårvatn	13.25	5½	Challenging	400	1175	210	810	1000	217
5 Kårvatn to Trollheimshytta	24	8	Very challenging	210	973	540	880	550	221
6 Snota summit	23.5	9	Very challenging	540	1669	540	1280	1280	224
7 Trollhøtta high traverse	19.75	9	Very challenging	540	1614	740	1350	1150	228
8 Jøldalshytta to Gjevilvasshytta	21	6½	Challenging	740	1072	710	550	580	232
Route 9: Trollheimen fells to fjord route									235
1 Gjevilvasshytta to Bårdsgarden	18	6	Moderate	710	828	625	280	365	236
2 Bårdsgarden to Innerdalen	23.75	8	Very challenging	625	1123	400	675	900	240
3 Innerdalen to Todalen	13	6	Challenging	400	1175	40	900	1260	244
Ryfylke									
Route 10: Lysefjord circuit									254
1 Øvre Espedal to Skåpet	10.5	3½	Moderate	120	610	610	585	95	256
2 Skåpet to Flørli	8.75	4	Moderate	610	810	85	340	865	259
3 Flørli to Langavatn	18.25	8	Very challenging	85	1104	945	1620	760	262
4 Langavatn to Øygardsstolen	12.5	6	Challenging	945	1143	645	580	880	266
5 Fyljesdalen to Songedalen	10	3	Moderate	650	670	390	385	645	269
6 Songedalen to Bakken	9.5	4	Challenging	390	390	175	730	945	272
7 Bakken to Preikestolhytta	15	7	Very challenging	175	630	270	1545	1445	275

APPENDIX B

Table of mountain huts and key services provided

For up-to-date information and seasonal opening dates, see https://english.dnt.no or https://ut.no; * DNT key needed out of season

Name of hut	Type of service	DNT key	Mobile coverage	Power	Dogs	Beds	Opening dates
Jotunheimen							
Gjendesheim	Lodge	No	No	220V	No	185	Seasonal as lodge
Memurubu Turisthytte	Lodge	n/a	No	220V	Allowed	150	Seasonal as lodge
Gjendebu	Lodge	No*	No	220V	Allowed	119	Seasonal as lodge
Fondsbu	Lodge	No	No	220V	No	100	Seasonal as lodge
Glitterheim	Lodge	No*	No	220V	Allowed	137	Seasonal as lodge
Spiterstulen	Lodge	n/a	No	220V	No	150	Seasonal as lodge
Leirvassbu	Lodge	n/a	No	220V	Allowed	185	Seasonal as lodge
Olavsbu	Self-service	Yes	No	No	Allowed	52	Seasonal
Skogadalsbøen	Lodge	No	Yes	220V	Allowed	87	Seasonal as lodge
Fannaråkhytta	Lodge	No	Yes	No	Allowed	34	Seasonal as lodge
Rondane							
Rondvassbu	Lodge	No*	No	220V	Allowed	128	Seasonal as lodge
Bjørnhollia	Lodge	No*	No	220V	No	90	Seasonal as lodge
Øvre Døralseter	Lodge	No*	Yes	220V	Allowed	100	Seasonal as lodge
Grimsdalshytta	Lodge	No*	No	220V	Allowed	54	Seasonal as lodge
Dovrefjell							
Reinheim	Self-service	Yes	No	No	Allowed	36	Seasonal

Name of hut	Type of service	DNT key	Mobile coverage	Power	Dogs	Beds	Opening dates
Åmotdalshytta	Self-service	No	No	No	No	34	Year-round
Gammelsetra	Self-service	Yes	No	No	No	32	Year-round
Vangshaugen	Lodge	No*	n/a	n/a	No	64	Seasonal as lodge
Snøheim	Lodge	No	Yes	220V	Allowed	80	Seasonal as lodge
Trollheimen							
Gjevilvasshytta	Lodge	No*	No	220V	Allowed	64	Seasonal as lodge
Trollheimshytta	Lodge	No*	No	220V	Allowed	80	Seasonal as lodge
Jøldalshytta	Lodge	No*	No	220V	Allowed	84	Seasonal as lodge
Vassendsetra	Self-service	Yes	No	No	Allowed	20	Year-round
Bårdsgarden	Self-service	No	Yes	220V	Allowed	20	Year-round
Innerdalshytta	Self-service	Yes	Yes	220V	Allowed	34	Year-round
Kårvatn	Self-service	Yes	No	220V	Allowed	20	Year-round
Todalshytta	Self-service	Yes	Yes	220V	No	8	Year-round
Eiriksvollen	Self-service	Yes	Yes	12V	No	17	Year-round
Ryfylke							
Flørli Turiststasjon	Not serviced	No	Yes	220V	Allowed	27	Year-round
Langavatn	Self-service	No	No	12V	No	28	Year-round
Lysefjorden Turisthytte	Lodge	No	Yes	220V	Allowed	80	Seasonal as lodge
Songedalen Fjellgard	Not serviced	No	No	No	No	16	Year-round
Bakken Gard	Not serviced	No	Yes	No	No	16	Year-round
Skåpet	Self-service	No	No	12V	Allowed	42	Year-round
Preikestolhytta / Preikestolen Fjellstue	Lodge	No	Yes	220V	No	150	Year-round

Hut phone numbers
(huts not listed here have no direct number)

Jotunheimen

Gjendesheim
tel +47 61 23 89 10

Memurubu Turisthytte
tel +47 46 01 61 00

Gjendebu
tel +47 47 61 15 33 (in season)
tel +47 915 74 965 (out of season)

Fondsbu
tel +47 970 74 218

Glitterheim
tel +47 900 15 529 or +47 994 25 915

Spiterstulen
tel +47 61 21 94 00

Leirvassbu
tel +47 61 21 12 10

Skogadalsbøen
tel +47 97 56 90 94 (in season)
tel +47 94 14 12 50 (out of season)

Fannaråkhytta
tel +47 48 15 22 44 (in season)
tel +47 48 09 59 45 (out of season)

Rondane

Rondvassbu
tel +47 612 31 866

Bjørnhollia
tel +47 901 11 380 (in season)
tel +47 61 23 43 08 (out of season)

Øvre Døralseter
tel +47 958 28 999

Grimsdalshytta
tel +47 452 98 155 (in season)
tel +47 970 13 264 (out of season)

Dovrefjell

Vangshaugen
tel +47 905 47 837

Snøheim
tel +47 47 96 22 86

Trollheimen

Gjevilvasshytta
tel +47 932 45 146 (in season)

Trollheimshytta
tel +47 73 51 52 75 (in season)
tel +47 916 50 661 (out of season)

Jøldalshytta
tel +47 73 50 50 01 (in season)

Bårdsgarden
tel +47 97 65 20 29

Innerdalshytta
tel +47 97 53 28 65

Kårvatn
tel +47 93 03 63 79

Todalshytta
tel +47 46 91 60 03

Ryfylke

Lysefjorden Turisthytte
tel +47 948 26 602 (in season)

Preikestolhytta/Preikestolen Fjellstue
tel +47 51 74 20 74

APPENDIX C

Useful websites and transport schedules

Note: when sourcing information on hikes, transport and other services, be aware that you might sometimes be looking at websites or blogs that contain (out) dated information. Always double check the reliability of your source. Where a website does not have a dedicated English-language version, it should be possible to find the information you need by using a free online translation tool such as that offered by Google Chrome.

Useful websites

General tourism information

Norwegian Directorate of Immigration – for information on visa requirements
www.udi.no/en

Country-specific requirements
www.norway.no/en

National tourism portals
www.visitnorway.com
www.fjordnorway.com

Local/regional tourism information

https://jotunheimen.com/en

www.nasjonalparkriket.no/en

www.regionstavanger-ryfylke.com

www.oppdal.com

www.florli.no

Weather forecast information

www.yr.no
best site with extensive information; English version and app available

www.varsom.no/en
general warnings for avalanches, floods, landslides and weather

Hiking and trekking information

www.dnt.no: the official website of the Norwegian Trekking Association (DNT). Extensive information on hiking and trekking; huts and trails that are supported by the DNT; packing list suggestions, gear and equipment; the Norwegian mountain code; and the rights and obligations of the 'Public right of access'. Note that the English-language site (https://english.dnt.no) is more limited than the Norwegian.
https://ut.no: extensive information on outdoor life in Norway, including huts (with booking); currently Norwegian-only
www.inatur.no: for information about fishing, including licences

Other regional hiking association sites relevant for this guide include:

www.dntoslo.no
Greater Oslo region

www.tt.no
Trondheim region

www.kntur.no
Kristiansund and Nordmøre region

www.stf.no
Stavanger region

Maps

Norwegian Mapping Authority
https://kartverket.no/en and
https://norgeskart.no
to create and print your own maps

www.kartbutikken.no
to buy maps, shipping worldwide; English site available

Norwegian Geological Survey
www.ngu.no/en

On maps, naming and distances

When searching for a location on a transportation, mapping or weather website, make sure you are looking at the correct area. Many names in Norwegian are spelled similarly or even the same; for example, looking for 'Trollhøtta' or even Preikestolen will give you three to four options across the country. In particular, be careful not to confuse:

- Skei in Surnadal with Skei in Jølster (the first is relevant for the exit at Todalen in Trollheimen)
- Oppdal town (in Trøndelag county; entry portal for Trollheimen) with Oppland county
- Otta in Oppland county with Odda in Hordaland county

Sometimes you might find references to a length measured in 'mil'. This refers to a Scandinavian mile and 1mil is 10km; translating apps might get this wrong by a factor of 10 and translate it to 1km, or 1 mile!

Public transport information

National and interregional

General portals
It is best to confirm schedules on the local transport sites. Check especially for exceptions during summer/school holidays (https://publicholidays.no/school-holidays).

www.rome2rio.com
for transport options from anywhere to anywhere – a great starting point

www.busradar.com
same as above but dedicated to bus travel

www.maps.google.com
very helpful in finding location of bus stops; often but not always reliable for schedules

www.entur.no
often in development and not always reliable, but improving

Main Norwegian airports
https://avinor.no/en
arrival/departure/airport information

www.flybussen.no
airport bus shuttles
(Oslo, Stavanger/Sandnes, Trondheim)

https://flytoget.no/en
airport train express (Oslo)

International buses
https://flixbus.com

National train network
www.vy.no/en
(especially the Oslo–Trondheim route servicing Ringebu, Otta, Kongsvoll, Hjerkinn and Oppdal)

National express buses
www.vy.no/en

www.lavprisekspressen.no

www/konkurrenten.no

www.nor-way.no/en
(especially the Valdresekspressen from Oslo to Gjendesheim/Leirvassbu in Jotunheimen)

https://kystbussen.no

National and international ferries
www.colorline.com

www.stenaline.com

www.fjordline.com/en

Local transport by area

Jotunheimen – Figure 1

Main entry points are Otta, Lom and Gjendesheim, all reachable by national bus or train. For local transport, visit www.innlandstrafikk.no. The summer routes to the mountain huts will only be posted on the website by late winter. Use the search function on www.innlandstrafikk.no/reise/rutetabeller and insert either the route number you are looking for, or the term *'sommerruter'*. For the boat across Gjende lake, a reservation is recommended through www.gjende.no/en. To exit at Fondsbu by boat over Bygdin lake to Bygdin village, see https://jvb.no/en.

Rondane – Figure 2

Main entry point is Otta, served by Innlandstrafikk (www.innlandstrafikk.no) for local transport. Busline 205 connects to the Spranget parking area, a short hike from Rondvassbu. Alternatively, busline 206 runs from Ringebu to Straumbu, a short hike from Bjørnhollia. Exit point is Hjerkinn. Otta, Ringebu and Hjerkinn have train stations (www.vy.no/en).

Dovrefjell – Figure 2

Main entry is Kongsvoll train station (see www.vy.no/en for local and regional trains). Fram (https://frammr.no) runs the regional express bus route 901 (Kristiansund to Oppdal, stopping at Fale Bru (Fale Bridge) for exit/entry to Eiriksvollen. See https://snoheim.dnt.no/eng for shuttle bus between Hjerkinn and Snøheim mountain hut.

Trollheimen – Figure 2

Main entry/exit point is Gjevilvasshytta. Visit https://atb.no/en – Trøndelag County public transport. Regional buses are at www.atb.no/en/bus-regions and there's a travel planner at www.atb.no/en/travel-planner. The relevant line is the 580 summer route from Oppdal to Gjevilvasshytta; this bus runs twice weekly, on Thursday and Sunday afternoon. Schedules for summer routes will normally be posted in late winter. Fram (https://frammr.no) runs the regional express bus routes 901 (Kristiansund to Oppdal, which stops at Fale Bridge for exit/entry via Eiriksvollen, and at Feste for access to Gjevilvasshytta) and 905 (Trondheim to Kristiansund, going past Skei in Surnadal for exit near Todalen).

Ryfylke – Figure 3

Ryfylke requires more careful planning, as there is a varied and fragmented offering of public transport. To start, see www.flybussen.no for airport shuttle from Sola airport to Sandnes (bus terminal) and/or Stavanger central bus terminal, as well as ferry terminal at Fiskepiren.

Kolumbus (www.kolumbus.no/en), local bus and ferry services company, including the Stavanger/Sandnes city buses and airport shuttle times. The local bus also connects the airport to the city (a lot cheaper, and a bit slower); currently line 42 from the airport to Sandnes, and line 42 from the airport to Jåsund with changeover to line 2 from Jåsund to Stavanger bus terminal. Stavanger Fiskepiren (ferry terminal) is a 15min walk from the bus terminal. Line 47 runs from Sandnes bus terminal to Lauvvik Quay on weekdays. See www.kolumbus.no/ruter/buss/ryfylke for the regional lines and ferries.

Kolumbus ferry line 560 (M/S Lysebotn) serves the Lysefjord ports. The ferry has peculiar schedules, so do study them carefully. Delays of up to an hour are possible in high season; nevertheless, be on time at the quay. It starts from Stavanger Fiskepiren terminal (1pm, Mon/Wed/Fri) or Lauvvik (Mon–Fri and Sun). For information on summer ferry schedules visit www.florli.no and www.lysefjorden365.com, operators and times may vary from year to year. From Revså quay you can walk up to Preikestolen Fjellstue and Preikestolen itself.

Note: advance booking for the ferries is recommended, to secure space and ensure the port is called, and necessary if you want to be picked up from one of the smaller quays such as Bakken. Booking at least a few hours ahead should be fine if you have only limited luggage and are not travelling in a large group.

Weekend ferry transfers into/out of the Lysefjord are currently only possible from/to Lauvvik, which is a 30min car drive from Sandnes and 45min from Stavanger. No public buses run from Sandnes or Stavanger to Lauvvik on weekends during summer school holidays. As a result, it is best to plan arrival on a weekday.

The entry point for the Lysefjord circuit (Route 10) is Øvre Espedal. Take the ferry to Forsand first. Kolumbus bus line 122 runs from Forsand to Øvre Espedal, but you have to call ahead (tel +47 51 74 02 40) to book at least two hours in advance of the regular departure time during the school holidays in summer; Mon–Fri only, once daily. This works perfectly well and is a reliable service, even for a single passenger. It may not run if no reservations are made, and it may leave early if all passengers that have reserved have shown up. Should you hike the Lysefjord circuit clockwise and end at Øvre Espedal, make sure you plan your final stage carefully to book and catch the bus. You can also order a taxi from or to Forsand (eg Strand taxi, tel +47 51 74 64 11 or +47 51 74 54 20 , or book through www.pellesreiser.no/en; around NOK 1100 in 2019).

The 7km road-walk between Øygardsstølen and Lysebotn at the end of Stage 4 can be avoided by pre-booking on the regular transfer service run by Stavanger Base Jump Club (SBK), tel +47 98 44 41 59.

The exit point for the Lysefjord circuit is Preikestolhytta. Transport to and from Stavanger is offered by many in a rather fragmented market, so details can vary often. Tide (www.tide.no/en) and Boreal (www.boreal.no/home) currently run very regular bus services between Stavanger and Preikestolhytta. See https://gofjords.com and www.pulpitrock.no/en. Pelles Reiser (www.pellesreiser.no/en) provides transport to/from Preikestolhytta and other locations in Ryfylke.

Finally, visit www.stf.no/buss-og-bat-til-fjells for information from the Stavanger Trekking Association on public transport options from the city to the mountains; and www.florli.no – an excellent commercial website – includes information on travel to and from Flørli and the Lysefjord as well as local attractions, with up-to-date ferry schedules.

APPENDIX D

Norwegian berries

Norway has a fantastic selection of berries in season, both on sale and wild on the mountainside. The long summer days seem to concentrate taste into the small berries, and locally grown **strawberries** (*jordbær*) are a revelation to those used to the more watery versions sold elsewhere. **Blackberries** (*bjørnebær*), **raspberries** (*bringebær*), **redcurrants** (*rips*) and **blackcurrants** (*solbær*) are all grown commercially and in gardens, and can be found wild along the roads in the warmer southern coastal areas. In the mountains there are a few wild berries that will give you tasty vitamins in season and provide for a great snack on the hike.

Bilberries (*blåbær, Vaccinium myrtillus*) are plentiful on the hillsides and in the forests. Their season, depending on altitude, is August to September, and foraging for them in autumn is a popular activity in Norway. A good patch can provide buckets full of them within a couple of square metres. The literal translation of *blåbær* is 'blue berry', but the true **blueberry** (*Vaccinium Cyanococcus*) is larger, commercially grown, and whitish on the inside. Bilberries are dark purple on the inside, rarely sold in shops, and they are a natural dye for hands and mouth! Although blueberries are native to North America, bilberries and blueberries may be found happily growing alongside each other on the Norwegian slopes.

Lingonberries (*tyttebær, Vaccinium vitis-idaea*, cowberry in North America) are similarly plentiful. These are bright red berries, growing on a short plant, with upright stems and leathery leaves, and clustered berries hanging from the stem. Lingonberries are in season from September and found on the mountainsides, often together with bilberries. This is the most commercial wild berry, and it is harvested widely to be eaten with any excuse for dinner. It is very commonly mistaken in name (and culinary use) with **cranberries** (*Vaccinium oxycoccus*); but the latter grow on creepers on the ground, with single berries on stems. **Bunchberries** (*skrubbær, Cornus suecica*) are easily mistaken for lingonberries, but have no taste. Pointy leaves, and the berries on top of the stem, are markers for bunchberries.

Cloudberries (*molte, Rubus chamaemorus*) are arguably the most precious berries to be found, from late July onwards depending on altitude and sun. These berries grow only in the wild, and are very fragile. They change from red to bright orange-yellow when ripe, and from sour-bitter to a very distinctive sweetish taste. Locations of good patches of cloudberries are kept as closely guarded family secrets. Such is their esteem that it is illegal to pick cloudberries that are not yet ripe; in fact picking cloudberries in northern Norway is not permitted at all except on your own property. Mixing fresh ripe cloudberries simply with cream makes for a great dessert.

Crowberries (*krekling* or *krøkebær, Empetrum nigrum*) are black, bitter, rather tough berries. They very commonly grow amongst the bilberries and lingonberries, and while the plant and leaves are distinctive, you should not mix them with your bilberries since folklore has it that they are a mild diuretic (hence also called *pissbær* in Norwegian). It is fact, however, that cooking them enhances the flavour and they are fine for jams and pies.

(Clockwise, from top left) lingonberry; bilberry; crowberry; redcurrant; bunchberry; blueberry; cloudberry

DOWNLOAD THE ROUTES IN GPX FORMAT

All the routes in this guide are available for download from:

www.cicerone.co.uk/975/GPX

as standard format GPX files. You should be able to load them into most online GPX systems and mobile devices, whether GPS or smartphone. You may need to convert the file into your preferred format using a conversion programme such as gpsvisualizer.com or one of the many other such websites and programmes.

When you follow this link, you will be asked for your email address and where you purchased the guidebook, and have the option to subscribe to the Cicerone e-newsletter.

CICERONE

www.cicerone.co.uk

LISTING OF CICERONE GUIDES

BRITISH ISLES CHALLENGES, COLLECTIONS AND ACTIVITIES

Cycling Land's End to John o' Groats
Great Walks on the England Coast Path
The Big Rounds
The Book of the Bivvy
The Book of the Bothy
The Mountains of England and Wales: Vol 1 Wales
The Mountains of England and Wales: Vol 2 England
The National Trails
Walking the End to End Trail

SHORT WALKS SERIES

Short Walks Hadrian's Wall
Short Walks in Arnside and Silverdale
Short Walks in Cornwall: Falmouth and the Lizard
Short Walks in Dumfries and Galloway
Short Walks in Nidderdale
Short Walks in Pembrokeshire: Tenby and the south
Short Walks in the South Downs: Brighton, Eastbourne and Arundel
Short Walks in the Surrey Hills
Short Walks Lake District – Coniston and Langdale
Short Walks Lake District: Keswick, Borrowdale and Buttermere
Short Walks Lake District: Windermere Ambleside and Grasmere
Short Walks on the Malvern Hills
Short Walks Winchester

SCOTLAND

Ben Nevis and Glen Coe
Cycling in the Hebrides
Cycling the North Coast 500
Great Mountain Days in Scotland
Mountain Biking in Southern and Central Scotland
Mountain Biking in West and North West Scotland
Not the West Highland Way
Scotland
Scotland's Best Small Mountains
Scotland's Mountain Ridges
Scottish Wild Country Backpacking
Skye's Cuillin Ridge Traverse
The Borders Abbeys Way
The Great Glen Way
The Great Glen Way Map Booklet
The Hebridean Way
The Hebrides
The Isle of Mull
The Isle of Skye
The Skye Trail
The Southern Upland Way
The West Highland Way
The West Highland Way Map Booklet
Walking Ben Lawers, Rannoch and Atholl
Walking in the Cairngorms
Walking in the Pentland Hills
Walking in the Scottish Borders
Walking in the Southern Uplands
Walking in Torridon, Fisherfield, Fannichs and An Teallach
Walking Loch Lomond and the Trossachs
Walking on Arran
Walking on Harris and Lewis
Walking on Jura, Islay and Colonsay
Walking on Rum and the Small Isles
Walking on the Orkney and Shetland Isles
Walking on Uist and Barra
Walking the Cape Wrath Trail
Walking the Corbetts
  Vol 1 South of the Great Glen
  Vol 2 North of the Great Glen
Walking the Galloway Hills
Walking the John o' Groats Trail
Walking the Munros
  Vol 1 – Southern, Central and Western Highlands
  Vol 2 – Northern Highlands and the Cairngorms
Winter Climbs in the Cairngorms
Winter Climbs: Ben Nevis and Glen Coe

NORTHERN ENGLAND ROUTES

Cycling the Reivers Route
Cycling the Way of the Roses
Hadrian's Cycleway
Hadrian's Wall Path
Hadrian's Wall Path Map Booklet
The Coast to Coast Cycle Route
The Coast to Coast Walk
The Coast to Coast Walk Map Booklet
The Pennine Way
The Pennine Way Map Booklet
Walking the Dales Way
Walking the Dales Way Map Booklet

NORTH-EAST ENGLAND, YORKSHIRE DALES AND PENNINES

Cycling in the Yorkshire Dales
Great Mountain Days in the Pennines
Mountain Biking in the Yorkshire Dales
The Cleveland Way and the Yorkshire Wolds Way
The North York Moors
Trail and Fell Running in the Yorkshire Dales
Walking in County Durham
Walking in Northumberland
Walking in the North Pennines
Walking in the Yorkshire Dales: North and East
  South and West
Walking St Cuthbert's Way
Walking St Oswald's Way and Northumberland Coast Path

NORTH-WEST ENGLAND AND THE ISLE OF MAN

Cycling the Pennine Bridleway
Isle of Man Coastal Path
The Lancashire Cycleway
The Lune Valley and Howgills
Walking in Cumbria's Eden Valley
Walking in Lancashire
Walking in the Forest of Bowland and Pendle
Walking on the Isle of Man
Walking on the West Pennine Moors
Walking the Ribble Way
Walks in Silverdale and Arnside

LAKE DISTRICT

Bikepacking in the Lake District
Cycling in the Lake District
Great Mountain Days in the Lake District
Joss Naylor's Lakes, Meres and Waters of the Lake District
Lake District Winter Climbs
Lake District:
  High Level and Fell Walks
  Low Level and Lake Walks
Mountain Biking in the Lake District
Outdoor Adventures with Children – Lake District
Scrambles in the Lake District – North
  South
Trail and Fell Running in the Lake District
Walking The Cumbria Way
Walking the Lake District Fells –
  Borrowdale
  Buttermere
  Coniston
  Keswick
  Langdale
  Mardale and the Far East
  Patterdale
  Wasdale
Walking the Tour of the Lake District

DERBYSHIRE, PEAK DISTRICT AND MIDLANDS

Cycling in the Peak District
Dark Peak Walks
Scrambles in the Dark Peak
Walking in Derbyshire
Walking in the Peak District –
  White Peak East
  White Peak West

SOUTHERN ENGLAND

20 Classic Sportive Rides in
South East England
South West England
Cycling in the Cotswolds
Mountain Biking on the
North Downs
South Downs
Suffolk Coast and Heath Walks
The Cotswold Way
The Cotswold Way Map Booklet
The Kennet and Avon Canal
The Lea Valley Walk
The North Downs Way
The North Downs Way Map Booklet
The Peddars Way and Norfolk
Coast Path
The Pilgrims' Way
The Ridgeway National Trail
The Ridgeway National Trail
Map Booklet
The South Downs Way
The South Downs Way Map Booklet
The Thames Path
The Thames Path Map Booklet
The Two Moors Way
The Two Moors Way Map Booklet
Walking Hampshire's Test Way
Walking in Cornwall
Walking in Essex
Walking in Kent
Walking in London
Walking in Norfolk
Walking in the Chilterns
Walking in the Cotswolds
Walking in the Isles of Scilly
Walking in the New Forest
Walking in the North Wessex Downs
Walking on Dartmoor
Walking on Guernsey
Walking on Jersey
Walking on the Isle of Wight
Walking the Dartmoor Way
Walking the Jurassic Coast
Walking the South West Coast Path
Walking the South West Coast Path
Map Booklets
– Vol 1: Minehead to St Ives
– Vol 2: St Ives to Plymouth
– Vol 3: Plymouth to Poole
Walks in the South Downs
National Park

WALES AND WELSH BORDERS

Cycle Touring in Wales
Cycling Lon Las Cymru
Great Mountain Days in Snowdonia
Hillwalking in Shropshire
Mountain Walking in Snowdonia
Offa's Dyke Path
Offa's Dyke Path Map Booklet
Ridges of Snowdonia
Scrambles in Snowdonia
Snowdonia: 30 Low-level and
Easy Walks
– North
– South
The Cambrian Way
The Pembrokeshire Coast Path
The Pembrokeshire Coast Path
Map Booklet
The Snowdonia Way
Walking Glyndwr's Way
Walking in Carmarthenshire
Walking in Pembrokeshire
Walking in the Brecon Beacons
Walking in the Forest of Dean
Walking in the Wye Valley
Walking on Gower
Walking the Severn Way
Walking the Shropshire Way
Walking the Wales Coast Path

INTERNATIONAL CHALLENGES, COLLECTIONS AND ACTIVITIES

Europe's High Points
Walking the Via Francigena
Pilgrim Route – Part 1

AFRICA

Kilimanjaro
Walking in the Drakensberg
Walks and Scrambles in the Moroccan
Anti-Atlas

ALPS CROSS-BORDER ROUTES

100 Hut Walks in the Alps
Alpine Ski Mountaineering
Vol 1 – Western Alps
The Karnischer Hohenweg
The Tour of the Bernina
Trail Running – Chamonix and the
Mont Blanc region
Trekking Chamonix to Zermatt
Trekking in the Alps
Trekking in the Silvretta and
Ratikon Alps
Trekking Munich to Venice
Trekking the Tour du Mont Blanc
Trekking the Tour du Mont Blanc
Map Booklet
Walking in the Alps

PYRENEES AND FRANCE/SPAIN CROSS-BORDER ROUTES

Shorter Treks in the Pyrenees
The Pyrenean Haute Route
The Pyrenees
Trekking the GR11 Trail
Walks and Climbs in the Pyrenees

AUSTRIA

Innsbruck Mountain Adventures
Trekking Austria's Adlerweg
Trekking in Austria's Hohe Tauern
Trekking in Austria's Zillertal Alps
Trekking in the Stubai Alps
Walking in Austria
Walking in the Salzkammergut:
the Austrian Lake District

EASTERN EUROPE

The Danube Cycleway Vol 2
The High Tatras
The Mountains of Romania
Walking in Hungary

FRANCE, BELGIUM AND LUXEMBOURG

Camino de Santiago – Via Podiensis
Chamonix Mountain Adventures
Cycle Touring in France
Cycling London to Paris
Cycling the Canal de la Garonne
Cycling the Canal du Midi
Cycling the Route des Grandes Alpes
Mont Blanc Walks
Mountain Adventures in
the Maurienne
Short Treks on Corsica
The Elbe Cycle Route
The GR5 Trail
The GR5 Trail – Benelux and Lorraine
The GR5 Trail – Vosges and Jura
The Grand Traverse of the
Massif Central
The Moselle Cycle Route
The River Loire Cycle Route
The River Rhone Cycle Route
Trekking in the Vanoise
Trekking the Cathar Way
Trekking the GR10
Trekking the GR20 Corsica
Trekking the Robert Louis
Stevenson Trail
Via Ferratas of the French Alps
Walking in Provence – East
Walking in Provence – West
Walking in the Ardennes
Walking in the Auvergne
Walking in the Brianconnais
Walking in the Dordogne
Walking in the Haute Savoie: North
Walking in the Haute Savoie: South
Walking on Corsica
Walking the Brittany Coast Path

GERMANY

Hiking and Cycling in the
Black Forest
The Danube Cycleway Vol 1
The Rhine Cycle Route
The Westweg
Walking in the Bavarian Alps

IRELAND

The Wild Atlantic Way and
Western Ireland
Walking the Wicklow Way

ITALY

Alta Via – Trekking in the Dolomites – Vols 1&2
Day Walks in the Dolomites
Italy's Grande Traversata delle Alpi
Italy's Sibillini National Park
Ski Touring and Snowshoeing in the Dolomites
The Way of St Francis
Trekking in the Apennines
Trekking the Giants' Trail: Alta Via 1 through the Italian Pennine Alps
Via Ferratas of the Italian Dolomites – Vols 1&2
Walking in Abruzzo
Walking in Italy's Cinque Terre
Walking in Italy's Stelvio National Park
Walking in Sicily
Walking in the Aosta Valley
Walking in the Dolomites
Walking in Tuscany
Walking in Umbria
Walking Lake Como and Maggiore
Walking Lake Garda and Iseo
Walking on the Amalfi Coast
Walking the Via Francigena Pilgrim Route – Parts 2&3
Walks and Treks in the Maritime Alps

MEDITERRANEAN

The High Mountains of Crete
Trekking in Greece
Walking and Trekking in Zagori
Walking and Trekking on Corfu
Walking in Cyprus
Walking on Malta
Walking on the Greek Islands – the Cyclades

NEW ZEALAND AND AUSTRALIA

Hiking the Overland Track

NORTH AMERICA

Hiking and Cycling the California Missions Trail
The John Muir Trail
The Pacific Crest Trail

SOUTH AMERICA

Aconcagua and the Southern Andes
Hiking and Biking Peru's Inca Trails
Trekking in Torres del Paine

SCANDINAVIA, ICELAND AND GREENLAND

Hiking in Norway – South
Trekking in Greenland – The Arctic Circle Trail
Trekking the Kungsleden
Walking and Trekking in Iceland

SLOVENIA, CROATIA, SERBIA, MONTENEGRO AND ALBANIA

Hiking Slovenia's Juliana Trail
Mountain Biking in Slovenia
The Islands of Croatia
The Julian Alps of Slovenia
The Mountains of Montenegro
The Peaks of the Balkans Trail
The Slovene Mountain Trail
Walking in Slovenia: The Karavanke
Walks and Treks in Croatia

SPAIN AND PORTUGAL

Camino de Santiago: Camino Frances
Coastal Walks in Andalucia
Costa Blanca Mountain Adventures
Cycling the Camino de Santiago
Cycling the Ruta Via de la Plata
Mountain Walking in Mallorca
Mountain Walking in Southern Catalunya
Portugal's Rota Vicentina
Spain's Sendero Historico: The GR1
The Andalucian Coast to Coast Walk
The Camino del Norte and Camino Primitivo
The Camino Ingles and Ruta do Mar
The Camino Portugues
The Mountains Around Nerja
The Mountains of Ronda and Grazalema
The Sierras of Extremadura
Trekking in Mallorca
Trekking in the Canary Islands
Trekking the GR7 in Andalucia
Walking and Trekking in the Sierra Nevada
Walking in Andalucia
Walking in Catalunya – Barcelona
Walking in Catalunya – Girona Pyrenees
Walking in Portugal
Walking in the Algarve
Walking in the Picos de Europa
Walking La Via de la Plata and Camino Sanabres
Walking on Gran Canaria
Walking on La Gomera and El Hierro
Walking on La Palma
Walking on Lanzarote and Fuerteventura
Walking on Madeira
Walking on Tenerife
Walking on the Azores
Walking on the Costa Blanca
Walking the Camino dos Faros

SWITZERLAND

Switzerland's Jura Crest Trail
The Swiss Alps
Tour of the Jungfrau Region
Trekking the Swiss Via Alpina
Walking in the Bernese Oberland – Jungfrau region
Walking in the Engadine – Switzerland
Walking in the Valais
Walking in Ticino
Walking in Zermatt and Saas-Fee

CHINA, JAPAN AND ASIA

Hiking and Trekking in the Japan Alps and Mount Fuji
Hiking in Hong Kong
Japan's Kumano Kodo Pilgrimage
Trekking in Tajikistan

HIMALAYA

Annapurna
8000 metres
Everest: A Trekker's Guide
Trekking in Bhutan
Trekking in Ladakh
Trekking in the Himalaya
Trekking in the Karakoram

MOUNTAIN LITERATURE

A Walk in the Clouds
Abode of the Gods
Fifty Years of Adventure
The Pennine Way – the Path, the People, the Journey
Unjustifiable Risk?
Unjustifiable Risk?

TECHNIQUES

Fastpacking
Geocaching in the UK
Map and Compass
Outdoor Photography
The Mountain Hut Book

MINI GUIDES

Alpine Flowers
Navigation
Pocket First Aid and Wilderness Medicine
Snow